THE ECONOMIC THEORY OF ENVIRONMENTAL POLICY IN A FEDERAL SYSTEM

NEW HORIZONS IN ENVIRONMENTAL ECONOMICS

General Editor: Wallace E. Oates, *Professor of Economics, University of Maryland*

This important series is designed to make a significant contribution to the development of the principles and practices of environmental economics. It includes both theoretical and empirical work. International in scope, it addresses issues of current and future concern in both East and West and in developed and developing countries.

The main purpose of the series is to create a forum for the publication of high quality work and to show how economic analysis can make a contribution to understanding and resolving the environmental problems confronting the world in the late twentieth century.

Recent titles in the series include:

Estimating Economic Values for Nature Methods for Non-Market Valuation
V. Kerry Smith

Models of Sustainable Development
Edited by Sylvie Faucheux, David Pearce and John Proops

Contingent Valuation and Endangered Species Methodological Issues and Applications
Kristin M. Jakobsson and Andrew K. Dragun

Acid Rain and Environmental Degradation
The Economics of Emission Trading
Ger Klaassen

The Economics of Pollution Control in the Asia Pacific
Robert Mendelsohn and Daigee Shaw

Economic Policy for the Environment and Natural Resources
Techniques for the Management and Control of Pollution
Edited by Anastasios Xepapadeas

Welfare Measurement, Sustainability and Green National Accounting A Growth Theoretical Approach
Thomas Aronsson, Per-Olov Johansson and Karl-Gustaf Löfgren

The Economics of Environmental Protection
Theory and Demand Revelation
Peter Bohm

The International Yearbook of Environmental and Resource Economics 1997/1998
A Survey of Current Issues
Edited by Henk Folmer and Tom Tietenberg

The Economic Theory of Environmental Policy in a Federal System
Edited by John B. Braden and Stef Proost

Economics of Ecological Resources
Selected Essays
Charles Perrings

The Economic Theory of Environmental Policy in a Federal System

Edited by

John B. Braden

Professor of Economics, University of Illinois, USA

Stef Proost

Research Fellow, Belgium National Fund for Scientific Research and Associate Professor of Economics, Katholieke Universiteit Leuven, Belgium

NEW HORIZONS IN ENVIRONMENTAL ECONOMICS

Edward Elgar

Cheltenham, UK • Lyme, US

Published by
Edward Elgar Publishing Limited
8 Lansdown Place
Cheltenham
Glos GL50 2HU
UK

Edward Elgar Publishing, Inc
1 Pinnacle Hill Road
Lyme
NH 03768
US

A catalogue record for this book is available from the British Library

Library of Congress Cataloguing in Publication Data
The economic theory of environmental policy in a federal system/
    edited by John B. Braden, Stef Proost.
        — (New horizons in environmental economics)
    Revised versions of papers presented at a conference held 14–16
June 1995 at the Catholic University of Leuven, Belgium, and
sponsored by the Catholic University, the University of Illinois at
Urbana-Champaign, and Wageningen Agricultural University.
    Includes index.
    1. Environmental economics—Congresses. 2. Environmental policy—
Economic aspects—Congresses. 3. Federal government—Congresses.
4. Business cycles—Political aspects—Congresses. I. Braden, John
B. II. Proost, S. III. Series.
HC79.E5E2737   1997
333.7—dc21   96–50094
                                                                 CIP

ISBN 1 85898 363 0

Printed and bound in Great Britain by
Biddles Limited, Guildford and King's Lynn

Contents

Tables

Contributors

Gregory S. Amacher, Assistant Professor in the Department of Forestry, Virginia Polytechnic Institute and State University, Blacksburg, USA.

John B. Braden, Professor in the Department of Agricultural and Consumer Economics and Director of the Water Resources Centre at the University of Illinois at Urbana-Champaign, USA.

Richard J. Brazee, Assistant Professor in the Department of Natural Resource and Environment Sciences at the University of Illinois of Urbana-Champaign, USA.

Klaus Conrad, Professor in the Department of Economics at the University of Mannheim, Germany.

Eliécer Feinzaig, Graduate Assistant in the Department of Economics at the University of Illinois at Urbana-Champaign, USA.

Thomas J. Miceli, Professor in the Department of Economics at the University of Connecticut, Storrs, USA.

Jeff Petchey, Postdoctoral Fellow at the Curtin University, Perth, Australia and Research Fellow at the Federalism Research Centre, Australian National University.

Stef Proost, Research Fellow of the Belgian National Fund for Scientific Research and Associate Professor in the Department of Economics of the K.U. Leuven.

Kathleen Segerson, Professor in the Department of Economics at the University of Connecticut, Storrs, USA.

Perry Shapiro, Professor in the Department of Economics at the University of California at Santa Barbara and Federalism Research Centre, Australian National University.

Thomas S. Ulen, Alumni Distinguished Professor of Law, College of Law, and Professor, Institute of Government and Public Affairs at the University of Illinois at Urbana-Champaign, USA.

Alistair Ulph, Professor in the Department of Economics at the University of Southampton, UK.

Lih-Chyi Wen, Research Assistant in the Department of Economics at the University of Connecticut, Storrs, USA.

Preface

The events of 1992 in Europe, and the changing political landscape in the United States have had important effects on the way relationships are defined between the central (federal or confederal) governments and the member states. In recognition of these trends, in 1990, the US Information Agency (USIA) issued a special call for transatlantic collaborations on economic and political integration. The seeds of this book were sown in that initiative.

The USIA selected the University of Illinois at Urbana-Champaign (USA), the Catholic University of Leuven (Belgium) and Wageningen Agricultural University (Netherlands) to conduct joint research on the consequences of integration for environmental policies. In an attempt to provide a forum for academic researchers from Europe and the USA to reflect upon these developments, the cooperating universities organized two symposia. The first, 'Environmental Policy with Political and Economic Integration: The European Union and the United States', took place between 30 September and 2 October 1993 at the University of Illinois in Urbana-Champaign. The papers from this conference were compiled in a book by the same name, edited by John Braden, Henk Folmer and Tom Ulen, and published by Edward Elgar Publishing, Ltd. The second symposium, 'Economic Aspects of Environmental Policy Making in a Federal System', took place between 14 and 16 June 1995, at the Catholic University of Leuven, Belgium. The collection of works presented in this volume emerged from the latter conference. It is a state-of-the-art scholarly assessment of the theoretical issues concerning environmental governance in a federal or confederal context. The chapters included here are substantially revised versions of those originally given at Leuven, the result of an effort by the contributing authors to incorporate the suggestions and comments of the participants and of reviewers since the summer of 1995. The empirical papers presented at the conference in Leuven will be grouped in a complementary volume, forthcoming from Edward Elgar Publishing, Ltd.

In addition to the scholarly symposium, several of the conferees participated in a seminar involving representatives of the European Commission, the Government of Belgium, and Belgian scientific and industrial groups, held at the Catholic University of Leuven's faculty club on 16 June 1995. This seminar was extremely helpful in exploring real world applications of the ideas presented in these papers.

The editors gratefully acknowledge the following organizations, without whose support this project would not have materialized:

- Directorate General for Science, Research and Development of the Commission of the European Communities – 'Human Dimensions of Environmental Change' Programme.
- Directorate General for Environment, Nuclear Safety and Civil Protection of the Commission of the European Communities.
- American Cultural Centre Brussels.
- United States Information Agency – University Affiliates Program (Project No. IA – ASPS–G1190234).
- Catholic University of Leuven.
  – Centre for Economic Studies.
- University of Illinois at Urbana-Champaign.
  – Institute for Environmental Studies
  – Illinois Agricultural Experiment Station (Project No. 05–0331)

We would also like to acknowledge the contributions of the following individuals: Jos Delbeke, Mathias Mors and William Watts, all in the service of the European Commission, and Wim Moesen, Chairman of the Department of Economics at the Catholic University of Leuven, who were instrumental in securing the funding and cooperated greatly with the symposium; Paul De Grauwe, Dirk Heremans, Knud Munk, Pierre Pestiau, Erik Schokkaert, Henri Tulkens, Patrick Van Cayseele and Klaus Conrad, who made the symposium livelier with their discussions of the theoretical papers presented in this volume; Domenico Siniscalco, Mathias Mors, Dieter Wellisch, and Andreas Pfingsten who also presented their work at the symposium; Camilla Mryglod who served as a technical editor for this volume; and Eva Crabbe and the other members of the secretariat of the CES, without whose able secretarial services the symposium would not have been possible.

1 Introduction

John B. Braden, Eliécer Feinzaig and Stef Proost

In a unitary government system, the design of environmental policy in general involves two steps, namely, setting policy goals and choosing the set of instruments to be used in achieving the goals. When those decisions are made in a federal context, issues of coordination arise in at least three dimensions: across levels of government (federal v. state v. local), across branches of government (executive v. legislative v. judicial), and across agencies at the same government level (for instance, EPA (Environmental Protection Agency) v. FDA (Food and Drug Administration) in the US) (Segerson 1996). Economists are not particularly concerned with the political, legal or constitutional implications of federation. Rather, they use the concept of federalism to refer to the analysis of, and to group, the issues surrounding governance and coordination between levels of government when a multi-layered or hierarchical system of government exists. In the words of Wallace Oates (1972, p. 17):

> The structure of government is ... of interest to [the economist] only to the extent that it carries with it implications for patterns of resource use and income distribution. From this perspective, decentralization of the public sector is of importance primarily because it provides a mechanism through which the levels of provision of certain public goods and services can be fashioned according to the preferences of geographical subsets of the population.

In recent years, interest in the process of policy-making in a federal system, and in particular in the environmental realm, has been sparked by a few events. The processes of political and economic integration in Europe, and the increasing demands in the US for a redefinition of the federal–state relationship are just two of them. However, as we argue above, the economic interpretation of federalism is quite broad. From that perspective, the Uruguay Round of GATT, the Rio accords from the 1992 Earth Summit and the creation of trade blocs such as the North American Free Trade Agreement (NAFTA) pose some interesting questions that are relevant to the field of federalism in general. Environmental issues have been an integral part of these developments, and in particular, the questions of coordination of environmental policies between countries and of assignment of legal and regulatory powers over the environment between the countries and the respective compact have received great attention. From the economic perspective, each one of these compacts can be thought of as a loose confederation with limited scope. The member countries yield limited powers to the compacts, usually on a single issue (generally trade), and retain sovereignty over all other aspects of their political existence. Environmental concerns are usually incorporated into these trade agreements, insofar as differences in environmental policies may explain trade flows or may constitute barriers to the free trade of goods and services. The results are, in general, limited coordination of environmental policy between countries and, to a lesser extent, the establishment of minimum environmental quality standards for production processes.

The events in Europe and the US, which are of central interest to this volume, reflect the relative differences in the stages of development of federalism on both continents. The birth of a confederation in Europe has meant that member states have yielded limited powers to the European Commission, whereas in the United States the restructuring of the relationship between the federal and state governments has resulted in (thus far) limited devolution of power from the higher to the lower levels of government. Recent court rulings[1] and the election of a Republican majority to the US Congress in 1994 have added momentum to, if not consolidated, the devolution process.

The differences between a federation and a confederation are not trivial. In a purely federal system, such as the US, the federal government has some direct power over its citizens, whereas in a confederation the central governing body has power only over its member states, and jurisdiction over citizens rests exclusively with the member states. Moreover, the scope of activities (and powers) of the federal government in the US is much broader than that of the Commission of the European Community, let alone regional compacts such as those mentioned above. Nevertheless, the process of environmental policy-making is conceptually similar under both arrangements, and thus is treated as one.

The chapters presented here all attempt to answer a common question under varying conditions: which level of government should be responsible for environmental regulation in a federal system? In other words, should environmental policy be assigned to the (con)federal government or to state and/or local authorities? Other important issues arise and are addressed by some but not all of the chapters:

- In what circumstances should federally uniform or regionally differentiated environmental policy instruments be used? Should the policy targets for environmental quality be uniform or regionally differentiated?
- Under what conditions will federal intervention in environmental policy-making result in welfare improvements compared to decentralized provision?
- Do necessary and sufficient conditions for federal intervention exist? That is to say, can we find a set of conditions under which policy-making at the federal level is clearly more efficient than at any other level?

- Can cooperation between member states in environmental policy design improve the welfare of the citizenry as compared to competition between states? If not, what are the conditions for cooperation?
- Which level of government should pay for the costs of environmental policies? What are the implications for policy choice at the federal and state levels of the federal government having the ability to impose mandates on the lower governments, but not the obligation to pay for the costs imposed?
- How are the answers to the previous questions altered when the various levels of government possess different information regarding costs and benefits of clean-up efforts and damage costs?
- What are the implications for natural resource stocks of environmental policy-making at different levels of government, with and without coordination between the different levels?

When it comes to environmental policy-making, the complexity of a multilayered government system yields a wealth of issues. In the present volume we are concerned mainly with the issues of coordination of environmental policy across levels of government, and this is a constant throughout the book. Compounding the problems that result from the existence of more than one level of government, other issues arise and are in turn dealt with in the different chapters. Even if there could be agreement as to which level of government should set environmental policy goals, the question of which level of government should pay the costs of implementing environmental policies needs to be addressed. This is done in the chapter by Kathleen Segerson, Thomas J. Miceli and Lih-Chyi Wen (Chapter 3). Furthermore, in a (con)federation, member states are linked in at least four ways that are relevant to environmental policy-making. First, states are linked through transboundary pollution, and this is treated in the chapters by Klaus Conrad (Chapter 5) and by Perry Shapiro and Jeff Petchey (Chapter 6). Secondly, member states can be linked through the trade of goods and services, and this is the focus of the chapter by Alistair Ulph (Chapter 4). Issues concerning trade are also considered in the chapter by Conrad. Thirdly, member states are linked through the migration of factors of production (capital and/or labour), and this is modelled in the first half of the chapter by Perry Shapiro and Jeff Petchey. Finally, member states may be linked through the existence of natural resources to which, given their characteristics, most or all states (or the federal government in lieu of them) may have claims of property even though they are fully contained in one state. This is analysed in the chapter by Gregory S. Amacher and Richard J. Brazee (Chapter 7).

The first elements of a theory of the costs and benefits of federalism date from Tiebout's (1956) and Oates's (1972) seminal contributions. These elements need further refinement in order to understand the present federal structures. One of the main sources of inspiration for these refinements is an economic analysis of the evolution of federalism over time.

The chapter by Thomas Ulen (Chapter 2) describes the evolution of federalism in the US since before the Civil War, and relates the historical shifts in power to and from the federal government to the real economic forces that create benefits and costs in a federation. It provides an analysis of these costs and benefits (an economic theory of federalism), and a public-choice theory of federal–state relations. This chapter is particularly useful in understanding why states are willing to yield some sovereignty to, and incur the costs associated with the formation and existence of, a higher level of government.

Ulen observes that in the US, the federal government sometimes takes a strong interest in regulating things that are of a purely local nature and sometimes leaves matters to the states where it could intervene. He notes that the relations between the federal and state governments in the US are not static. Historically they have changed in response to economic, social and political conditions and to the electorate's perceptions of the problems that most need addressing. As an example of the more recent changes in the balance of power, he mentions that in 1994 the US Supreme Court ruled that the federal government may compel states to implement federal policies if it pays for their costs of compliance. Otherwise it has to give the states options of non-compliance. Furthermore, for the midterm elections of 1994, the Republican Party ran on a platform that called for reducing the size of the federal government and returning decision-making power to the states and the individuals. Ulen points out that, as a result of the Republican takeover of both chambers of the US Congress in November 1994, the movement to reduce the size of the federal government and to place more sovereignty in the states gained ground.

One example of US legislation enacted after the 1994 political watershed is the Unfunded Mandate Reform Act of 1995, which limits the extent to which the federal government can impose mandates on state and local governments without providing the funds necessary to implement the mandate. The Act imposes procedural restrictions when the aggregate cost burden on state and local governments of a federal mandate exceeds $50 million, designed to make passage of such a mandate more difficult. The Act is of considerable significance for federal environmental regulation, since the $50 million threshold is not very high at the national level. In this sense, the Act appears to create an obstacle to environmental regulation since the costs of compensation would be borne nationally while many benefits accrue locally.

Further complicating matters, the states may have more complete information than the federal government regarding the costs and benefits of implementing certain mandates. Information asymmetries in general lead to adverse selection or moral-hazard problems. The former arises when a party to a trade or transaction enters an exchange with another party who has better information. More relevant to our discussion, moral hazard occurs when one party to a contract has the ability to shift the cost of his or her behaviour onto another party. If a central government were to have the same level of information as a lower government and the same policy instruments, it might do as well as the local government or it could control and guide them perfectly to the federal optimal solution. But with asymmetric information, the states can over-report their implementation costs and shift the burden of the mandate onto the federal government.

In Chapter 3, Kathleen Segerson, Thomas J. Miceli and Lih-Chyi Wen take on the issue of unfunded mandates and differential information, providing one example of moral-hazard analysis in the context of environmental governance. They focus on the question of which level of government should pay for the cost of implementing policies that are mandated by the federal government on the states and localities when the states and the federal government do not have the same information. Notice that we do not say here that one level of government has better information than the other. Segerson, Miceli and Wen assume that each party has private information, which leads to a double moral-hazard problem. They provide a principal agent model that incorporates the interactions between the federal government and a state government in environmental policy-making. The presence of an interjurisdictional externality is assumed to give rise to the possibility of a federal role in setting policy goals. However, by modelling a single state, the authors do not explicitly consider the interactions between states and the possibility of interjurisdictional differences and competition. The model is used to analyse the impact of decisions taken at the federal level regarding the funding of mandates on the policy choices of both the federal and state governments.

In general, Segerson, Miceli and Wen find that a funding rule that promotes efficiency in the policy choices of both levels of government must accomplish the following:

- eliminate the moral-hazard problem for the federal government (if it incurs no cost, it has an incentive to over-regulate);
- eliminate the moral-hazard problem for the states (if the federal government must always provide the funding for compliance with its mandates, the states have an incentive to exceed the mandate beyond the efficient level, or they will not try to find and use the least-cost way to meet the mandate); and
- solve the interjurisdictional externality problem (which provides states with an incentive to under-regulate in the absence of a federal standard).

Segerson, Miceli and Wen show that the double moral-hazard problem and the externality problem can be dealt with successfully using a threshold rule that identifies the conditions under which mandates would be funded, with the threshold being established on a case-by-case basis. They also conclude that an arbitrary rule, such as the $50 million threshold imposed by the Unfunded Mandate Reform Act of 1995, will only be efficient when the cost of the mandate is exactly $50 million.

The unfunded mandates of the US have a European parallel in the directives and regulations imposed by the European Commission on the member states. Interestingly, in the European context, the costs of compliance with these directives and regulations are borne entirely by the member states.[2] This was the rule in the US prior to the Unfunded Mandate Reform Act of 1995, and it remains in effect below the $50 million threshold.

Another source of potential information asymmetry in the context of environmental governance in a (con)federation results from the presence of eco-dumping. Differentiated environmental policies between states may lead to specialization in more pollution-intensive goods by the states with the laxest environmental policies, while the stricter regions specialize increasingly in less pollution-intensive goods and services. In a competitive environment governments may be concerned about the competitive impact of imposing tougher environmental policies than other countries (states), which may lead them to act non-cooperatively and to relax their environmental policies, relative to the policies they would choose if they acted cooperatively. In Chapter 4, Alistair Ulph tackles this interesting issue with a model of imperfect competition and no-factor mobility, where the countries differ only in their damage costs. He assumes two countries that produce a homogeneous commodity and export to third markets, not to each other. It should be stressed here that policy relaxation (or eco-dumping) in this context results from trade concerns, not from the existence or lack of internalization of external costs imposed by transboundary pollution. The chapter focuses on the instruments available to the federal government to correct ecological dumping in the absence of transboundary spillovers.

The results of Ulph's enquiry are quite interesting. The non-cooperative solution to ecological dumping is characterized and used as a benchmark for evaluating cooperative solutions. First, some previously known results are confirmed, namely that, with full information, when damage costs are sufficiently different between countries, harmonization (of either environmental standards or taxes) will not Pareto-improve upon the non-cooperative outcome. That this is the case follows from the standard economic theory; under the conditions described, harmonization of policies requires that both member states engage in 'environmentally friendly' activities up to a prescribed point, rather than allowing for these activities to take place where they can be carried out at the lowest cost. Ulph's next result, however, contradicts previously found conclusions: under the same conditions, minimum environmental standards will not secure a Pareto-improvement either. This is because in this context more stringent standards adopted by one country (required to meet the minimum standard) are met with a relaxation of standards in another that already exceeds the standard. It should be noted that binding minimum environmental standards offset the trade benefits perceived by countries that specialize in the production of pollution-intensive exportable goods and services. Ulph also finds that minimum environmental taxes in this context do have a ratchet effect, and thus can obtain 'modest' Pareto-improvements over the non-cooperative outcome.

Nevertheless, Ulph's major contribution has to do with the consequences of the lack of full and perfect information. When countries have different damage costs and the (con)federal government has perfect information, the federal government can implement the cooperative solution via state-specific rules. There are two reasons, however, why the federal government may not be able to implement the cooperative solution. The first is political: the federal government simply may not have the right to implement state-specific policies. The second reason is of more interest here. It is that the federal government may have incomplete information: it simply may not know whether a state has low or high pollution-damage costs. The general conclusion is that when the Commission lacks information about the damage costs of individual countries, such asymmetries warrant setting less differentiated policies across countries than would be the case with full information. This finding may be explained by the presence of a moral-hazard problem for the countries resulting from the information asymmetry. In other words, when the federal government lacks information, a member state with low damage costs is able to report costs that are higher than the actual, bringing its reported costs closer to those of the high-cost country, and fooling the federal government into setting more uniform policies.

The existence of pollution that crosses borders presents yet another set of problems for environmental decision-makers in a federation or confederation as well as another source of potential information asymmetries. Spillovers between jurisdictions represent an externality, and it is commonly argued that when the costs of it are not fully internalized by the state (or country) that generates it, non-cooperative behaviour may lead to inefficient policies, which are less stringent than would be arrived at in a cooperative arrangement. This can be used as an argument for federal intervention in environmental policy-making. The conclusion does not go unchallenged; it is argued by opponents that federal policies that do not take into consideration differences in preferences, characteristics and environmental-damage costs between regions need not result in improvements over non-cooperative outcomes or over cooperative arrangements without federal intervention (such as the formation of regional compacts). The problems of transboundary pollution are dealt with in the chapters by Perry Shapiro and Jeff Petchey, and by Klaus Conrad.

In Chapter 5, Conrad uses a homogeneous duopoly model that allows for intra-industry trade and for transboundary pollution. Each firm is in a different country. Countries, which can be different in economic terms (damage costs, private-good demand, preferences over environment) as well as in ecological terms (strictly local pollution, symmetric and asymmetric transboundary spillovers), choose environmental taxes as strategies. Reductions in emissions come at a cost in terms of output foregone, that, when unmatched by the trading partner, result in domestic loss in consumer surplus. Thus, this model is different from the one presented by Ulph in that it allows for transboundary pollution and for trade between the two countries involved. As an alternative to the non-cooperative solution, Conrad considers only cooperative arrangements without federal intervention. In particular, the goal in Conrad is to find conditions that result in non-prisoner's dilemma situations, where cooperation can be prevented by one party when side-payments are not possible.

Not surprisingly, Conrad finds that under symmetry of conditions (economic and environmental), prisoner's dilemma type situations generally arise, allowing for binding agreements between parties without side-payments and/or federal intervention. Yet when asymmetries are modelled, the results change. When asymmetric pollution (e.g., upstream–downstream) is present, one country will generally be better off in the non-cooperative Nash equilibrium than under any agreement without side-payments, even if the economic characteristics of the two countries are identical. Under these circumstances international or interstate agreements are not to be expected. Another interesting finding is that when economic conditions and pollution flows between the two countries are different, the welfare benefits of a cooperative solution are lower than when economic conditions are different, but pollution flows are the same or when no pollution crosses the border. Furthermore, welfare loss increases with the intensity of the spillover in the cooperative (prisoner's dilemma) outcome, stressing the need for cooperation in emission policies.

The chapter by Shapiro and Petchey (Chapter 6) is concerned with whether the existence of transboundary pollution constitutes a necessary and sufficient condition for federal intervention in environmental regulation. They present two models to show that interstate spillovers are neither necessary nor sufficient for federal intervention. The first model considers two states that choose environmental policies strategically when factors of production are mobile. In this case, the states are interrelated through the migration of labour, rather than through trade or spillovers. The mobile factor is assumed to have no say in the policy choice of the state, and it does not contribute to the maintenance of environmental quality. In the non-cooperative Nash equilibrium, states maximize the utility of the immobile factor subject to a budget constraint. They find that, under these conditions, cooperation between the states is likely, as it will result in welfare gains to the immobile factors on both sides of the border.

However, coordination in this case amounts to collusion between the immobile-resource owners of both states to extract surplus from the mobile resources. Federal intervention may be necessary, even in the absence of transboundary pollution, to protect the interests and welfare of the mobile-resource owners. This notwithstanding, it is also shown that federal uniform standards will result in welfare losses for at least one of the immobile factors as compared to the unconstrained treaty. Furthermore, a non-cooperative equilibrium with uniform standards is shown to be possible only if the two states are identical, leading to the conclusion that if the federal government wants uniform standards across states, it must allow states to cooperate in a treaty. The implicit assumption throughout is that the federal government has full and perfect information regarding state preferences and environmental damages. This contrasts with the conclusions of Ulph where, in the case where countries within a confederation were linked through trade rather than factor migration, some degree of policy harmonization resulted in Pareto-improvements over the non-cooperative solution when the (con)federal authority lacks full and perfect information and damages differ across states.

In the second part of the chapter by Shapiro and Petchey, a model is presented in which two states decide initially on whether to form a treaty with an externality causing neighbour. The terms of the agreement are assumed to be such that if a treaty is signed, both states will abide by it during the first year, and will decide whether to continue to abide by it in the second. It is assumed that the two states share a common airshed and that both contribute to air pollution as a byproduct of their respective production processes. It is further assumed that states cannot perfectly observe the decisions of their partner, but can obtain estimates of the quantities of pollution they generate (given that total pollution in the air basin must be equal to the sum of pollution generated by both states plus or minus a random variable). The moral-hazard problem arises again in this context, due to incomplete and (potentially) asymmetric information resulting from imperfect monitoring.

Shapiro and Petchey find a set (or cluster) of conditions which, if met, would imply that interstate cooperation is possible and can guarantee efficient policies without the need for federal intervention. These conditions are: (1) that states have sufficient trust in one another's morality; (2) that their estimates of their partner's policies reveal perfect information or that there is no uncertainty (i.e., that states are fully informed about the policy choices of their treaty partners); or (3) that the benefits of cooperation are sufficiently high relative to the rewards of defection. These conditions are hard to find in real situations, but the point is nevertheless made: the existence of interstate externalities is not sufficient justification for federal intervention in environmental regulation. Yet, even if the three conditions are met, there may be a role for the federal government to play. If the states decide to cooperate in a treaty but there is uncertainty about the policy followed by each participant, and if the federal government has superior monitoring capabilities, it may pursue a policy of publicly disclosing its findings to reduce or eliminate that uncertainty. Notice, however, that this is different from federal participation in choice of environmental policies.

When the political units are large enough to fully internalize the costs and benefits of their environmental choices, there is little dispute that independent local policy-making is the way to go. However, transboundary spillovers in this context present a basic problem. Environmental events (e.g., generation of pollution, abatement activities) and the design of environmental policy in one region will have effects on other areas, because political boundaries need not coincide with the spatial dimension of different environmental events. On economic efficiency grounds, there seems to be a need for regionally differentiated policies. The assimilative capacities of different regions may vary, and the differences in population size and density across regions imply that the environmental damages and benefits of economic activity accrue differently to different areas. State and local governments have the advantage of being better suited to identify the preferences of the population through the local political process. However, when the environmental problems transcend the boundaries of the political sub-units of a (con)federation, state and local governments do not fully internalize the costs of those environmental problems and thus lack proper incentives to correct the externality. In the Coasean tradition, one can argue that in a decentralized system, these inefficiencies can be overcome by voluntary cooperation among states. Coordination will, however, remain relatively inefficient in the presence of private information so that externalities have to be large before agreements become sufficiently valuable to overcome transaction costs (Klibanoff and Morduch 1995). The presence of transfrontier pollution combined with equity considerations (such as the demand for similar living conditions among member states), suggests the need for federal participation in setting environmental policy goals, and perhaps for some level of uniformity of environmental policies in a (con)federation. It is this perceived conflict between environmental policy goals when different levels of government participate in the policy-making process that the contributing authors address in this volume. The seemingly contradictory[3] results of Conrad and of Shapiro and Petchey reflect the complexity of the issues at hand.

The matter of transboundary externalities has a loose parallel in the potential for preferences to cross boundaries, in particular, for unique environmental assets. Different states or regions within a federation may be interrelated in the sense that the quality of certain environmental amenities present in one state may be incorporated into the welfare function of other states. This is certainly the case with unique natural resources, which can be thought of as immobile assets owned by the entire population of the federation, rather than by the state in which they are physically contained. The inhabitants of the rest of the federation (and elsewhere) may place an existence value on those assets, and to the extent that they do, coordination between member states and/or the formulation of policy at a higher level of government may be called for, even when the amenity is entirely contained within the jurisdiction of a specific member state.

Gregory Amacher and Richard Brazee (Chapter 7) explore the governance implications of transboundary preferences. They provide a model that is used to investigate policy design when various governments (at the same or different levels) coordinate or compete, taking into account specific characteristics of natural resource markets. In particular, they assume that the higher-level government owns and manages the public resource, which can be developed or conserved (partial conservation is an option), whereas the lower-level government collects revenues by taxing productive activities of firms that fall within their jurisdiction and which use the public capital as an input. The different governments face different constituencies, and thus have different incentives. The federal government faces a national audience that values 'existence' benefits (of the *in situ* resource stock), whereas states face both local consumers that value 'existence' and firms that use the public capital as an input in their productive process.

The results of Amacher and Brazee have important practical implications. They find that *in situ* resource stocks are larger when governments behave strategically than when they coordinate, and this occurs because in the coordination process the preferences of the private firms are taken into account. In the non-cooperative outcome, the federal government allocates a smaller portion of the public capital stock for consumption by private firms (which are assumed to be constituents of the lower-level governments only). Consumers of *in situ* benefits are therefore worse off when governments coordinate in policy design, and this is further magnified (i.e., *in situ* stock is even lower) as the higher government becomes less concerned with lower government's revenues. With increasing pressure in the United States being placed on lower-level governments to fund their own as well as mandated projects, natural resource stock reductions can be expected.

Amacher and Brazee also find that cooperative bargaining between governments reduces the inefficiencies that arise from uncooperative policy design. But it is only when public goods have substantial local values, or one lower government has a large constituency, and revenue is shared among different levels of government that bargaining will lead to the perfect coordination outcome.

As our discussion has indicated, the coordination of environmental policy across levels of government in a (con)federation is complicated by the presence of information asymmetries, which lead to problems of adverse selection and/or moral hazard. Members of a (con)federation may have private information when the costs and benefits of environmental activities in which they engage are distributed differently across regions. This is of particular importance in shaping the relationship between the central authorities and state or local governments, and in defining the nature of the relationship between the member states of a (con)federation. Furthermore, the costs of the environmental activities in which members of a (con)federation engage may be shifted to other members and/or the (con)federal authorities.

The presence of information asymmetries gives rise to a wealth of issues, and the implications for policy-making in a (con)federal context are pervasive. Information asymmetries may also result from the existence of transboundary pollution, interregional trade, mobility or migration of factors of production, and transfrontier preferences (as in the case of unique natural assets). Many of these issues are treated in the ensuing chapters.

Can the central government play a fruitful role in the policy-coordination process? To what extent should it be involved? Given that members of a (con)federation may have differential information, under what conditions can cooperation between states (with or without the intervention of the central authority) yield welfare improvements over decentralized policy design? The results obtained in this volume support the notion that the (con)federal government can indeed play an important role. Even when its direct intervention results in no welfare improvements for the member states, it still can effect a considerable impact on the results of bilateral or multilateral negotiations between the states by disclosing information it may possess, or by creating and enforcing the legal framework to facilitate the sharing of information. This notwithstanding, the works presented in this volume also show that information asymmetries combined with the intrinsic differences (economic, technological and demographic conditions or social preferences) between regions create considerable room for direct negotiations and policy coordination between the lower-level governments. There is no contradiction here. Given the proper conditions, cooperation between member states in the design of environmental policy works. When the conditions are such that member states lack the proper incentives to negotiate and/or coordinate, under many circumstances we can expect federal intervention to result in welfare improvements for the states and the citizenry. Moreover, federal activities can create the proper environment for direct interstate negotiations and agreements. We conclude that economic integration through a (con)federation can result in better and more efficient environmental policy design.

Notes
1. For a summary of the most important rulings see Ulen, Thomas, 'The Economic Cycles of Federalism', Chapter 2 in this volume.
2. Neither directives nor regulations are entirely identical to mandates, but in principle all three represent decisions of the central government that must be carried out by the member states.

For a more detailed discussion and comparison of European versus North American institutions, see the introduction to Braden et al. (1996).

Europe also has a different set of problems. Although the unfunded character of these directives and regulations is not a major issue, the European Commission lacks the enforcement and monitoring capabilities of the US federal government, and the US Courts have stronger remedial powers than their European counterparts. See the introduction to John B. Braden, Henk Folmer, Thomas S. Ulen (eds.), *Environmental Policy with Political and Economic Integration: the European Union and the United States,* 1-16, Edward Elgar Publishing, Cheltenham, UK.

3. Recall that Conrad (Chapter 5 in this volume) finds that when the spillover is asymmetric, agreements between states or countries can be effectively prevented by one of them, perhaps requiring the participation of a higher authority, such as the (con)federal government. Shapiro and Petchey (Chapter 6 in this volume), in the second part of their chapter, find conditions under which interstate cooperation is possible and will result in efficient policies and welfare improvements without federal intervention.

References

Braden, J.B., Folmer, H. and Ulen, T.S. (eds.) (1996), *Environmental Policy with Political and Economic Integration: The European Union and the United States*, Aldershot: Edward Elgar Publishing.

Klibanoff, P. and Morduch, J. (1995), 'Decentralization, Externalities and Efficiency', *Review of Economic Studies*, 62, 223–47.

Oates, W. (1972), *Fiscal Federalism*, New York: Harcourt Brace Jovanovich.

Segerson, K. (1996), 'Issues in the Choice of Environmental Policy Instruments', in J.B. Braden, H. Folmer and T.S. Ulen (eds), *Environmental Policy with Political and Economic Integration: The European Union and the United States*, Aldershot: Edward Elgar Publishing, pp. 149–74.

Tiebout, C.M. (1956), 'A pure theory of local expenditures', *Journal of Political Economy*, 64, 416–24.

2 The economic cycles of federalism

Thomas S. Ulen

Introduction

Federalism describes the arrangement under which a group of equally sovereign states combine to form a union in which they cede some sovereignty to a central government but retain some sovereignty, too.[1] To use an economic analogy, the formation of a federation is like the merger of independent firms. But the analogy is not precise. Some economic mergers are of limited scope and duration (e.g., for the purpose of pursuing a joint advertising campaign for a few months) while others are complete (e.g., the extinction of the independent firms and the creation of an entirely new business entity). Political mergers are usually between these extremes: the members of the federation do not disappear but retain some measure of sovereignty and the arrangement is meant to last for an indefinite (usually, long) period.[2]

Presumably, when independent countries first form a federation, they perceive the benefits of the arrangement to exceed the costs. And, presumably, they establish the particular institutions of the federation (the representation rules, jurisdictional competence, voting rules, and the like) so as to maximize the excess of benefits over costs. However, the affairs of the union and of the constituent states may change over time such that either the costs of remaining united will *temporarily* exceed the benefits or the benefits of union can only be realized under a different institutional structure. The ideally designed federal system will anticipate these periods, distinguish between those episodes that call for dissolution of the federation and those that call for restructuring, and provide sufficiently flexible institutions so as to adjust optimally to the changes.

The purpose of this chapter is to offer a tentative explanation of some of the dynamic forces facing a federation. I shall do this by elaborating an economic theory of federalism. By identifying the economic forces that create costs and benefits in a federation, I seek to suggest how real factors cause those costs and benefits to change over time and, therefore, give rise to pressures to amend (or dissolve) the federation. The central focus will be on the appropriate division of governmental responsibility between the constituent states and the federal government. And I hope also to show that as the factors that explain this appropriate division change, the assignment of governmental responsibilities ought to change. Thus, there may be periods in which the central government in the federation is weak and its duties narrowly defined and other periods in which the central government is strong and its powers wide. This suggests that, even in an ideally defined federation, the relationship between the central government and the constituent state governments cannot be immutably fixed. The appropriate division of responsibility should, instead, vary between the centre and its constituents.[3]

In the following section, an economic theory of federalism will be presented and how this theory can explain shifts in the appropriate division of authority between the central government and the states will be shown. Then, the next section will briefly review the history of federalism in the United States to show that the federal experiment has seen periodic changes in the division of responsibility between the national and state governments and that these changes can be explained using the economic theory of federalism. The concluding section summarizes the argument and shows its application to some of the issues facing the European Union.[4]

An economic theory of federalism

Law and economics has been one of the most important and productive innovations in legal scholarship of the 20th century. Yet its contributions to the issues of constitutional law, including federalism, are relatively modest. Many of the early efforts to look at federal–state relationships from an economic perspective focused on tax matters but did not take a broader view.[5]

In this section I shall develop an economic theory of federalism. First, I examine the anticipated benefits of forming a federal union as seen from the perspective of the member states. Then I look at the costs of the federation, with particular attention to the public-choice aspects of a federal system. Next I use the economic theory to explain the dynamics of federalism – i.e., how changes over time in the costs and benefits of being federated can cause changes in the appropriate assignment of governmental responsibilities as between the different layers of government. I conclude with an account of two recent proposals for restructuring federal–state relations in the United States.

The benefits of a federal structure of government

Any theory of federalism should explain two central things: first, why constituent states would willingly cede some degree of sovereignty to a superior government and retain some independent sovereignty for themselves, and, secondly, which governmental responsibilities ought to be assigned to the central government and which to the member-state governments.[6] Presumably, when independent countries form a union, they do so because they perceive the benefits of union to exceed the costs. This section seeks to specify those benefits.[7] The anticipated costs will be examined in the next section.

Economic analysis suggests four benefits to the member states from forming a federal union:

1. minimizing costs and maximizing benefits that cross jurisdictional borders;
2. realizing economies of scale in the provision of governmental services;
3. minimizing the monopolistic distortions of government; and
4. implementing optimal redistributive policies.

The first economic factor that might lead independent states to consolidate is cross-jurisdictional costs or benefits. For example, suppose that production in Country A generates pollution that imposes uncompensated costs on those in Country B.[8] Clearly the polluters are beyond the reach of the regulators in Country B, and, from the point of view of the citizens in Country B, there will be too much pollution by those in Country A.

Alternatively, suppose that employment opportunities are slim in Country B but good in Country A and that there is labour mobility between the two countries. If there is a publicly funded job-training programme in Country B, the beneficiaries of that programme would include the employers and citizens in Country A. The taxpayers of Country B would be paying more than they need to do for job-training, while the taxpayers and employers in Country A would be paying less. Following the usual economic logic, the governments of both countries would have incentives not to provide the appropriate amount of job-training.

In both examples, Countries A and B can reduce the inefficiencies by somehow *internalizing* these externalities. One method of doing so would be through a Coasean bargain. Thus, in the pollution example, Country B could pay Country A's polluters not to pollute, and, in the job-training example, employers in Country A could pay the government in Country B to provide training programmes. To pursue the economic analogy introduced earlier, the countries could enter into a contractual arrangement with respect to, say, pollution or job-training programmes. This contract would be a limited merger for a specific activity and, probably, for a limited duration. Indeed, there are many such limited intergovernmental contracts (regional compacts in the United States with regard to lotteries and hazardous-waste disposal are examples, as are the early compacts of the European Steel and Coal Community).

While these bargaining solutions to the cross-jurisdictional externality problem are possible, often they are not practicable. The costs of negotiating and enforcing such bargains may be so high as to make them impossible. Moreover, intergovernmental contracts do not amount to federal unions. What, then, is the connection between cross-jurisdictional externality problems and the formation of a federation? One possibility is that the externality generating activities are so pervasive (because of, for instance, geography and custom) in both directions that it would be simpler for the countries to consolidate than to have a series of contractual arrangements dealing with each external cost or benefit. Thus, we might tentatively conclude that where cross-jurisdictional externality problems are numerous, the consolidation of the two governments may be the optimal means of resolving the inefficiencies. A corollary of this conclusion would be that intergovernmental cooperation through quasi-contracts would be an optimal means of dealing with limited cross-jurisdictional externalities.

Thus far, I have been focusing on the *formation* of a federal union. But we may invoke these same considerations about cross-jurisdictional externalities to explain how governmental responsibilities ought to be assigned once a federal union has been established. Thus, if the costs and benefits of an action, whether public or private, stray across jurisdictional lines, then the highest level of government that can fully internalize the costs and benefits of the action ought to take responsibility. Only then will a governmental authority have the appropriate incentives to regulate the externality generating activity.[9]

As a final example of this point, consider the regulation of interstate commerce. The temptations of state governments to favour their own citizens over foreign interests are strong so that state governments tend to confer benefits on their own citizens and to impose costs on citizens of other states. To internalize these costs and benefits to a trading area, responsibility for interstate commerce should lie with the national government and not with lower-level governments.[10]

A second economic factor that might lead independent states to consolidate is economies of scale in the provision of governmental services. Suppose that there is some governmental function – say, tax collection – for which there are economies of scale, in the sense that the greater the number of taxpayers, the lower the average cost of collecting taxes. If these economies would be realized for a population that is greater than that of any one country, then it may make sense for the function to be performed by a consolidated government of the independent countries. As was the case with cross-jurisdictional externalities, the countries do not necessarily have to form a federal union in order to realize these economies of scale. Rather, they could maintain their independence and agree to form a joint taxation authority.[11]

As was the case with cross-jurisdictional externalities, we need to distinguish between a situation in which independent states realize economies of scale in the provision of governmental services through a series of intergovernmental agreements from one in which they can do so only through consolidation in a federation. And as before, the distinction must lie in the fact that when the number of governmental services for which economies of scale are large, consolidation is superior to mere intergovernmental cooperation. It may also be posited that intergovernmental cooperation through quasi-contracts would be the superior means of dealing with economies of scale in governmental services when there are only a few such services for which the average cost of provision continually falls.

As before, it is necessary to distinguish between the formation of a federation and the assignment of responsibilities once the federation has been created on other grounds. Once a federation is in place, efficiency argues for assigning particular governmental responsibilities to that level of government where it can be most efficiently performed – whether the member state or the federal government. When the members of a federation negotiate the assignment of a governmental responsibility, they will have an incentive to take economies of scale (as well as other factors) into account.

A third economic factor to consider in forming a federation is the minimization of monopolistic distortions from governing. Every government has monopolistic elements, and one of the economically interesting aspects of a federal system is that it minimizes the monopolistic distortions attributable to the government. Federalism does this by replacing a single government with multiple governments – i.e., by introducing competition among governing units.[12] How does this consideration help to explain the formation of a federation? Perhaps independent states recognize the distortions of monopolistic government and the benefits of competition and affirmatively choose a federation so as to minimize the distortions and maximize the benefits. Additionally, once a federal structure is in place, this economic factor can help to determine to which level of government certain governmental responsibilities should be assigned. For instance, if the social benefits of government can be just as efficiently secured from placing a governmental responsibility at any level of the federal system, then that responsibility should be assigned to the level at which the monopolistic distortions will be minimized. Generally speaking, and again subject to the assumption that the governmental service can be equally efficiently supplied by any level, the monopoly distortions at the federal level are worse than those at the member-state level. If a state abuses its monopoly position – by, say, imposing a confiscatory tax – some of those adversely affected can migrate to other states with less burdensome taxes. (And, of course, the knowledge that citizens may leave in response to bad policy will serve to ameliorate the monopolistic impulses of local governments.) By contrast, this corrective migration is not nearly as likely in response to a bad policy at the federal level. People may be willing to move from Illinois to Wyoming to avoid what they consider to be the depredations of the Illinois government, but it is unlikely that they would be willing to move to another country in response to a similarly burdensome policy from Washington, DC.

There is also a positive aspect to placing authority at the member-state level. It is not just that competition among the states (combined with free migration) will minimize the possibilities of monopoly distortion. In addition, there are all the positive benefits of competition. In the United States, the states constitute 50 different experiments designed to attract taxpayers and jobs.[13] As they frame policies to accomplish that attraction, the states are promoting national economic growth and expansion. They are also searching for the most efficient solutions to common problems, such as tort reform, welfare reform and health care reform.[14]

The final economic consideration in the formation of a federation and in the efficient division of authority between member states and the federal government is that of optimal redistributive policies. As we saw above, states (even those not affiliated in a federation) compete among themselves to attract taxpayers and jobs. Thus, the immigration of investment and jobs is desirable. However, the immigration of welfare recipients from other states is a drain on the community's resources.[15] Generous welfare benefits paid for by high taxes will drive out the wealthy and bring in the poor. Thus, 'the level of redistribution in a decentralized system is likely to be lower even if there is virtually unanimous agreement among the citizens that higher levels would be desirable'(Oates 1972, p. 7). For that reason, there is an economic justification for independent states who care deeply about redistribution and who otherwise compete for resources to affiliate in a federation. Moreover, once the federation is established, there is an economic reason for giving responsibility for redistributive policies to the federal government, rather than leaving them to the member-state governments.[16]

The costs of a federation

Assume that a group of independent states perceive that the benefits of federation are substantial. What costs can they anticipate bearing? These costs may be classified as either fixed or variable. The fixed costs are those of negotiating and drafting the original agreement to form a federal union. While these may be considerable, they are, nonetheless, fixed costs and, therefore, should not affect the ongoing operations of the federal system. The variable costs are those that depend on the scope of the federation's activities, and of these costs, the largest element is that of coordinating the relations between the sovereign member states and the federal government.

There are several reasons for believing these costs to be particularly important. First, in the founding document of the federation the division of authority between the federal government and those of the member states will probably not be exact but rather specified according to general rules. There will be uncertainty about what is and is not allowed to the various levels of government, and this uncertainty will cause mistakes by both levels of government. In some instances a government will over-reach its authority, and in others it will refrain from exercising authority when it might legitimately do so. Either mistake will impose costs on the federation. Secondly, there must be some ongoing means of resolving these disputes about legitimate authority. For example, in the United States the Supreme Court serves as the ultimate arbiter of federal–state disputes; in other federal systems, the political process may serve this role.[17] The costs of this dispute resolution can be large.

These considerations apply even to an ideal federal system, one in which the member states have devised an ideal arrangement for realizing their joint goals and continue to act in good faith. In a federation that is less than ideal, the variable costs of resolving problems are heightened.

Consider two examples. First, suppose that political constituencies are so powerful at the member-state level that they distort policies away from socially desirable goals and toward their own ends. Those political interest groups may be less powerful at the federal level, and, therefore, it may be less distorting to assign governmental responsibility at the federal level, even though other considerations would seem to argue for assignment to the member-state governments.[18] Secondly, interstate competition may not always be desirable. There may be instances in which competition among the constituent states leads not to experimentation that produces the best outcome but rather to a 'race to the bottom'. That is, there might be so much competition among the member states that the result is a minimal set of governmental activities that is less than socially optimal. Central rules precluding interstate competition may prevent this race to the bottom. It is difficult to distinguish *ex ante* those circumstances in which interstate competition is good from those in which it is bad. Nonetheless, this difficulty is an example of the practical difficulties that may beset even a reasonably well-crafted federation.

A public-choice theory of federal–state relations

In the previous section I suggested that the power of political constituencies at the member-state level may argue for assignment of governmental responsibility to the federal level. This consideration raises the more general issue of the impact of politics on the optimal design of a federation. To see the impact of this consideration on the issues of federalism, we must turn to public-choice theory. That theory explains political behaviour (of constituents, bureaucrats and politicians) using the same rational-choice models that economists use to model economic behaviour. Public-choice theory sees statutes, for example, as the result of forces of supply and demand in the political marketplace. Some interest groups demand favourable legislation, and some politicians supply it.[19]

How might the insights of public-choice theory apply to the issues of the design of a federation? The literature could be read to suggest that, taking the case of the United States, the federal government would almost always exert its power, under the Supremacy Clause,[20] to preempt local law (either by regulating or failing to regulate) so as to receive the political and other benefits of providing services for constituents. This prediction notwithstanding, in the United States there *is* a division of responsibility between the federal and state governments in which the federal government willingly abstains from regulation, leaving the field to those state governments, when, in fact, the federal government *could* exert its authority. The actual division of regulatory responsibility is not one that obeys the predictions of the economic theory of federalism outlined above. Rather, in the United States at least, the federal government sometimes takes a strong interest in regulating things that seem purely local. For example, the federal government issues charters to banks that are not going to do business across state lines. At other times, the federal government leaves regulatory authority to the states in areas in which one might say that there was a strong national interest. An example is Delaware's preeminence in United States corporate law. Because the economic theory of federalism cannot easily explain these phenomena, we need an alternative theory.

To begin, consider that the interest groups who demand regulation prefer, in general, federal regulation to state regulation. This is because it is generally cheaper to obtain passage of one federal bill rather than 50 separate ones. In addition, even if a regulatory bill is passed at the state level, support must still be obtained from the federal level to forbear from regulating. In contrast, a federal regulation clearly preempts the field. A third reason that demanders of regulation prefer the federal solution is that federal law is generally considered to be of higher quality than state law.[21] Lastly, federal law is more difficult to avoid than is state law (as was seen in a previous section). Thus, parties adversely affected by regulation may escape state regulations but cannot escape federal law. Why should the *demanders* of regulation prefer that state of affairs? Sometimes the purpose of regulation is to 'raise rivals' costs' by requiring them to provide a higher quality output or to do so in a more expensive fashion than they otherwise would. If that tactic is successful, the rivals may be forced from the market. For all these reasons, interest groups generally prefer federal to state regulation.

Nonetheless, federal regulators sometimes defer to state regulators. Why? Clearly the answer must be that the preemptive suppliers of regulation (the Congress) gain more from deference than from satisfying the demands of the political interest groups. In all cases it must also be true that those who demand regulation prefer that regulation be done at the state level. Macey (1990) identifies three sets of conditions under which federal deference to the states is likely to occur:

1. where 'interest groups have made an expropriable investment in a particular set of local regulations' and the value of that investment would be dissipated by federal regulation (pp. 274–5);
2. where 'the political-support-maximizing solution for a particular regulatory issue differs markedly from jurisdiction to jurisdiction' (p. 275); and
3. when Congress can escape subsequent adverse political reaction by delegating a controversial set of decisions to the states (p. 268).[22]

As an example of this theory,[23] consider the provision of corporate law by state legislatures. There are two different views about the efficiency of federal versus state regulation of corporations. Those in favour of state regulation argue that competition among the states produces efficient corporate law that maximizes the value of firms and of shareholder wealth.[24] Those in favour of a federal law (which would, in the United States system, probably preempt state law) argue that competition among the states for corporate-chartering revenues will lead to a 'race to the bottom' – i.e., to a set of minimally acceptable corporate laws that will tend to transfer wealth from shareholders to managers.[25]

In point of fact, the competition among the states for corporate charters is over. Delaware is the winner. More than 40 per cent of the companies listed on the New York Stock Exchange are chartered in Delaware. Of those firms who decide to reincorporate for whatever reason, 82 per cent of them do so in Delaware. Why? It is not the case that Delaware's corporate code is vastly superior to or more lenient than those of other states. In fact, it is indistinguishable from those of many other states. Delaware's predominance in corporate law is due to another, unexpected, factor – its small size. Delaware obtains about 16 per cent of its state revenues from franchise taxes on corporate chartering. This is such a high percentage of Delaware's budget that it constitutes a credible bond of the state's promise not to alter its corporate law precipitously (Romano 1985). The bar in Delaware is highly specialized with particular competence in corporate law, and the judiciary in the state is also well acquainted with corporate law. There will be no or few surprises in litigation over corporate-law matters in that state.[26]

Interest groups in the state of Delaware – the bar, Delaware corporations, investment bankers, the state and others – have a very strong stake in maintaining this regulatory regime as it is. In Macey's terms, they do not want the value of 'their specific capital investments ... destroyed if the federal government enacted a pervasive system of federal corporate law that preempted the field' (Macey 1990, p. 279).

Contrast this explanation for the division of federal and state responsibilities with that of the economic theory of previous sections. That theory of federalism suggests that state regulation would dominate where there are no externalities. But, as seen earlier, state regulation – at least in the case of corporate-chartering laws – sometimes predominates even where there are externalities. 'The [economic theory of federalism mistakenly] assumes that the full costs and benefits of a particular legal regime to the public is what motivates the local decisionmaker, while the [public-choice] model ... focuses on the fact that interest groups have a strong incentive to press for local solutions to their regulatory problems' (Macey 1990, p. 264).

The economic dynamics of federalism

All the pieces are now in place to speculate on how *real forces* might cause changes in a federation constructed according to the principles of the previous sections. By 'real forces' I mean such things as technological change; changes in the average size of economic enterprises; changes from an agricultural to a manufacturing to a service economy; changes in production techniques that generate, for the first time, toxic and hazardous wastes and that make air and water pollution more harmful; and so on. I seek to stress the impact of these forces in causing alterations in federalism in contrast to alterations attributable to ideological forces. I would suggest that the dominant view of changes in federalism is that alterations in the strength of central government versus member-state governments in a federation are due to political and ideological factors. Thus, to take an example from the United States, most observers would ascribe the apparent current trend toward a weaker federal government and stronger state governments[27] to a change in the prevailing ideology of voters: to simplify, voters are more conservative than in the recent past and generally favour a relatively smaller federal government and relatively stronger state and local governments. By contrast, I would assert that, if a trend toward weaker central government exists, that trend is a response to underlying real factors that alter the costs and benefits of assigning governmental responsibilities in the federation. In the last subsection of this part and again in the next section there is a survey of the broad sweep of changes in federal–state relations in the United States in an attempt to attribute these changes to real forces. In this section I merely want to identify those forces that, I assert, *really* cause changes in the efficient structure of a federation.

The efficient structure of a federation should change when the benefits and costs of federal affiliation change in response to real forces. Some examples can be sketched. Consider, first, external costs and benefits. Recall that the economic theory suggested that cross-jurisdictional external costs and benefits would create an incentive for independent states to affiliate and that the more pervasive those externalities were, the stronger the case for a more complete affiliation. Moreover, in an existing federal system, member-state governments should handle local externalities (including public goods), while the central government should handle cross-jurisdictional externalities. Suppose that up to a certain time pollution (an external cost) is local so that member-state governments can optimally regulate the externality generators. There would be no central regulation of pollution. But now suppose that changes in the technology of production cause new forms of pollution to appear that stray across state borders or that changes in the scale of production generate much more conventional pollution, which, in these increased amounts, drifts across state borders. Under these changed circumstances, the appropriate locus of regulation for the pollution has passed from the member states to the federal government. One can imagine these circumstances reversing themselves, too. A technological change could so reduce the amount of pollution from stationary sources that pollution effectively becomes, once again, a local rather than a cross-jurisdictional problem. In keeping with the economic theory of federalism, the locus of regulation would then devolve from the federal back to the member-state governments. Finally, the population's taste for pollution might change in such a way as to create a demand for stricter regulation of polluters – even those who are not polluting across state borders but are harming something in another state that people have come to value, such as a beautiful natural resource.[28]

As another example, consider the effect of changes in the efficient scale of production of governmental services. These changes might occur because of either a change in the technology of producing the services or a change in population. For instance, the rapid drop in the prices of large-scale computing may so lower the average cost of information gathering as to move the appropriate locus of some governmental function from the member state to the federal level.[29]

Finally, what about the political considerations raised in the previous section? Might they change so as to play a role in restructuring a federation? Recall from the previous section that the public-choice theory of federalism predicted a different division of governmental responsibility between member-state governments and the federal government than the economic theory did. Specifically, the public-choice theory predicted that the starting point in making the division might be that the federal government would regulate everything; deviations from that prediction would be due to political considerations of constituent interest groups and politicians. If the logic of public-choice theory with respect to federalism is followed, then changes in the assignment of governmental responsibility would occur only when there are changes in the strength and breadth of political interest groups. If interest groups are primarily local – i.e., they do not cross jurisdictional lines – then they will be content with local regulation. However, if the concerns of interest groups cross jurisdictional borders, then they will prefer federal regulation. Thus, changes in the strength of member-state and federal government will result from changes in the strength and breadth of political interest groups.

Two proposals for reforming federal–state relations
Two recent studies by public-policy scholars lend support to the economic theories of federalism outlined in the previous sections. Both studies also make recommendations about restructuring the federal system that are in line with the economic theory.

The first study, by Peterson (1995), examines how the states and the federal government have specialized in the provision of services in the federal system. He asserts that states and localities generally should control physical and social infrastructure – roads, education, mass transit systems, public parks, police and fire services and sanitation systems. He calls these *developmental* policies. By contrast, the federal government should be in charge of distributional matters, transferring resources from those who have to those who have not. He calls these policies *redistributive*.[30]

Against this rough normative theory of governmental responsibility in a federation, Peterson evaluates recent trends in the United States. He finds that since 1962 state and local spending on developmental matters has been double what it has been at the federal level. The total amount spent on development by all levels of government, as a percentage of Gross Domestic Product, has increased over the last 30 years, but the relative shares of the various segments of government have been constant. By contrast, the division of redistributive expenditures has changed dramatically. State and local expenditures on those in need have steadily declined, while federal-government redistributive expenditures have more than doubled as a percentage of GDP: from 4.9 per cent in 1962 to 10.3 per cent in 1990.

Peterson holds that these trends were not the result of ideological differences but rather were the result of non-political, perhaps economic, forces. He discounts ideology as a causal influence because, during the period that these trends developed, Democrats controlled the state legislatures, the governorships and the national legislature. Because Democrats generally prefer redistributive policies, their control of state government should have led them, all other things being equal, to *increase* state expenditures on redistribution. That this did not occur suggests that other factors determined the trends in the division of redistributive authority between states and the federal government over the last 30 years.

Why are state and local governments particularly efficient at providing developmental infrastructure? For all the reasons elaborated in the economic theory of federalism. States and localities are sensitive to local business interests and to their residents. If voters and businesses like local policies, they will stay or in-migrate. If they do not, they will go elsewhere. Thus, if a state or local government finds an attractive policy innovation, other state and local governments will copy, and the innovation will spread. If they implement a new policy that does not work, other governments will *not* follow. This does not necessarily mean that policies will be uniform across all members of a federation. Because citizen tastes and preferences differ from region to region, state and local governments can be sensitive to these differences and accommodate their policies to them.

Peterson sees the national government as the natural provider of redistributive policies (just as the economic theory did). Therefore, he thinks that sending welfare back to the states (as has recently been proposed by the new Republican Congressional leadership) is a very serious mistake. The evidence supports Peterson's and the economic theory's prediction that member-state governments will under-provide redistributive policies. State 'Aid to Families with Dependent Children' (AFDC, the principal US welfare programme) benefits are jointly funded by the national and state governments. AFDC was set up in 1937, and for its first 33 years federal aid was relatively generous and federal controls were relatively strong. As a result, states raised the real value of the benefits continuously. The mean benefit paid to a family (in real 1993 dollars) in the average state was $287 in 1940, $431 in 1950, $520 in 1960, and $608 in 1970. Then in 1970 the federal government allowed the states much more freedom to set AFDC benefit levels and they became relatively less generous. From 1970 on, welfare benefits have declined. They fell in real terms to $497 in 1975, $437 in 1980, $409 in 1985, $379 in 1990, and to $349 in 1993.

State-level welfare reform has generally been nothing more than the reduction of benefits. The federal government in the 1988 Family Support Act gave the states the opportunity to experiment with AFDC. Not surprisingly, the first three proposals to come to the Department of Health and Human Services all proposed new restrictions on welfare benefits. For example, Wisconsin and New Jersey asked, among other things, to withhold the increase in benefits that normally comes with the birth of an additional child. California wanted an immediate 25 per cent reduction in benefits for all welfare recipients and a second reduction for all families remaining on welfare after six months, and a restriction that limited the level of benefits to newcomers to the level in the state from which they came. In summer 1994, Wisconsin said that 20 per cent of its new welfare recipients were newcomers to the state, mostly from Illinois, a state with lower welfare benefits. They asked the federal government for permission to restrict payments to these newcomers for their first six months to the level of benefits they would have received in their previous state of residence.[31]

Peterson sees the natural division of responsibility in the federal system to be one in which the states take on developmental efforts and the federal government takes on redistributive policies. He suggests that US federalism needs to be restructured so as to send developmental programmes back to the states from the national government while transferring redistributive policies back to the federal government from the states. This assignment of governmental responsibility as between the national and state governments would certainly be in keeping with the efficiency suggestions of the economic theory of federalism.

Rivlin (1992) has proposed a restructuring of the federal–state division of responsibilities. The central reform she proposes is that the 'states should take primary responsibility for a productivity agenda involving education, work force skills, and public infrastructure, while the federal government should retreat from these areas [and that] a new system of common shared taxes ... should be adopted to help put state financing on a more secure and less unequal footing' (Rivlin 1992, p. 8). She gives four reasons for restructuring federalism:

1. increasing global interdependence, which requires the United States economy to become more productive in order to thrive;

2. the need for less top–down reform (i.e., reform dictated from the federal government) and more bottom–up reform (i.e., reform that results from a multitude of experiments at the state level);
3. the need for more tax revenue, which the states are reluctant to provide but which the federal government can provide; and
4. general dissatisfaction with government, in large part because the federal government seems so distant.

Rivlin proposes that the restructuring should have the states taking charge of the public investment needed to raise productivity and incomes. It has already been demonstrated that an argument in favour of devolution is that the states can serve as experimental laboratories for different policies.[32] In the recent past, a frequent argument against devolution was that the states did not have the abilities or the revenues to take on new governmental duties, even if economic considerations otherwise argued for devolution. Rivlin says that this argument against a shift in federal responsibilities is no longer true. In the past the federal government was, relatively speaking, far more competent than state governments. Governors had very short terms and few powers. Legislatures met for only a few weeks every other year. Members served part-time and had almost no staff. Rural areas dominated these state legislatures, in some cases preventing reapportionment. For instance, Tennessee had no reapportionment between 1901 and 1962; by the early 1960s eight other states had not redistricted in 50 years. Then, partly under the compulsion of Supreme Court decisions, the states undertook serious legislative reform in the 1960s.[33] Governors were typically given more power. In 1955 only 29 governors had four-year terms. By 1988 there were 47 who had such terms. During that same time period the number of states that barred a second term for their governor dropped from 17 to 3. The general trend in the 1960s and 1970s was toward more professional and better-qualified governors. Similarly, the quality of state legislators improved. As the workload on state legislatures increased, the part-time state legislator gave way to the full-time legislator with a small but professional staff.

States have also found new sources of revenue. The traditional sources of state- and local-governmental revenues have always been property and sales taxes. Whatever other arguments could be made against the property tax, it was not very flexible, so that as long as that tax was the main source of revenue, states could not increase their revenues to take on new responsibilities. But sales taxes now bring in more revenue to the states than property taxes, and income taxes are an increasing source of revenue. Between 1960 and 1990 property taxes dropped from 37.7 per cent to 21.8 per cent of state- and local-government revenue. Individual income taxes rose from 5.7 per cent to 14.8 per cent of state revenues, and fees and charges grew from 16.8 per cent to 28.9 per cent (Advisory Commission on Intergovernmental Relations 1991, p. 132). As a result, state and local revenues, exclusive of federal grants, have gone up from 7.6 per cent of GDP in 1960 to 10.3 per cent in 1990 (*Budget of the US Government* 1991, table 15.1).

There have been two prior, recent efforts to restructure the division of responsibilities between state and federal governments. In the early 1970s Nixon's New Federalism envisioned a stronger federal role in income maintenance and health care but a weaker federal role in almost every other governmental duty. Under that plan, there would have been fewer categorical grants from the federal government to the states, and the federal government would have given that financial aid to the states with fewer restrictions.[34] But the New Federalism failed. The beneficiaries of the existing categorical programmes fiercely resisted the proposal. In the end only two block grants were enacted – the Comprehensive Employment and Training Act of 1973 and the community development block grant.

The second recent effort to restructure the federal relationship was President Reagan's 'swap proposal' in the mid-1980s. The federal government would have taken over some responsibilities from the states if the states would have taken over some from the federal government. For example, the federal government would have taken over the full costs of the Medicaid programme in exchange for devolution of AFDC and the food-stamp programmes to the states. Most governors stoutly resisted the proposal (although, in retrospect, most of their states would have been better off financially if they had accepted). In addition, the proposal called for the devolution of 125 separate categorical grants to the states in exchange for the phasing-out of some federal taxes (alcohol, tobacco, telephone, part of the federal gasoline tax and the windfall profits tax on oil and gas sales). Revenues from those taxes would have been put in a federal trust fund for the use of the states between the time of the implementation of the proposal and the elimination of the taxes in 1991. States would thereafter have had to raise their own taxes to pay for the programmes or terminate them. The states were not at all enthusiastic about the proposal, and it died.

Rivlin suggests that if a restructuring leads to many programmes being sent back to the states, it is unlikely that the states will raise taxes in order to pay for those programmes. States are reluctant to impose new taxes for two reasons. First, they have unequal resources. Some may be wealthy and willing to raise taxes; others may be poor and unwilling to raise taxes. Secondly, interstate competition generally precludes the states from imposing new taxes unless everyone does.[35] Because of this reluctance on the part of states to raise taxes, Rivlin proposes common shared taxes between federal and state governments. No doubt she is correct that this supra-state source of revenue will be necessary in order to restructure the federal–state relationship. However, whatever economic sense there may be to restructuring federalism, its political prospects are not bright.

The dynamics of federalism in the United States

Woodrow Wilson said in 1911 that there was no single, immutable answer to the appropriate balance of authority between the federal and state governments. The balance, he wrote, changes according to the social and economic conditions, the electorate's perceptions of the problems that most need addressing, and the prevailing political values (Wilson 1911). This section traces the history of federal relations in the United States Supreme Court to illustrate Wilson's contention.[36] The account of Supreme Court federalism jurisprudence here is sparse and stylized, but I submit that it illustrates that the broad changes in federal–state relations are attributable to the real forces identified earlier.

The antebellum period[37]

In the antebellum period there were five background issues against which the Supreme Court sought to determine, by reference to the Constitution, the appropriate division of authority between the national and state governments. The first of these was the common understanding that the American Revolution had been fought to free the colonists from an unfair and arbitrary power exercised from afar. This understanding made the revolutionary generation extremely sceptical of consolidated power. A second background issue was an ambiguity left over from the ratification debates. Everyone agreed that the national government was to be one of limited powers, that the Constitution enumerated these powers and that the ratification process through the states gave these powers to the federal government. There were, however, ambiguities. How broad were these enumerated powers to be? What was the extent of 'sovereignty' in the states as constituent units within the larger system? To what extent would this 'sovereignty' ensure elements of state jurisdiction against any encroachments by the central government? James Madison recognized that the result of the Constitutional Convention's work in 1787 was 'a novelty and a compound' because it perpetuated the states as political units but established a federal authority that acted directly on the people rather than (as in the Confederation period) only upon the states. But Madison said that he could not perceive how to mark out an 'inviolable sovereignty' for the states. Thus, there was a legacy of ambiguity.[38] The third issue was that of secession from the Union. Could the states resume an independent existence or were they bound to the Union forever? The fourth issue was that the division of responsibility between the national and state governments needed to be specified. The states were obviously equipped to do much of the work of government. Thus, the scope of governmental work that was to be reserved to the national government was relatively small. Finally, there was the issue of slavery. The Constitution avoided the subject directly, with three exceptions: the decision to count slaves as three-fifths of a person for the purposes of determining population for representation in the House of Representatives;[39] the decision to allow Congress to terminate the importation of slaves 20 years after the end of the Constitutional Convention;[40] and the fugitive slave clause.[41]

Scholars frequently characterize the antebellum period as one of 'judicial nationalism', in which the Supreme Court, led by Chief Justice John Marshall, established the authority of the federal government. They did this by broadly construing the enumerated powers granted to the national government in the Constitution.[42] This trend toward a stronger national government notwithstanding, the Court, at times during the antebellum period, also restrained the federal government. For example, in *United States* v. *Hudson and Goodwin* (7 Cranch (11 US) 32 (1812)),[43] the Court said that the federal judiciary did not have a common-law jurisdiction over crimes. Its jurisdiction in the criminal area was restricted to explicit statutory authority. The Court also adopted rulings that made clear that the state courts had the authority to construe their own state constitutions and statutes and to perpetuate many rules of common law.

Another important legacy of this period was what has come to be called 'dual federalism' or 'dual sovereignty'. Under that theory, the Constitution is a compact made by the sovereign states and the people of those states for the limited purpose of giving the new national government a range of explicitly enumerated powers; the states otherwise retained all the authority of sovereign states, had 'reserved' powers and were fully supreme within the sphere of those powers as the national government was within its own sphere of enumerated powers. Chief Justice Marshall articulated this theory forcefully in *Cohens* v. *Virginia* (6 Wheat. (19 US) 264 (1821)), where he said that 'these States ... are members of one great empire – for some purposes sovereign, for some purposes subordinate'.[44] Then, in *Gibbons* v. *Ogden* (1824), Marshall asserted national power over commerce but recognized explicit state police powers as embracing elements of authority 'not surrendered to the general government'. The Court broadened that view in *Willson* v. *Blackbird Creek Marsh Co.* (1829), where it enunciated the dormant commerce power.[45] The most important case of the period in terms of decentralizing the nation's governance was *Barron* v. *Baltimore* (1833). There the Court held that the Bill of Rights had never been intended to apply as a check upon state governments, but only upon the federal government.

In the later part of the antebellum period, the Court, under Chief Justice Roger B. Taney, sought to reduce the breadth of the national government's enumerated powers and to draw brighter lines between the appropriate realms of the national and state government. For example, the Court held in *Cooley* v. *Board of Wardens* (1852) that the Constitution did not grant an exclusive right to regulate interstate commerce to the federal government. Rather, some aspects of commerce required a uniform national rule, while others required diversity among the states. Therefore, the constitutionality of state regulation of commerce needed to be assessed on a case-by-case basis.

The Court's jurisprudence in the antebellum period saw an expansion of the national government's powers under Marshall and a retreat under Taney. These swings were the result of both a new federation's working out the practicalities of federal–state responsibilities, a profound dispute between those eager for a stronger central government and those deeply sceptical of centralized power, and a response to the economic realities of the growing nation.

Post-Civil-War federalism jurisprudence

After the Civil War the Court had to reestablish the federal relationship that had come apart in the war. At the same time, it had to wrestle with how the Constitution allowed the national and state governments to regulate the new economic forces and their social consequences of the late 19th century. In *Munn* v. *Illinois* (1877) the Court upheld a strong regulatory intervention in private decision-making on the ground that government could legitimately regulate 'business affected with a public interest'. But the Court also asserted that neither the states nor the federal government could go too far. There were limits to regulation on both levels. For example, one of the most famous holdings of this period was the Court's invalidation (under the Contract Clause) of the State of New York's regulation of the maximum hours of employment of bakery workers in *Lochner* v. *New York* (1905). The Court also restricted the scope of Congressional authority when it thought that Congress exceeded its constitutional authority. In 1879 the Court struck down an Act of Congress protecting trademarks. In *Pollock* v. *Farmers' Loan & Trust Co.* (1895) the Court declared the federal income tax unconstitutional.

The Court took a swerving path through the issues of federalism during this period. On the one hand, the Court seemed to rely upon the notion of dual federalism or dual sovereignty when it refused to extend federal procedural guarantees in the criminal justice area to the states. And in *Hammer* v. *Dagenhart* (1918) the Court overturned an Act of Congress that would have banned the products of child labour from interstate commerce. This, clearly, was an attempt to revive the notion of dual federalism and to restrict the federal government to its specifically enumerated powers. On the other hand, in 1897 the Court held that the Fourteenth Amendment incorporated the 'takings' clause of the Fifth Amendment to the states.

The New Deal revisions to federalism

The New Deal era saw a dramatic clash between the desires of the federal government to deal with an economic emergency and the limitations imposed through dual federalism. The hallmark of this period was a shift in the balance of power away from the states and toward the federal government. By the early 1940s there was very little perceptible limit on the federal government's powers relative to those of the states. Some commentators say that the government had become unitary rather than federal.

Early in the decade, the Court reiterated its dual federalism limits on the national government. In *A.L.A. Schecter Poultry Corp.* v. *US* (295 US 495 (1935)), the Court declared the National Industrial Recovery Act to be unconstitutional. In his concurring opinion in *Schecter Poultry*, Justice Cardozo said

> There is a view of causation that would obliterate the distinction of what is national and what is local in the activities of commerce. Motion at the outer rim is communicated perceptibly, though minutely, to recording instruments at the center. A society such as ours is an elastic medium which transmits all tremors throughout its territory; the only question is of their size.'[46]

The reach of the Commerce Clause, he said, was not so broad as to 'reach all enterprises and transactions which could be said to have an indirect effect upon interstate commerce'. If it did, there would be nothing beyond the reach of Congress, and then 'the authority of the State over its domestic concerns would exist only by sufferance of the federal government'.[47]

The Roosevelt administration was so frustrated by this and other decisions that the famous Court-packing controversy ensued.[48] In a series of important decisions between 1937 and 1941, the Court changed course and began to find constitutional warrant for the expansive federal programmes of the New Deal.[49] A case that is frequently taken to be the indication of the turning point is *NLRB* v. *Jones & Laughlin Steel Corp.* (301 US 1 (1937)). In determining whether or not a particular Congressional regulation was within the proper scope of the Commerce Clause, the Court held in *Jones & Laughlin Steel* that the answer would always necessarily be a matter of degree.[50]

As a final indication of how expansive the Court's Commerce Clause jurisprudence had become by the close of this period, consider *Wickard* v. *Filburn* (317 US 111 (1942)).[51] Filburn operated a small farm in Ohio, on which, in the year concerned, he grew 23 acres of wheat. He sowed winter wheat in the Fall, harvested it in July, and sold a portion of the harvest, fed part to poultry and livestock on his farm, used some of it to make flour for home consumption and saved the remainder as seed crop. The Secretary of Agriculture imposed a penalty on Filburn under the Agricultural Adjustment Act because he had planted 12 acres more than he had been allotted to plant under the Act.[52]

By 1941 the Commerce Clause no longer served as an effective limitation on congressional regulatory power, and the Tenth Amendment no longer effectively constrained the reach of the federal government.

Federalism after the New Deal

Since the New Deal, federalism has expanded in some areas and, more recently, contracted in others. Under Chief Justice Earl Warren the Court completed the incorporation of the Bill of Rights to place limits on state action so as to achieve uniform national minimum standards. This occurred most dramatically in civil rights and voting rights.

The Burger and Rehnquist Courts have reasserted, to a degree, the dual federalism views. In 1971 Justice Hugo L. Black wrote for a majority in *Younger* v. *Harris* that when a state defendant applied for relief on civil rights grounds, there must be 'a proper respect for state functions, a recognition of the fact that the entire country is made up of a Union of separate state governments' (44); and that 'the National Government will fare best if the States and their institutions are left free to perform their separate functions in their separate ways' (44). In *National League of Cities* v. *Usery* (1976) the Court for the first time in 40 years overturned an Act of Congress regulating economic relationships: it held unconstitutional a Congressional statute that applied minimum wage and maximum hours limitations to state- and local-government employees. This decision marked the beginning of an unsettled period in federalism jurisprudence.

The Supreme Court reversed the *Usery* decision ten years later in *Garcia* v. *San Antonio Metropolitan Transit Authority*.[53] Why did the Supreme Court change its mind? The reason was that the Court discovered and applied a new model of federalism in the period between *Usery* and *Garcia*. The new theory is sometimes referred to as the 'federal process' model.[54] That model holds that the Constitution protects the federal–state balance through political institutions and that, therefore, the Supreme Court does not need to become involved through judicial review in the thorny political issue of 'enforc[ing] limits on the scope of national regulatory power' (Merritt 1994, p. 1566). For instance, the United States Senate protects state interests by guaranteeing equal representation to each state. Additionally, the states control electoral qualifications for the House of Representatives (but see below) and for electors for President and Vice-President.

Applying the federal-process model, one could argue that the Court erred in *Usery*. Debate in Congress and state representation in the Senate adequately represented state interests. Because the Senate (and House, of course) passed the statute, the *ex post* objections of the states to the statute should be discounted.

This plausible argument notwithstanding, the Supreme Court then reversed the field again in *New York* v. *United States* in 1992, rejecting the federal-process model.[55] Why? Further reflection convinced the Court that federal political institutions did not serve as an adequate protection against federal infringement on state sovereignty. For example, the composition of the Senate generally protects private citizens from the less-populous states, not state governments *per se*.[56] Another problem with the federal-process model is that Congress responds to conflicting interests, not just to state interests. Congressional representatives, for instance, may perceive a conflict between their own political interests and the institutional interests of state governments. If pressed to achieve some national goal, Congress will try to do so without raising taxes by, perhaps, imposing unfunded mandates on the states. In *New York* the Supreme Court held that these and other flaws of the federal-process model were fatal. Instead the Court opted for a federal–state relationship in which the federal government may compel the states to implement federal policies if it pays for them or gives the states options of non-compliance.

Recent developments in federalism jurisprudence

Late in its 1994 term, the United States Supreme Court handed down two opinions that illustrate how alive the issue of federalism still is. The matter was most forcefully joined in *U.S.* v. *Lopez* (1995 WL 238424 (US)).[57] At issue was the constitutionality of the Gun-Free School Zones Act of 1990. In that Act Congress made it a federal offence 'for any individual knowingly to possess a firearm at a place that the individual knows, or has reasonable cause to believe, is a school zone'.[58] The defendant Lopez, a twelfth-grade student at Edison High School in San Antonio, Texas, arrived at school with a .38 calibre handgun and five bullets. The authorities, acting on an anonymous tip, arrested and charged him under Texas law with firearm possession on school premises. The following day the state dropped its charges after federal agents charged Lopez with violating the Gun-Free School Zones Act. The District Court found him guilty and sentenced him to six months' imprisonment and two years' supervised release. Lopez appealed on the ground that the Act violated Congress's power to legislate under the Commerce Clause. The Court of Appeals for the Fifth Circuit agreed and reversed the respondent's conviction.

The US Government appealed. The Government justified the Act as falling within the Commerce Clause in the following way: firearms in or near schools may lead to violent crime, and violent crime affects the national economy in three ways. First, the costs of violent crime are large and are spread across state lines, principally by insurance markets. Secondly, violent crime makes some areas of the country less attractive and therefore reduces travel across state lines. And thirdly, firearms in or near schools damage the educational environment and that will lead to a less productive labour force and, therefore, a less healthy national economy.[59]

In finding the Act to be unconstitutional for a closely divided Court, Chief Justice Rehnquist dismissed this line of reasoning. Under the government's theory, he argued that the government could regulate anything that would cause violent crime to increase, virtually without regard to its connection to interstate commerce. Thus, the government's argument recognized no limits on the Congress's commerce-power jurisdiction. Chief Justice Rehnquist said that the Court has recognized three activities that Congress may legitimately regulate under the Commerce Clause. First, it may regulate the use of the avenues of interstate commerce, such as navigable waters. Secondly, it may regulate the 'instrumentalities of interstate commerce', as when Congress regulates vehicles that might engage in interstate commerce. And thirdly, it may regulate those activities that are substantially related to interstate commerce. Chief Justice Rehnquist proposed that 'the proper test [of the appropriate reach of the Commerce Clause] requires an analysis of whether the regulated activity *substantially affects interstate commerce*' [my emphasis].'[60]

State objections to federal regulation

When the Republicans took control of the House and the Senate in November 1994, the movement to reduce the size of the federal government and to place more sovereignty in the states gained ground. The manifestations of this movement may be seen outside the Supreme Court. For instance, in 1994 four states – Colorado, Hawaii, Illinois and Missouri – passed 'sovereignty' resolutions, whose purpose was to remind the federal government that the states have their own claims on sovereignty and are not mere agents of the national government. Several other states are contemplating similar resolutions this year. There is a political movement to create something called the 'Conference of the States'. The Conference would be an ongoing convention that would propose amendments to the United States Constitution. Two such amendments that the organizers of the Conference have proposed are one that allows the states to bypass Congress and to suggest amendments of their own and another that allows the states the power to veto some federal laws by a three-fourths vote. A model resolution calling for the convening of the Conference is before all 50 state legislatures.

Among other complaints, the states object to unfunded mandates from the federal government. A United States Conference of Mayors survey recently found that ten of these mandates account for an average of 11.7 per cent of city budgets. The City of Chicago claims to spend $190 million per year complying with federal mandates (Reuben 1995).

Some states have brought actions against the federal government for imposing costs on them through these unfunded mandates.[61] For example, the State of California has filed an action against the federal government – *California* v. *United States* (94-0674K(CM)) – to recover the cost of increased services that the state must provide to illegal immigrants, who have arrived, the state alleges, because the federal government is not doing an adequate job of policing the borders. Additionally, California, Pennsylvania and Illinois originally refused to pass legislation to implement the federal Motor Vehicle Registration Act of 1993, called the 'motor voter' law.[62] Both chambers of the new Republican-dominated Congress have passed bills in 1996 to limit unfunded mandates.

Neither bill is retroactive and permits future unfunded mandates so long as they do not impose costs in excess of $50 million per state per year.

This activity clearly indicates that the federal relationship is in flux. This uncertainty has caused passions to run high on both sides.[63] Issues of federalism are still alive in the United States, pushed both by ideological fervour and by real forces.

Conclusion

For countries and regions that are implementing or, as in the European Union, redesigning federal systems, the lessons of the economic theory of federalism are clear. First, there are economic factors that determine the benefits and costs of affiliating in a federation. These factors arise both from straightforward microeconomic theory and from public-choice theory. No federation should ignore these factors in devising its institutions and the rules governing them. Thus, the Intergovernmental Conference of 1996–98 in the European Union should carefully consider how its principles – e.g., subsidiarity – fit into the economic framework of federalism. Secondly, real forces of change in the political, economic and social fabric of the nations in a federation will cause changes in the costs and benefits of affiliation in a federation and in the particular institutions of the federation. No one should expect the relationship between the central government and the constituent state governments in a federal system to be immutable. There will be changes. The economic theory of federalism can help to identify the circumstances under which the rules and institutions of the federation will and ought to change. A federal system that does not prepare for these changes may be subject to periodic constitutional crises when underlying economic and other forces call for a change in the appropriate division of authority.

Acknowledgements

I would like to thank Christine Pfeffer, Stefan de Boeck, and Dean Gournis for their very helpful research assistance, and Lee Alston, Ian Ayres, Dirk Heremans, Larry Kramer, Jim Pfander, Stephen Ross and Earl Clay Ulen, Jr for their valuable comments and suggestions.

Notes

1.   There are also examples in which the nation-state *precedes* the federation. For example, both Belgium and Germany were nation-states that created governmental sub-entities that then shared power with the central government.
2.   Secession or the orderly dissolution of the federation would be analogous to the break-up of a firm into constituent parts.
3.   There is no reason to posit that the division of authority should change monotonically; that is, in a well-crafted federal system, no level of government should amass power and responsibility over time. Nonetheless, some scholars have argued that there *was* a tendency for power in the United States to flow to the national government. 'The erosion of local

autonomy may well have been inevitable, given the constitutional structure. Whatever the founders' intentions, the rules they wrote are skewed in favor of national power. In cases of conflict between state and federal law, federal law wins. If there is disagreement over constitutional rules, a department of the federal government, the courts, serves as umpire. And the principal structural protection for federalism, the direct representation of state legislatures in the Senate, was eliminated by the seventeenth amendment' (McConnell 1987, p. 1488).

4. I shall not discuss the particular federal institutions of the European Union. There is a superb summary of those institutions (and of United States' federal institutions), and a comparison between the federal institutions of the United States and the European Union, by Pfander (1996). To give the flavour of the importance of this comparative study, a paradox to which Pfander draws attention may be noted. The Supreme Court of the United States has steadfastly refused to allow Congress to instruct the states to adopt and enforce environmental regulations, and yet the European Union, which has a weaker federal structure and more jealously-guarded state sovereignty, implements environmental regulations by the routine use of directives (which require each Member State to enact Union obligations into positive national law), precisely like those that the US Supreme Court forbids.

5. See, for example, Tullock (1969), Oates (1972), and Rose-Ackerman (1981). An exception is Posner (1985, 1992). Nonetheless, Posner's analysis is as much about the optimal size of the nation-state as it is about the division of governmental responsibilities among different layers in a federation. I elaborate on this distinction in this section of the chapter.

6. This second issue is known to Europeans as 'subsidiarity'. The Treaty of Rome and the Maastricht Treaty define subsidiarity as follows: '[T]he Community shall take action … only if and in so far as the objectives of the proposed action cannot be sufficiently achieved by the Member States.'

7. The thought experiment focused on here imagines equal, independent states to be contemplating federal union. I shall not consider here the important question of how an existing union decides whether or not to add a new member and, if so, on what terms.

8. If the polluter's actions impose external costs only within the jurisdiction of a single country, then that country has the appropriate incentives to regulate the polluter's behaviour. The benefits of so doing will accrue to the citizens of that country. But if some of the costs spill across state lines, then this diminishes the governmental incentive to regulate the polluter because some of the benefits will accrue outside the jurisdiction.

9. For the argument that these interstate externalities are neither a necessary nor a sufficient condition for federal control, see Shapiro and Petchey (Chapter 6 in this volume).

10. This is the economic justification for the Commerce Clause in the United States Constitution and for the dormant Commerce Clause, both of which I discuss in the next section. For an economically minded discussion of the Commerce Clause, see Epstein (1987). Note that independent countries need not form a federation in order to take advantage of the cooperative regulation of trade. They could do so through Coasean bargaining leading to a limited contractual arrangement. Indeed, the World Trade Organization (and its predecessor, GATT) is precisely a multilateral contract well short of federal union that establishes rules on inter-country commerce and an equivalent dormant Commerce Clause restriction on the members of the WTO. Arguably, the European Union, prior to the 1980s, was simply a limited contractual arrangement among independent nations rather than a federation.

11. Or they could agree to hire a private firm to collect all their taxes.

12. Note that this factor is the *only* one thus far considered that specifically addresses the novelty of a *federal* government. All the other factors heretofore considered address the optimal size of the nation-state as much as they address the optimality of a federal structure.

13. Justice Brandeis wrote in dissent in *New State Ice Co.* v. *Liebmann* (285 US 262, 311 (1932)): 'It is one of the happy incidents of the federal system that a single courageous state may, if its citizens choose, serve as a laboratory, and try novel social and economic experiments without risk to the rest of the country.' Rose-Ackerman has argued that this may be an overly optimistic view of the role of constituent states in a federation (Rose-Ackerman 1980, 1981). She examines the incentives for individual politicians to develop innovative policies in three different governmental structures: a highly centralized government, a decentralized multiple-government setting, and a federal government that is between these extremes. In neither of the extremes is there much of an incentive for a politician intent on being re-elected to adopt

innovative policies. A two-tiered system like that in a federation improves matters but not much. In a federal system politicians may choose to innovate in order to run for federal office or to be appointed to a federal office. Additionally, in a federation low-level elected office is more attractive than in a more simple governmental structure. The winner of a local election can try for a higher office. Thus, there is more competition for lower-level offices and the returns to risk-taking innovation are generally greater. One last improvement in federalism is that politicians who aspire to higher office have an incentive to adopt policies that may generate benefits across jurisdictions. Clearly this incentive is not as strong in the alternative governmental systems considered. But Rose-Ackerman finds that these effects still may not produce as much innovation as would be deemed socially optimal. To get closer to that result, she suggests that the central government in a federation may wish to give grants to local governments in order to subsidize innovation. The policy would be mutually beneficial to the politicians in addition to improving social efficiency: federal politicians would get credit for encouraging innovation, and the local politicians would get credit for innovation without having to induce local taxpayers to increase taxes to make risky innovations.

14. For an argument in favour of state experimentation in product liability, see Rice (1985).

15. Most people seem to believe that a state is better off it if discourages in-migration by welfare recipients from other states. This is not necessarily true. It may be that welfare recipients (like many recent international immigrants) will eventually be productive, tax paying citizens after a transition period on welfare. Nonetheless, for the purposes of the argument in the text, assume the in-migration of welfare recipients from other states to be undesirable.

16. There are, of course, compelling non-economic reasons for increasing redistributive policies and for placing them at the federal level. For example, in the United States there is now general agreement that uniform national rules on civil rights and civil liberties are preferable to disparate state rules on those matters. See Stewart (1985).

17. As we shall see in the next section, there are those who argue that in the United States the federal political process, not judicial review by the Supreme Court, is the best arbiter of federal–state relations.

18. This is, of course, an economic gloss on James Madison's most important contribution to the ratification debate. Madison argued, principally in Federalist 10 (Madison et al. 1987), that individual liberties, such as property rights and freedom of religion, are best protected at the *national* level, not the state level. Madison held that the most serious threat to individual liberty is the tyranny of a majority faction and that factions have more effect in the locality in which they are concentrated. In the nation as a whole, they are a small minority. Therefore, factional tyranny is more likely in the state (or local) government and least likely in the national government.

19. For an excellent summary of the literature, see Farber and Frickey (1991). For an application of public-choice theory to federalism, see Macey (1990), on which much of this section relies.

20. U.S. Const., Art. VI, § 2.

21. Alexis de Tocqueville remarked on this matter in *Democracy in America* (1832): '[T]he business of the Union is incomparably better conducted than that of any individual state. ... It has more prudence and discretion, its projects are more durable and more skillfully combined, its measures are executed with more vigor and consistency' (p. 158). James Madison in Federalist 10 (Madison et al. 1987), noted that the federal government would probably have better-qualified officials than would the state governments. See the further discussion on pages 24–28 about the relative competencies of federal and state regulators.

22. This is an extension of Fiorina's observation that Congress can sometimes avoid political fallout for difficult decisions by delegating them to an administrative agency. See Fiorina (1982) and Aranson et al. (1983).

23. Macey (1990) calls this theory a 'franchise theory of federalism'. He draws an analogy between Congress's delegation to the states to regulate and a business's decision to franchise its operation. Under a franchise agreement the business owner refrains from operating a business himself, choosing instead to license to another firm the rights to market, sell and produce his product.

24. See, for example, Easterbrook and Fischel (1990) and Winter (1977). The literature frequently describes this competition as a 'race to the top'.

25. See, for example, *Louis K. Liggett Co.* v. *Lee* (288 US 517, 559 (1933)) (in which Brandeis, J., in dissent, describes the competition among the states for corporate charters as a race 'not of diligence but of laxity'); and Cary (1974) (in which the competition for corporate charters is described as a 'race for the bottom').

26. Indeed, Macey and Miller have argued that Delaware has the further attraction that it channels corporate litigation into the state's courts. See Macey and Miller (1987).

27. See the next section.

28. There is evidence that as a society's Gross Domestic Product increases so does its taste for a cleaner environment. Grossman and Kreuger (1995).

29. When a change in the optimal scale of governmental service occurs so that a particular governmental function ought to be transferred to another level in the federal system, Coasean bargaining among the levels may lead to voluntary reassignment of the responsibility. That is, if the function could be more efficiently performed at another level, it could be in the interests of *all* the levels to have the duty transferred. Congress could be conceived of as an institution that, among other things, facilitates these Coasean bargains among states or regions. Indeed, the First Congress made a large number of such deals in which representatives acted principally as state advocates.

30. Peterson (1995a, 1995b).

31. There are important issues of federalism involved in these restrictions. For several decades many states have attempted to limit welfare and other governmental benefits for new migrants to their states. Those thereby disadvantaged have challenged those state limitations as unconstitutional restrictions on the right of United States citizens to travel. Thus far, the United States Supreme Court has always found these restrictions to be unconstitutional.

32. Two arguments against this were noted above. First, Madison felt the states would be more likely to be in the thrall of tyrannical factions than would the national government. Secondly, there may be circumstances in which national uniformity is more important than is satisfying local preferences.

33. In *Baker* v. *Carr* (1962) the Court held that legislative malapportionment was violative of the Fourteenth Amendment and that state legislative districts should be apportioned according to the principle of 'one person, one vote'. *Reynolds* v. *Sims* (1964) held that the Fourteenth Amendment required *both* houses of state legislatures to be apportioned according to population.

34. Under the proposal 129 separate programmes (or 'categorical grants') would have been lumped into six block grants with very few constraints on how the state-recipients spent that money.

35. For example, Florida attempted to impose a tax on services in 1987. The tax went into effect, but businesses then boycotted Florida as a place for conventions. The impact was so great that the governor and legislature agreed to repeal the tax within six months of its implementation.

36. There is an extensive literature in the law and in political science on federalism. For leading examples in the political science literature, see Ostrom (1987) and Beer (1993). Some leading examples in the law literature on federalism are Wechsler (1954); Choper (1980); Amar (1987); Merritt (1988, 1994).

37. This section owes much to Scheiber (1992).

38. Consider the Ninth and Tenth Amendments. The Ninth Amendment says, 'The enumeration in the Constitution, of certain rights, shall not be construed to deny or disparage others retained by the people.' And the Tenth Amendment, about which there is a great deal of interest today, says, 'The powers not delegated to the United States by the Constitution, nor prohibited by it to the States, are reserved to the States respectively, or to the people.' That latter amendment reflects a view of the relationship between the federal government and the states that James Madison put this way: 'The powers delegated by the proposed Constitution to the federal government are few and defined. Those which are to remain in the State governments are numerous and indefinite' (Rossiter 1961, pp. 292–3).

39. US Const., Art. I, § 2, cl. 3. This provision was superseded by § 2 of the Fourteenth Amendment.

40. US Const., Art. I, § 9, cl. 1.

41. US Const., Art. IV, § 2, cl. 3. That clause was superseded by the Thirteenth Amendment after the Civil War.

42. The Court accomplished 'judicial nationalism' principally through its interpretations of the Supremacy Clause (US Const., Art. VI, § 2), the Commerce Clause (US Const., Art. I, § 8, cl. 3), and the Contract Clause (US Const., Art. I, § 10, cl. 1; this clause applies to the states, not to the federal government).
43. Barzillai Hudson and George Goodwin were indicted in 1806 and 1807 for common-law seditious libel. They had published a report that President Thomas Jefferson and Napoleon Bonaparte were conspirators. Federal courts had been upholding such convictions, but the Republicans claimed that the federal courts had no constitutional authority to create or enforce common-law crimes. This was part of the Republican contention that the federal government had only those powers explicitly granted by the Constitution.
44. Philip and Mendes Cohen sold lottery tickets in Virginia under the authority of an Act of Congress for the District of Columbia. Virginia banned such lotteries and charged the Cohens with violating state law. The Cohens' defence was that because of the Supremacy Clause, federal law should prevail. Chief Justice Marshall used the decision to accomplish two ends: he reasserted the federal judicial power but held that the federal lottery statute applied only in the District of Columbia.
45. The Commerce Clause gives Congress the power '[t]o regulate Commerce with foreign Nations, and among the several States, and with the Indian Tribes'. The *dormant* Commerce Clause is the term given to the view that the states may not regulate commerce in such a way as to interfere with interstate commerce, whose regulation is the exclusive preserve of Congress.
46. 295 US, at 554 (quoting *United States* v. *A.L.A. Schecter Poultry Corp.*, 76 F. 2d 617, 624 (CA2 1935) (L. Hand, J., concurring).
47. Ibid. at 536. Note how closely Chief Justice Rehnquist echoes this view, even these words, in the majority opinion in *US* v. *Lopez*, discussed below.
48. See Leuchtenberg (1995).
49. Some scholars believe that well before the Court-packing controversy there had been mixed signals from the Court about what the state and federal governments could legitimately do. For example, in *Nebbia* v. *New York* (1934) the Court had abandoned the *Munn* distinction between ordinary business and that 'affected with a public interest'. Also in 1934 in *Home Building and Loan Association* v. *Blaisdell* the Court upheld a state moratorium on payments of mortgages, thus setting aside the Contract Clause limits on state action. The Court held that emergency conditions warranted the intervention. Chief Justice Charles Evans Hughes called these decisions 'excursion tickets', good for a day, without any lasting or reliable guidance as to the law.
50. 301 US, at 37. Justice Kennedy says in concurrence in *Lopez* (discussed below) that '[t]he case that seems to mark the Court's definitive commitment to the practical conception of the commerce power is [*Jones & Laughlin Steel*]'. At 12.
51. The opinion has an excellent discussion of Commerce Clause jurisprudence at 121.
52. The Act's purpose was to limit the amount of wheat grown and traded in interstate and foreign commerce so as to raise the market price, eliminate surpluses and shortages and, thus, to reduce market-price fluctuation.
53. 469 US 528 (1985).
54. One of the seminal pieces in this literature is Choper (1980). An important part of Choper's argument is that the Court should avoid politically charged issues whenever it can, that federalism is a politically charged issue, and that the Court can safely leave the resolution of federal–state controversies to the political process. See also Merritt (1994, pp. 1566–70).
55. 112 S. Ct. 2408.
56. The connection between the Senate and the states *per se* was stronger until the early part of this century. Until the passage of the Seventeenth Amendment in 1913 state legislatures, not citizens, elected Senators.
57. The other case was *US Term Limits, Inc.*, v. *Ray Thornton* (1995 WL 306517 (US)), decided on 22 May 1995. At issue was the constitutionality of an amendment to the Arkansas Constitution that restricted the ability of a candidate to appear on the ballot for Congress if that person, although otherwise eligible to serve, had already served three terms in the House of Representatives. The Supreme Court held, 5–4, that neither Congress nor the states could determine the conditions of eligibility of Congressional candidates. Those conditions are fixed

by the Constitution; the Constitution allows the states (through US Const., Art. I, § 4) to determine only the time, manner and condition of elections for Congress.

58. 18 USC § 922(q)(1)(A) (1988 ed., Supp. V). The Act defined a 'school zone' as 'in, or on the grounds of, a public, parochial or private school' or 'within a distance of 1,000 feet from the grounds of a public, parochial, or private school'.

59. Justice Breyer's dissent found much to admire in the federal-process model. He felt that Congress had felt that the effects of handguns in schools were deleterious, that there was adequate protection for the states in the Congressional debate and representation, and that, in light of these things, the Court should show extreme deference to Congress in these matters.

60. 1995 WL 238424 (US) at 6 (emphasis added). In dissent, Justice Souter said that the appropriate standard that the Court should apply is whether or not Congress had a rational basis for regulating the activity in question. This is a far more deferential standard toward Congress than the one that the majority approved in *Lopez*.

61. For an excellent discussion of the economic issues in unfunded mandates, see Segerson, Miceli and Wen (Chapter 3 in this volume).

62. Pennsylvania and Illinois originally refused to pass implementing legislation. California passed such legislation, but Governor Pete Wilson, who sought the Republican nomination for President in 1996, vetoed the bill and sued the federal government for a declaration that the law was unconstitutional. California estimated that it would cost the state $20 million per year to implement the motor voter law. A public-interest group sued the governor of Illinois for failure to comply with the law. In *Association of Community Organizations for Reform Now (ACORN)* v. *Edgar*, 1995 WL 329726 (7th Cir. (Ill.)), decided 5 June 1995, Judge Richard A. Posner held that the federal mandate to provide voter registration as part of motor vehicle registration was not violative of the US Constitution. The State of Illinois chose not to appeal the decision. However, its announced scheme of implementation of the motor voter law may itself be challenged. The state will have employees of the Department of Motor Vehicles inform applicants for a driver's licence that they may register for an election for *federal* office and will assist them to do so but will not inform or assist them in registering for state and local elections.

63. As an example of this passion, consider this excerpt from Schlesinger (1995): 'The Republican Party has apparently embarked on a crusade to destroy national standards, national projects, and national regulations and to transfer domestic governing authority from the national government to the states. A near majority of the Supreme Court even seems to want to replace the Constitution by the Articles of Confederation. There has not been so basic an assault on the national government since the Civil War.'

References

Advisory Commission on Intergovernmental Relations (1991), *Significant Features of Fiscal Federalism*, vol. 2: *Revenues and Expenditures*, Washington: US Govt.

Amar, Akhil R. (1987), 'Of Sovereignty and Federalism,' *Yale Law Journal*, 96, 1425.

Aranson, P., Gellhorn, E. and Robinson, G. (1983), 'A Theory of Legislative Delegation', *Cornell Law Review*, 68, 1

Beer, Samuel (1993), *Make a Nation: The Rediscovery of American Federalism*, Cambridge, MA: Harvard University Press.

Budget of the United States Government, Fiscal Year 1992 (1991), Washington: US Govt.

Cary, William (1974), 'Federalism and Corporate Law: Reflections Upon Delaware', *Yale Law Journal*, 83, 663.

Choper, Jesse (1980), *Judicial Review and the National Political Process*, Chicago, IL: University of Chicago Press.

de Tocqueville, Alexis (1990), *Democracy in America*, 2 vols., New York: Vintage Classics.

Easterbrook, Frank and Fischel, Daniel (1990), *The Economic Structure of Corporate Law*, Cambridge, MA: Harvard University Press.

Epstein, Richard (1987), 'The Proper Scope of the Commerce Power,' *Virginia Law Review*, 73, 1387.

Farber, Daniel A. and Frickey, Philip (1991), *Law and Public Choice: A Critical Introduction*, Chicago, IL: University of Chicago Press.

Fiorina, Morris (1982), 'Legislative Choice of Regulator Forms: Legal Process or Administrative Process?', *Public Choice*, 39, 33.

Grossman, Gene and Kreuger, Alan B. (1995), 'Economic Growth and the Environment', *Quarterly Journal of Economics*, 110, 353.

Leuchtenburg, William (1995), *The Supreme Court Reborn: The Constitutional Revolution in the Age of Roosevelt*, New York: Oxford University Press.

McConnell, Michael W. (1987), 'Federalism: Evaluating the Founders' Design', *University of Chicago Law Review*, 54, 1481.

Macey, Jonathan R. (1990), 'Federal Deference to Local Regulators and the Economic Theory of Regulation: Toward a Public-Choice Explanation of Federalism', *Virginia Law Review*, 76, 265.

Macey, Jonathan and Miller, Geoffrey (1987), 'Toward an Interest-Group Theory of Delaware Corporate Law', *Texas Law Review*, 65, 469.

Madison, J., Hamilton, A. and Jay, J.(1987), *The Federalist Papers*, London: Penguin Books Ltd.

Merritt, Deborah J. (1988), 'The Guarantee Clause and State Autonomy: Federalism for a Third Century', *Columbia Law Review*, 88, 1.

Merritt, Deborah J. (1994), 'Three Faces of Federalism: Finding a Formula for the Future', *Vanderbilt Law Review*, 47, 1563.

Oates, Wallace (1972), *Fiscal Federalism*, New York: Harcourt Brace Jovanovich.

Ostrom, Vincent (1987), *The Political Theory of a Compound Republic*, Lincoln: University of Nebraska Press, NE, 2nd edn.

Peterson, Paul E. (1995a), 'Who Should Do What?', *The Brookings Review* 13, (2) (Spring), 17.

Peterson, Paul E. (1995b), *The Price of Federalism*, New York: The Twentieth Century Fund, Inc.

Pfander, James E. (1996), 'Environmental Federalism in Europe and the United States: A Comparative Assessment of Regulation Through the Agency of Member States', in John Braden, Henk Folmer, and Thomas S. Ulen (eds), *Environmental Policy with Political and Economic Integration: The European Union and the United States*, London: Edward Elgar Publishers, pp. 59–131.

Posner, Richard A. (1985), *The Federal Courts: Crisis and Reform*, Cambridge, MA: Harvard University Press.

Posner, Richard A. (1992), *Economic Analysis of Law*, Boston, MA: Little, Brown and Company, 4th edn.

Reuben, Richard (1995), 'The New Federalism', *American Bar Association Journal* 76–81 (April), 34.

Rice, David A (1985), 'Product Quality Law and the Economics of Federalism,' *Boston University Law Review*, 65, 1.

Rivlin, Alice M. (1992), *Revivng the American Dream: The Economy, the States and the Federal Government*, Washington, DC: Brookings Institution.

Romano, Roberta (1985), 'Law as a Product: Some Pieces of the Incorporation Puzzle', Yale Law School, Center For Studies in Law, Economics, and Public Policy, Working Paper/Civil Liability Program, no. 33, New Haven, CT.

Rose-Ackerman, Susan (1980), 'Risk Taking and Reelection: Does Federalism Promote Innovation?', *Journal of Legal Studies*, 9, 593.

Rose-Ackerman, Susan (1981), 'Does Federalism Matter? Political Choice in a Federal Republic', *Journal of Political Economy*, 89, 152.

Rossiter, Clinton (ed.) (1961), *The Federalist Papers*, New York: New American Library.

Scheiber, Harry N. (1992), 'Federalism', in Kermit T. Hall, James W. Ely, Jr., Joel Grossman, and William M. Wiecek, (eds), *The Oxford Companion to the Supreme Court of the United States*, New York: Oxford University Press, pp. 278–87.

Schlesinger, Jr., Arthur (1995), 'In Defense of Government,' *Wall Street Journal*, 7 June, A14, col. 3.

Stewart, Richard B (1985), 'Federalism and Rights', 19 *Georgia Law Review*, 918.

Tullock, Gordon (1969), 'Federalism: Problems of Scale', *Public Choice*, 6, 19.

Wechsler, Herbert (1954), 'The Political Safeguards of Federalism: The Role of the States in the Composition and Selection of the National Government', *Columbia Law Review*, 54, 543.

Wilson, Woodrow (1911), *Congressional Government: A Study in American Politics*, Boston, MA: Houghton Mifflin.

Winter, Ralph K. (1977), 'State Law, Shareholder Protection, and the Theory of the Corporation', *Journal of Legal Studies*, 6, 251.

3 Intergovernmental transfers in a federal system: an economic analysis of unfunded mandates

Kathleen Segerson, Thomas J. Miceli and Lih-Chyi Wen

Introduction

A considerable amount of debate has centred around the question as to which level of government should set environmental policy goals.[1] The advantages of centralized (e.g., federal) decision-making include the ability to internalize interjurisdictional externalities, to ensure uniformity and a 'level playing field', and to take advantage of economies of scale in policy design and administration. On the other hand, decentralized (e.g., state-level) decision-making allows policies to be tailored to local conditions and preferences.

In practice, environmental policies are often set at both the federal and the state level. In some cases, both the federal and state governments control the same variables. For example, in the United States there are federally set standards on automobile emissions.[2] While states can sometimes set their own standards, they are constrained to be at least as stringent as the federal standards.[3] Alternatively, in some cases the federal government sets goals and then leaves it to the states to implement policies for achieving those goals (e.g., Freeman 1990; Portney 1990). An example is non-point source pollution in the United States. The Clean Water Act requires states to develop and implement plans for reducing non-point pollution to achieve federally specified goals (Freeman 1990).

While the economics literature has addressed the question of the appropriate division of authority between different levels of government,[4] relatively little attention has been given to the question as to which level should pay for the cost of implementing policies.[5] When the federal government imposes mandates on the states (or local governments) that require the states to meet minimum standards or environmental quality goals, the states must incur the costs of complying with the mandates. Often the federal government does not provide the states with additional funding to meet the requirements imposed by the mandate. Moreover, the number of unfunded mandates is growing rapidly. The United States Congress has passed 72 mandates since the late 1980s, compared with just 19 between 1970 and 1986 (Hosansky 1994). State and local governments have claimed that such unfunded mandates impose heavy burdens on them. Concern about the burden has grown recently, since state and local governments have been less able to absorb the costs of mandates as their own budget problems grew during the mid-1980s (US House of Representatives, Committee on Government Reform and Oversight 1995).[6] For example, city officials in Columbus, Ohio claimed that in 1991 costs associated with unfunded mandates comprised 10 per cent of its operating budget. By 2000, the city estimates that nearly one-fourth of the city's budget will be used to comply with all federal environmental unfunded mandates (*National Journal* 1995).

Table 3.1: Estimated costs of unfunded federal mandates to cities (Hours and costs in thousands)

Mandates	Fiscal year 1993				Fiscal years 1994–1998
	Estimated annual staff hours (inc. overtime)	Estimated annual staff costs ($)	Estimated annual direct/ indirect budget costs ($)	Total costs ($)	Projected total costs ($)
Underground Storage Tank Regulations (UST)	862	23 393	137 755	161 148	1,040 627
Clean Water Act (CWA)/Wetland	57 378	1,185 549	2,426 984	3,619 533	29,303 379
Clean Air Act(CAA)	12 138	195 526	208 294	403 820	3,651 550
Solid Waste Disposal/RCRA	9 680	173 384	708 191	881 575	5,475 968
Safe Drinking Water Act (SDWA)	4 444	94 549	467 783	562 332	8,644 145
Asbestos (AHERA)	898	19 554	109 754	129 308	746 828
Lead-based Paint	374	7 875	110 342	118 217	1,628 228
Endangered Species	252	6 934	30 024	36 958	189 488
Americans with Disabilities Act	4 701	114 935	240 746	355 681	2,195 808
Fair Labor Standards Act (Exempt Employee & Other Costs)	1 227	22 765	189 358	212 123	1,121 524
Total	91 954	1,844 464	4,629 231	6,473 695	53,997 545

Source: Price Waterhouse for the US Conference of Mayors

The possible repercussions on environmental laws are extremely broad. Many environmental laws have been cited as particularly burdensome at the local level, including the Clean Air Act (CAA), Clean Water Act (CWA), Safe Drinking Water Act (SDWA), and Superfund.[7] An October 1993 Price Waterhouse study for the United States Conference of Mayors contained a survey on the costs incurred by cities to implement unfunded Federal mandates (see Table 3.1). The most costly mandate was the Clean Water Act, with an estimated cost for fiscal year 1993 of $3.6 billion. The estimated cost was $403.8 million for the Clean Air Act and $562.3 million for the Safe Drinking Water Act (US House of Representatives, Committee on Rules 1995).

In response to outcries from state and local officials, the United States Congress recently passed the Unfunded Mandate Reform Act of 1995, which limits the extent to which the federal government can impose mandates on state and local governments without providing the funds necessary to implement the mandate.[8] Specifically, the law imposes procedural restrictions when a federal unfunded mandate would impose an aggregate cost burden on state and local governments in excess of $50 million.[9]

The debate over unfunded mandates has centred around a number of concerns. A major concern of the opposition is that, if unfunded mandates are allowed, the federal government will not adequately consider the costs of its actions when deciding on the stringency of environmental policies. This is essentially an argument that unfunded mandates create a moral hazard problem for the federal government that leads to over-regulation.[10] On the other hand, proponents of unfunded mandates argue that, if all federal mandates are funded, states will not face proper incentives for innovation and cost-minimization, in that they will have no incentive to try to implement the mandate in a least-cost way (e.g., Dana 1995). Thus, they would argue that funding mandates creates a moral hazard problem for the states. In addition, in the absence of the federal mandate, states may choose environmental standards that are 'too lax' due to interjurisdictional externalities or budgetary and other constraints.

The double moral hazard problem associated with the funding of federal mandates is similar to the incentive problems that exist in other contexts in which a transfer payment is made from one party to another. For example, in economic models of accidents where both injurers and victims can take care to reduce expected damages (i.e., bilateral care models), a liability rule under which the injurer always pays the victim for damages (strict liability) creates a moral hazard problem for the victim. Conversely, a rule of no payment (no liability) creates a moral hazard problem for the injurer (Shavell 1987). Similarly, in economic models of regulatory takings where the government imposes land-use restrictions that reduce the private value of the land, a rule of always compensating for such 'takings' creates a moral hazard for the landowner, whereas a rule of never requiring compensation creates a moral hazard problem for the regulator (Blume et al. 1984). However, it has been shown in these other contexts that the double moral hazard problem can be 'solved' by using a threshold rule that identifies certain conditions under which payment will be required.[11]

In this chapter, we develop a simple model that captures the basic interaction between the federal government and a representative state[12] in the formulation of environmental policy.[13] We then use the model to examine the impact of higher level decisions regarding the funding of federal mandates on the environmental policy choices of both the federal government and the state.[14] The model incorporates the double moral hazard problem associated with the funding of federal mandates, as well as the potential for states to set environmental regulations that are 'too lax' if a federal mandate does not exist. We show that, as in other contexts, the double moral hazard problem can be solved by using a threshold rule that identifies the conditions under which mandates would be funded. Interestingly, such a rule also simultaneously eliminates any incentive for states to under-regulate, i.e., it solves the interjurisdictional externality problem as well. It thus ensures efficient decisions by both the federal government and the states. Moreover, as the Unfunded Mandate Reform Act includes a type of threshold rule, we use the model and our results to evaluate the efficiency of this recently passed legislation.

An overview of the model

Assume that the state government chooses an n-dimensional vector y of specific environmental policies that yield a (scalar) level of environmental quality $R(y)$ where the elements of y are measured such that $R_i > 0$ (subscripts denote partial derivatives). The federal government chooses a target level of environmental quality x. A federal mandate takes the form of a specific level of environmental quality that must be met by the states. Thus, the federal government chooses a level of x and mandates that the states choose a vector y such that $R(y) \geq x$.[15] If the federal government and the states are choosing the same variable (for example, automobile emission standards) so that $n = 1$ and $R(y) = y$, the mandate simply takes the form $y \geq x$. Alternatively, if the federal government is setting the goal and the states are choosing how to achieve that goal, then y represents a vector of implementation policies and the state must choose a set of policies that satisfy the constraint $R(y) \geq x$. Note that in either case the state is free to choose y such that the resulting level of environmental quality exceeds the federal goal, in which case the constraint imposed by the mandate would not be binding.[16]

The social benefits of environmental quality are given by $b[R(y)]$, which is assumed to be strictly concave. However, we assume that the benefits to the state differ from the social benefits. Specifically, let the state's benefits be $b[R(y)]$, where $b(R) < B(R)$ and $b'(R) < B'(R)$ for all R. The difference between the social benefits and the state's benefit could stem from an interjurisdictional externality or from the state's concern about non-efficiency objectives such as interstate competition and jobs.[17] For ease of exposition, we simply refer to this effect in terms of an interjurisdictional externality. The costs associated with a policy vector y are given by $C(y)$, where $C_i > 0$ and C is convex.

The socially efficient choice of y (denoted y^*) maximizes net social benefits, i.e., it solves the following problem:

$$\text{Max } B[R(y)] - C(y). \tag{1}$$

Since both benefits and costs depend on y rather than on the target level of environmental quality, the choice of x does not affect net social benefits. Nonetheless, we let $x^* = R(y^*)$ denote the level of environmental quality that would be achieved by the efficient choice of y.

The actual choice of y by the state depends both on the federal mandate that it faces and on whether or not that mandate will be funded by the federal government. Let $T(y) \geq 0$ denote the transfer that the federal government makes to the state to pay for the cost of meeting the mandate. Given the mandate (x) and the funding rule, the state then chooses y to solve the following problem:

$$\text{Max } b[R(y)] - C(y) + T(y) \tag{2}$$
$$\text{subject to } x \leq R(y).$$

The solution to this problem yields the state's reaction function $y(x)$.

We assume that at the time that it chooses the mandate, the federal government is aware of the state's reaction function. Thus, the federal government is a leader in a Stackelberg game. Furthermore, we assume that the federal government suffers from 'fiscal illusion', i.e., it does not consider the costs incurred by the states when making its mandate decision. It does, however, consider any 'out-of-pocket' costs in the form of funding that it must provide to the states in conjunction with the mandate. The federal government thus chooses x to solve the following problem:[18]

$$\text{Max } B\{R[y(x)]\} - T[y(x)]. \tag{3}$$

This simple model captures three important concerns that have arisen in the unfunded mandate debate. The first is the fear that, if the federal government is not required to fund mandates, it will over-regulate. Specifically, if $T = 0$, (3) implies that the federal government will directly consider only the benefits of a mandate and not the associated costs.[19] This reflects the federal government's moral-hazard problem when funding is not required. The second concern is the possibility that, in the absence of a federal mandate, the state would choose a level of environmental quality that is 'too low'. In the model, the difference between the social benefits (B) and the state's benefits (b) implies that the state would, in fact, under-protect the environment without the federal mandate (and any funding that might go with it). This can be seen by comparing (1) and (2) (without the constraint) for the case where $T = 0$. This reflects the impact of the external benefit the state's choice confers on other jurisdictions. Finally, it captures concerns that federal funding will reduce the state's incentive to innovate and implement the mandate in a least-cost way. Specifically, even if the state's benefits equal the social benefits (so that $b = B$), if the federal government imposes a mandate but always fully funds it (so that $T = C(y)$), the state will choose a level of environmental quality that is 'too high' since it will reap benefits from further increases in environmental protection without incurring any additional costs. This reflects the state's moral hazard problem associated with fully funded mandates.[20] When both the interjurisdictional externality and the state's moral hazard problems exist, whether the state will choose on net to over- or under-protect the environment depends on the relative magnitude of the two effects and the extent of the federal mandate. We consider below whether there is some rule regarding the funding of mandates (i.e., some function $T(y)$) that will ensure that the state always chooses the efficient y (y^*) given the federal government's mandate decision.

Unconditional funding rules

We begin by considering two 'unconditional' rules. Under the first rule, all federal mandates are required to be fully funded,[21] i.e., unfunded mandates are *never* allowed. Under the second rule, no federal mandates are required to be funded, i.e., unfunded mandates are *always* allowed. We show that neither rule is generally efficient (although the first rule will be efficient in some cases). Specifically, both rules can lead to over-protection of the environment. When all mandates must be funded, the over-protection stems from the state's moral-hazard problem. When funding is never required, it stems from the federal government's moral hazard problem, i.e., its tendency to over-regulate (impose too stringent a mandate) when it is not required to pay the cost of meeting the mandate. Furthermore, we show that, unlike other contexts (e.g., Rose-Ackerman 1989), the state's moral hazard problem when funding is required cannot be 'corrected' simply by fixing the level of compensation at the cost of meeting the mandate in an efficient way (so that the payment to the state becomes lump-sum).

For simplicity, we rely on a graphical illustration of the results for the case when $n = 1$ (i.e., y is a scalar). Without loss of generality, we assume $R(y) = y$ so that the federal government and the state are effectively choosing the same variable. This allows us to use the same axis to represent both x and y.[22] We define the following values of y:

$$\hat{y} \quad \text{maximizes } b(y) - C(y) \tag{4}$$
$$y^* \quad \text{maximizes } B(y) - C(y) \text{ (as defined previously)} \tag{5}$$
$$y_s \quad \text{maximizes } b(y) \text{ and} \tag{6}$$
$$y_f \quad \text{maximizes } B(y) \tag{7}$$

Thus, $\hat{y}$ is the level of y that would be chosen by the state if there were no mandate (and no funding) from the federal government; y^* is the efficient level of y; y_s is the level of y that would be chosen by the state if it did not have to pay the costs associated with y; and y_f is the level of y that would be chosen by the federal government if it did not have to pay the costs associated with y. Since B' > b', clearly $\hat{y} < y^*$ and $y_s < y_f$. This reflects the interjurisdictional externality. In addition, $\hat{y} < y_s$ and $y^* < y_f$, which reflects the moral hazard problems that exist if the state (federal) government does not bear the costs of its decision. If the state's moral hazard effect is stronger than the effect of the interjurisdictional externality, then $y_s > y^*$. Otherwise, $y_s < y^*$.

Figure 3.1 depicts the effect of a rule under which federal mandates are never required to be funded, i.e., $T = 0$ always, for the case where $y_s > y^*$. The top graph shows the benefit functions for the federal and state governments ($B(y)$ and $b(y)$) as well as the associated net benefit functions ($B(y) - C(y)$ and $b(y) - C(y)$). As mandates are never funded, the state will always pay the costs associated with its choice of y. It thus faces the curve $b(y) - C(y)$. Given this, the bottom graph depicts the state's reaction function to a federal mandate. If the federal government imposes a mandate less than $\hat{y}$ (i.e., requires that the state choose a level of y that is greater than or equal to some $x < \hat{y}$), then the state will choose y to maximize $b(y) - C(y)$ subject to the lower bound on y. Clearly, for any lower bound less than $\hat{y}$, the solution to this will be to choose $\hat{y}$. Thus, for $x \le \hat{y}$, the state chooses $\hat{y}$. Note that when the federal government chooses an x in this range, the constraint on the state will not be binding since the state will voluntarily choose a level that is higher than the mandate. In contrast, if the federal government imposes a mandate that exceeds $\hat{y}$, then, as $b(y) - C(y)$ is downward-sloping in this range, maximizing $b(y) - C(y)$ subject to the lower bound on y will always cause the state to choose the lower bound, i.e., the constraint will be binding. Thus, in this range the state's reaction function is simply the 45° line, as shown in the bottom of Figure 3.1.

Given the state's reaction function, $y(x)$, the heavy curve in the top graph in Figure 3.1 shows the federal government's payoff from different levels of the mandate. For all $x \le \hat{y}$, the state will choose $\hat{y}$ and the federal government's payoff will be simply $B(\hat{y})$ (given $T = 0$), as shown by the horizontal part of the heavy line in the top of Figure 3.1. However, for any $x > \hat{y}$, the state will choose a y equal to that x. As a result, in this range the federal government's payoff is $B(y)$. Clearly, to maximize its payoff the federal government will choose $x = y_f$, and in response the state will choose $y = x = y_f$. While the graphs in Figure 3.1 assume $y_s > y^*$, the results are identical when $y_s < y^*$. Thus, under a rule where the federal government is not required to fund any mandates, it will impose a mandate that exceeds the efficient level and the state will be forced to implement the overly stringent regulation.

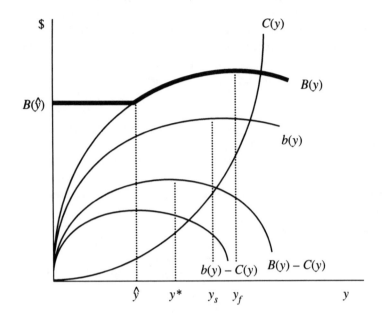

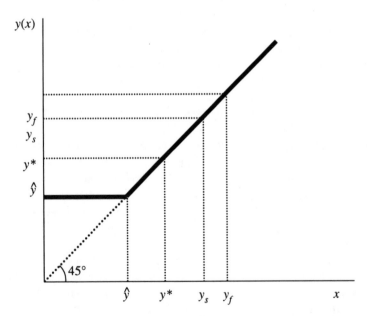

Figure 3.1

Consider next the case under which all mandates must be funded, i.e., $T = C[y(x)]$.[23] Figure 3.2 depicts the effect of this rule when $y_s > y^*$, while Figure 3.3 shows the case where $y_s < y^*$. When all mandates must be funded, the state's payoffs are defined by the curve $b(y)$ since it does not bear the cost of y. Thus, if the federal government imposes a mandate less than or equal to y_s, the state will choose y_s. This is shown by the horizontal segment of the reaction function in the bottom of Figures 3.2 and 3.3. However, when the federal government imposes a mandate that exceeds y_s, as $b(y)$ is downward-sloping in this region, the state will simply choose to implement the lower bound defined by the mandate. Thus, when $x > y_s$, the reaction function is simply the 45° line.

When funding is always required, the federal government's payoffs will be determined by $B(y) - C(y)$. The shape of the payoff function depends on whether $y_s > y^*$ or $y_s < y^*$. Consider first the case where $y_s > y^*$. If the federal government chooses a level of x less than or equal to y_s, the state will choose y_s and the federal government will receive a payoff of $B(y_s) - C(y_s)$, giving the horizontal segment of the heavy curve in the top of Figure 3.2. Alternatively, if it chooses a level of x that exceeds y_s, the state will simply implement the mandate, i.e., the state will choose y equal to x. The federal payoff will then be $B(y) - C(y)$ in this range, as shown in Figure 3.2. The federal government's payoff function determines the level of the mandate that will be chosen. It is clear from Figure 3.2 that under a rule where the federal government must always fund its mandates, if $y_s > y^*$, then the federal government will choose some level of $x \leq y_s$ and the state will respond by choosing y_s. Since $y_s > y^*$ here, the resulting outcome will be inefficient. In contrast to the previous case where mandates were never funded, here the inefficiency arises not because the federal government necessarily over-regulates; rather, it occurs because the state does not face the costs associated with its choice of y and thus chooses a level of environmental protection that exceeds the efficient level. Thus, when the state's moral hazard problem exceeds the effect of the interjurisdictional externality (so that $y_s > y^*$), a rule of always funding federal mandates will lead to over-protection. However, the inefficiency does not exist if the interjurisdictional externality effect is stronger (so that $y_s < y^*$), as shown in Figure 3.3. In this case, the federal government will choose $x = y^*$, as shown in the top graph in Figure 3.3, and the state will respond by choosing y^*. The outcome is efficient in this case because the mandate is binding on the state at y^*, given $y_s < y^*$.

In some contexts, the moral hazard problem associated with compensation can be overcome by making the payment lump-sum, i.e., independent of the decisions of the recipient. For example, in economic models of accidents in which both injurers and victims can take care to reduce expected damages, the inefficiency associated with victim compensation can be eliminated by setting the award equal to damages evaluated at the optimal level of victim care rather

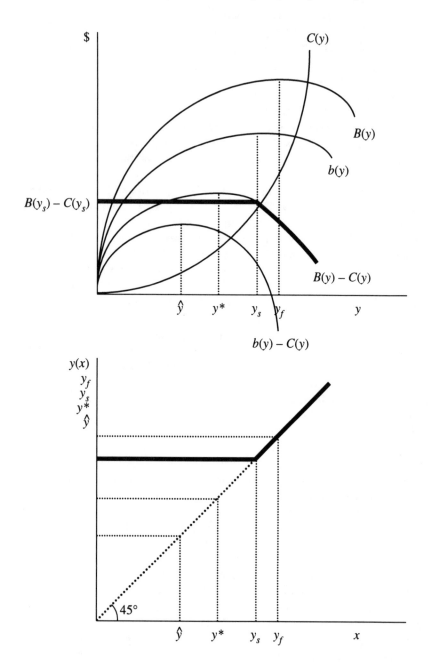

Figure 3.2

than the actual level (Rose-Ackerman 1989). In our context, this would be equivalent to requiring the federal government to fund the cost of meeting the mandate efficiently rather than the actual cost. (The actual cost would exceed the cost of meeting it efficiently if, as a result of the moral hazard problem, the state chose a level of environmental quality that exceeded the mandate.) However, we show below that here the use of a lump-sum payment does not eliminate the inefficiency.

Specifically, consider a rule under which $T = C[y^*(x)]$, where $y^*(x)$ is the solution to:

$$\text{Minimize } C(y) \tag{8}$$
$$\text{subject to } x \leq R(y).$$

When $n = 1$ and $R(y) = y$ (the special case considered here), $y^*(x) = x$ and thus $T = C(x)$. In other words, under this rule the federal government is required to fund the cost of just meeting the mandate but is not required to fund the cost of exceeding it.

Figure 3.4 shows the effect of this rule on the decisions of the federal government and the state for the case where $y_s > y^*$ (the case where compensating for actual costs led to inefficiency). Given that the compensation to the state is lump-sum, i.e., unaffected by its actual choice of y, the state will choose y to maximize $b(y) - C(y) + T(x)$, or equivalently $b(y) - C(y)$, subject to $y \geq x$. Thus, the relevant curve for determining the state's reaction function in Figure 3.4 is $b(y) - C(y)$. Clearly, if the federal government imposes a mandate less than or equal to $\hat{y}$, the state will choose $\hat{y}$; whereas if the federal government imposes a mandate in excess of $\hat{y}$, the state will simply choose to implement the mandate. This is reflected in the reaction function shown in the bottom of Figure 3.4.

The top graph in Figure 3.4 shows the federal government's payoff function, given the reaction function of the state. If the federal government chooses a mandate less than or equal to $\hat{y}$, the state will choose $\hat{y}$. The payoff to the federal government will then be $B(\hat{y}) - C(x)$, where x is the level of y chosen by the federal government. Note that in this payoff the benefits are determined by the state's actual choice of y ($\hat{y}$), while the costs are determined by the level of the mandate (x). Since over the range where $x \leq \hat{y}$, the federal government's benefits remain constant but its costs increase as x increases, the payoff is a decreasing function of x in this range, as shown in Figure 3.4. If the federal government chooses an $x > \hat{y}$, the state will simply choose y equal to x. Over this range, the federal payoff is then simply $B(x) - C(x)$ (or, equivalently, $B(y)$ $- C(y)$). It should be clear from Figure 3.4 that, if $B(\hat{y}) > B(y^*) - C(y^*)$ (as shown), then the federal government will choose $x = 0$. Given the federal government's decision, the state will in turn choose y equal to $\hat{y}$. Thus, in this case, lump-sum compensation does not eliminate the inefficiency but instead leads to a level of

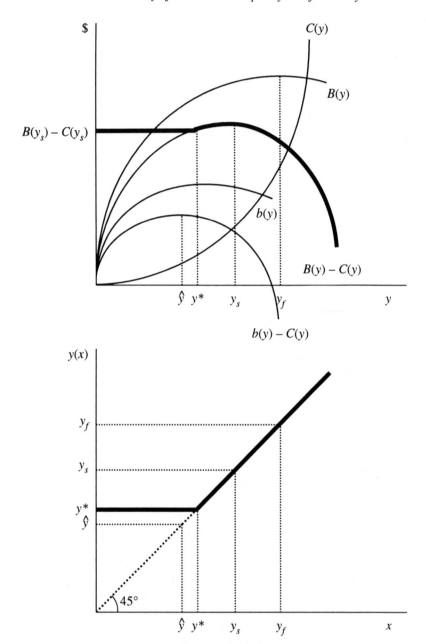

Figure 3.3

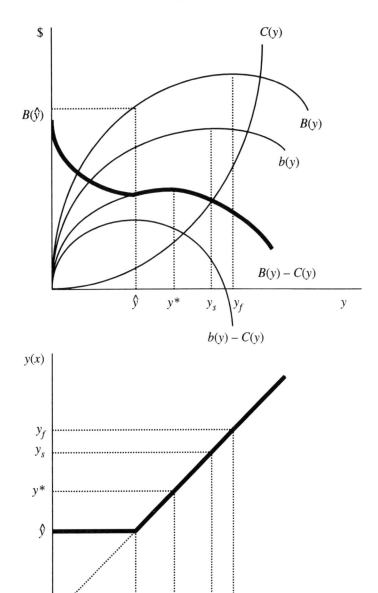

Figure 3.4

environmental protection that is 'too low', i.e., below the efficient level. While the lump-sum compensation can solve the state's moral-hazard problem, it does not eliminate the effect of the interjurisdictional externality. Specifically, it does not induce the federal government to impose a mandate that ensures that the state chooses an efficient level of y despite the interjurisdictional externality. Hence, limiting funding to the cost of efficiently meeting the mandate, thereby making the payment lump-sum to the state, does not ensure efficiency.

An efficient funding rule

As shown above, the rules of requiring all mandates to be fully funded or never requiring funding do not ensure efficient levels of environmental protection, even when the funding is made lump-sum to the state. In this section, we propose a funding rule that does ensure efficiency. It is a threshold rule of the type discussed by Miceli and Segerson (1994) in the context of regulatory takings. Under the proposed rule, the federal government would be required to provide funding whenever it imposes a mandate that exceeds x^*, but it would not be required to fund mandates that are less than or equal to x^*. Thus, it would be required to fund inefficient mandates, but would not have to fund efficient mandates. We show below that such a rule ensures efficiency.[24]

Specifically, let:

$$T = C(y) \text{ if } x > x^* \text{ and} \qquad (9)$$
$$0 \text{ if } x \leq x^*$$

where $x^* = R(y^*)$.[25] The effect of this rule for our special case where $R(y) = y$ and hence $x^* = y^*$ is shown in Figure 3.5 (when $y_s > y^*$) and Figure 3.6 (when $y_s < y^*$). Consider first the derivation of the state's reaction function when $y_s > y^*$. If the federal government imposes a mandate less than $\hat{y}$, then it will not have to fund the mandate since $\hat{y} < y^*$. Thus, in this range the relevant curve for determining the state's decision is $b(y) - C(y)$. Clearly, for any $x < \hat{y}$, maximizing $b(y) - C(y)$ subject to $y \geq x$ yields $\hat{y}$ as the solution, giving the first horizontal segment of the reaction function in the bottom graph of Figure 3.5. If the federal government imposes a mandate between $\hat{y}$ and y^*, the state will still face $b(y) - C(y)$ since the mandate will still not exceed y^* but in this range maximizing $b(y) - C(y)$ subject to $y \geq x$ will yield x as its solution, i.e., the state will choose simply to implement the mandate. This gives the first segment along the 45° line in the bottom graph of Figure 3.5. If the federal government imposes a mandate that exceeds y^*, it will have to fund the mandate. Thus, for x's in this range, the relevant curve for determining the state's reaction is simply $b(y)$. As long as the mandate is less than or equal to y_s, the state will choose y_s. If the mandate exceeds y_s, the state will choose just to implement the mandate since $b(y)$ is downward-sloping in this range. This gives the last two segments of the reaction function in Figure 3.5.

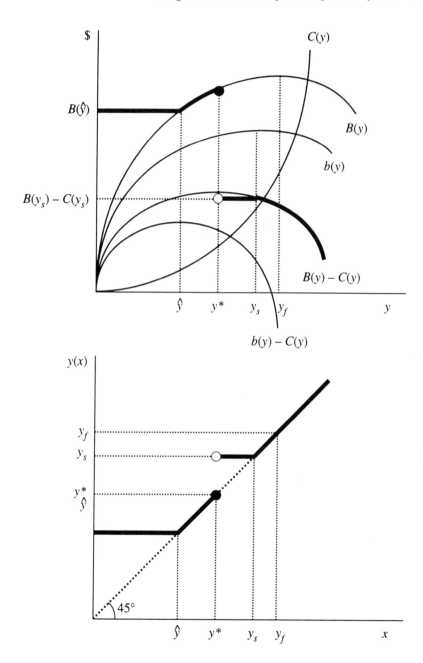

Figure 3.5

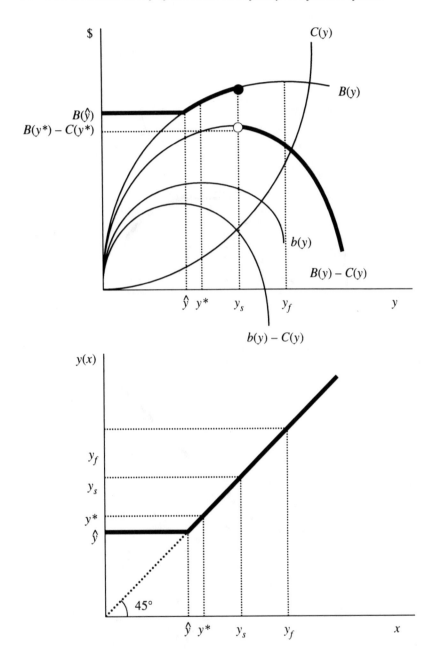

Figure 3.6

Given the state's reaction function, we can now determine the payoffs to the federal government for the different choices of x. If the federal government imposes a mandate less than $\hat{y}$, the state will choose $\hat{y}$ and the payoff to the federal government will be $B(\hat{y})$ since it will not have to fund the mandate (since $\hat{y} < y^*$). If the federal government imposes a mandate between $\hat{y}$ and y^*, the state will choose just to implement the mandate, and the federal payoff will be $B(y)$ (as funding will still not be required). If the federal government chooses a level of x between y^* and y_s, the state will choose y_s. However, now the federal government will have to fund the mandate since it exceeds y^*. Thus, the payoff to the federal government is $B(y_s) - C(y_s)$. Finally, if it imposes a mandate that exceeds y_s, the state will simply implement the mandate. Again the federal government will have to fund the mandate, implying that the payoff in this range of x is $B(y) - C(y)$.

The heavy curve in the top graph of Figure 3.5 depicts the resulting payoff function for the federal government. Note that the discontinuity in the funding rule in (9) creates a discontinuity in the payoff function at y^* (or equivalently x^*).[26] It is clear from Figure 3.5 that the choice of x that maximizes the federal government's payoff function is $x = x^*$, which implies that $y = y^*$. Thus, when $y_s > y^*$, the outcome is efficient. Figure 3.6 shows that efficiency also results when $y_s < y^*$. Thus, the funding rule in (9) ensures efficiency. It induces the federal government to impose the mandate at the efficient level, and the state reacts by choosing y^* as well.

Interestingly, the funding rule in (9) is able to solve simultaneously the three potential sources of inefficiency identified above: (1) the federal government's moral hazard problem (i.e., tendency to over-regulate) when it does not have to fund mandates; (2) the state's moral hazard problem (i.e., tendency to choose too high a level of environmental quality) when all of its costs are covered through federal funding; and (3) the tendency of the state to under-protect the environment because of the existence of the interjurisdictional externality. The threat of having to fund inefficient mandates solves the federal government's moral hazard problem and prevents it from over-regulating. As a result, the federal government will choose x^* and not have to fund the mandate. The fact that the federal government chooses a level of x that does not result in funding solves the state's moral hazard problem as in equilibrium it will bear the costs associated with its choice of x. Finally, the mandate prevents the state from choosing a level of environmental protection that is too low. It thus solves the inefficiency that would otherwise be created by the interjurisdictional externality.

An analysis of the Unfunded Mandate Reform Act

The above analysis, which was purely normative, implies that the threshold rule in (9) ensures an efficient level of environmental protection by requiring the federal government to provide funding when it imposes an inefficiently high mandate. The Unfunded Mandate Reform Act of 1995 also includes a threshold-based funding rule. Under the Act, any unfunded mandate that would impose new costs that exceed a fixed level ($50 million) would be subject to a 'point of order' which would disallow further consideration of the proposal unless overridden by a majority vote. To avoid a possible point of order, the proposal would have to provide funding sufficient to cover the additional costs imposed.[27] This type of policy can be represented by a funding rule of the following form:

$$T = C[y^*(x)] - C(\hat{y}) \text{ if } C[y^*(x)] - C(\hat{y}) > C_o \text{ and} \qquad (10)$$
$$0 \text{ if } C[y^*(x)] - C(\hat{y}) \le C_o.$$

Given the monotonicity of C and the fact that $y^*(x) = x$ when $n = 1$, this is equivalent to a rule of the form:

$$T = C(x) - C(\hat{y}) \text{ if } x > x_o \text{ and} \qquad (11)$$
$$0 \text{ if } x \le x_o$$

where $x_o = C^{-1}[C(\hat{y}) + C_o]$. We show below that this rule can lead to too much or too little environmental protection, depending on the level of x_o. However, if $x_o = x^*$, the resulting level will be efficient.

As above, we limit consideration to a particular case in order to illustrate the possible inefficiency that can result. Specifically, consider the case where $y_s > y^*$ and $B(\hat{y}) > B(y^*) - C(y^*)$. (An analogous analysis could be conducted for the opposite cases.) Under these conditions, the effect of the rule in (11) is different for different values of x_o. If the threshold x_o is set at an amount less than $\hat{y}$, it can be easily shown that the federal government will choose some level of x less than or equal to x_o. (The actual amount that will be chosen is indeterminate since the value of x that maximizes the payoff function is not unique in this case.) In response, the state will choose $\hat{y}$, which is less than the efficient level. In contrast, if $\hat{y} \le x_o \le y_f$, the federal government's optimal choice is to impose a mandate just equal to the threshold x_o and the state's optimal reaction is simply to implement the mandate, i.e., choose y equal to x_o. When $x_o > y_f$, the federal government will set the mandate equal to y_f. Again, the optimal response of the state is simply to implement the mandate, i.e., the state chooses y_f as well.

Figure 3.7 maps the optimal choices[28] for the federal government and the state as a function of the value of x_o for the case considered here ($y_s > y^*$ and $B(\hat{y}) > B(y^*) - C(y^*)$). It is clear from Figure 3.7 that in this case the outcome will be efficient, i.e., the state will choose y^*, if and only if $x_o = x^*$. In other words, for all x_o not equal to x^*, the outcome will be inefficient. Thus, basing the funding on whether the cost of the mandate exceeds some arbitrary level will in general be inefficient. In the context of the Unfunded Mandate Reform Act, this implies that unless the optimal mandate happens to correspond to an incremental cost

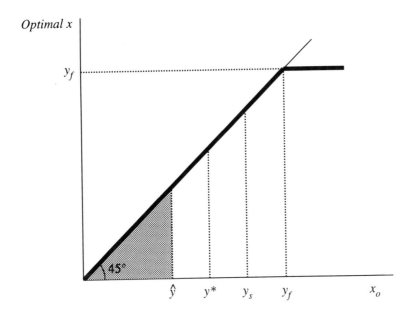

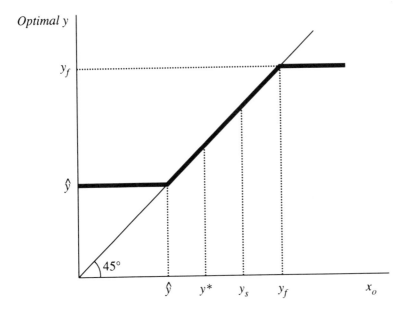

Figure 3.7

of $50 million, using $50 million as a threshold for determining when funding will be required will generally lead to inefficient decisions.[29] In cases where the efficient mandate size involves an incremental cost in excess of $50 million, i.e., when $x_o < x^*$, the result will be under-protection of the environment, that is, the choice of y will be less than y^*. Likewise, when the efficient mandate size involves a cost that is less than $50 million, i.e., when $x^* < x_o$, the level of environmental protection will be 'too high', that is, the choice of y will exceed y^*.

Conclusion

This chapter provides an economic analysis of the incentives for the federal and state governments created by rules regarding funding of federal mandates. A simple model of federal and state environmental policy-making is used to examine the impact of alternative rules. The model captures the double moral hazard problem associated with the funding decision, as well as the potential for states to under-protect the environment if they perceive their own benefits from environmental protection to be less than those perceived by society as a whole.

The results of our analysis suggest that both a rule of always requiring funding, i.e., never allowing unfunded mandates, and a rule of never requiring funding will be inefficient. Always requiring funding creates a moral hazard problem for the state, which leads states to choose a level of environmental protection that exceeds the efficient level. This problem cannot be corrected simply by making a lump-sum payment to the state. Similarly, never requiring funding creates a moral hazard problem for the federal government, causing it to over-regulate, i.e., impose inefficiently stringent mandates. We show that this double moral hazard problem can be solved by a funding rule that relies on a threshold for determining whether a given mandate will be funded. Specifically, a rule under which the federal government would be required to fund mandates that exceed the efficient mandate but would not be required to fund those that are less than the efficient mandate ensures an efficient outcome. While the Unfunded Mandate Reform Act uses a threshold to determine whether funding is required, the threshold is set at an arbitrary level ($50 million) for all types of mandates rather than being tailored to the benefits and costs of different levels of the mandate in a particular context. As a result, the outcome is likely to be inefficient. It can lead to either over- or under-protection of the environment, depending on how the cost of the efficient mandate compares to the $50 million threshold.

Acknowledgements

We acknowledge the useful comments of Terry Dinan, Perry Shapiro, and participants in the Symposium on Economic Aspects of Environmental Policymaking in a Federal System, Leuven, Belgium, June 1995.

Notes

1. See, for example, Oates (1996), Olson (1969), Peltzman and Tideman (1972), Davis and Lester (1989), Revesz (1992), Rose-Ackerman (1995), and Smets and Van Cayseele (1995).
2. See Crandall et al. (1986) for a description of regulation of automobile emissions in the United States.
3. For example, the State of California has set automobile emission standards that are more stringent than the federal standards. See Krier and Ursin (1977) for a description of the development of the California standards.
4. See references in note 1.
5. There is some legal literature related to this issue. See, for example, Pfander (1996) and Dana (1995), and the references therein. The only economic study of which we are aware is Dinan (1994).
6. Federal aid to state and local governments dropped from $47 billion in 1980 to $19.8 billion in 1990. On average, in 1979, the federal contribution to state and local government revenues was 18.6 per cent. By 1989, however, the federal share had dipped to 13.2 per cent before climbing back to 14.3 per cent in 1991.
7. The National Association of Counties constructed the following list of the 12 unfunded mandates considered most 'burdensome and costly': Underground Storage Tanks, Clean Water Act, Clean Air Act, Subtitle D of the Resource Conservation and Recovery Act, Safe Drinking Water Act, Endangered Species Act, Comprehensive Environmental Response, Compensation and Liability Act (Superfund), Americans with Disabilities Act, Fair Labor Standards Act, Davis–Bacon Act, Arbitrage (municipal bonds), and the Immigration Act. See US House of Representatives, Committee on Rules (1995).
8. See Pfander (1996) and Dana (1995) for discussions of judicial restrictions on the use of unfunded mandates.
9. Any unfunded mandate whose cost exceeds $50 million would be subject to a separate 'point of order' vote, which would presumably make passage much more difficult.
10. Technically, the term 'moral hazard' is used in the context of asymmetric information where one party cannot observe, and hence directly control, a decision of a second party that somehow affects the first party. Here we use the term more loosely to refer to a situation where the inability to control directly the actions of the second party may stem from reasons other than lack of observability (for example, institutional constraints). In the formal analysis in the text, information asymmetries are not considered. For a model of unfunded mandates that has the more traditional form of moral hazard, see Miceli and Segerson (1996).
11. In the context of accidents, a simple negligence rule, a negligence rule with a defence of contributory negligence and a strict liability rule with a defence of contributory negligence, all ensure efficient behaviour by both injurers and victims by appropriately conditioning payment on the actions of one or both of the parties (see Cooter and Ulen 1988). Miceli and Segerson (1994) propose compensation rules that are analogous to these negligence-based rules that ensure efficient behaviour by both landowners and regulators in the context of regulatory takings.
12. Throughout we focus on a single state. Thus, in this chapter, we do not address questions of competition among states or heterogeneity across states (see, for example, Oates and Schwab 1988). In addition, we do not specifically consider the role of firms. Hence, we do not consider the common agency problem that can arise from firms' interactions with both the state and federal governments (see, for example, Smets and Van Cayseele (1995)). While these issues are clearly important, they are left for future research.
13. We do not explicitly consider the question of the appropriate division of authority between the federal and state governments. However, the assumed presence of an interjurisdictional externality provides a rationale for a federal role in choosing environmental quality standards. States are then assumed to have a role in implementing policies. The justification for this role is not explicit in the model considered in the text. For a model that explicitly incorporates the role of the state, see Miceli and Segerson (1996).
14. We assume that the funding rule is imposed by some higher authority, for example, a Supreme Court or Constitution. Alternatively, the federal government could impose the rule on itself

as a form of self-discipline. The latter appears to have been the motive for passage of the Unfunded Mandate Reform Act in 1995.

15. We assume that the level of environmental quality is observable by the federal government so that compliance with the mandate is verifiable. In the simple case discussed below, this also implies that y is observable. Thus, there is no asymmetric information. The role of asymmetric information is examined in Miceli and Segerson (1996).

16. Alternatively, in Miceli and Segerson (1996), the constraint is always binding but the state is allowed to choose the level of 'effort' used in implementing the mandate.

17. Two possible explanations for this type of behaviour by states are the 'race to the bottom' and 'local capture'. See Dana (1995) for a discussion of these in the context of unfunded mandates. The implications of local capture are also discussed in Smets and VanCayseele (1995).

18. More generally, the federal government could suffer from some degree of fiscal illusion. In this case, (3) would become:

$$\text{Max } B\{R[y(x)]\} - kC[y(x)] - (1-k)\,T[y(x)]$$

where $k = 1$ implies no fiscal illusion and $k = 0$ corresponds to full or complete fiscal illusion under which the federal government completely disregards costs that are not out-of-pocket. While we consider the extreme case of $k = 0$, our results hold qualitatively for any $k < 1$.

19. Of course the costs will enter indirectly through the state's reaction function.

20. If the mandate takes the form of an equality constraint, as in the model in Miceli and Segerson (1996), then this effect is manifested not in over-protection of the environment but rather in the state's choice of an effort level that is inefficiently low.

21. An alternative would be to require partial funding, for example, some fixed percentage of costs would have to be provided by the federal government. It can be easily shown that such a rule would not be efficient.

22. More general proofs of all results are available from the authors.

23. More generally, under partial funding $T = sC[y(x)]$ for some $0 < s < 1$. An alternative funding rule would tie the amount of funding to the interjurisdictional externality, i.e., $T(y) = B(y) - b(y)$. It should be clear that, while such a rule would correct the state's interjurisdictional externality problem and hence induce efficient behaviour by the state, it would not provide correct incentives for the federal government if the government has some degree of fiscal illusion.

24. Thus, we show that a first-best rule exists. Moreover, the analysis in this section implies that, of the threshold-type rules discussed here, the proposed rule is a unique first-best rule.

25. Note that implementation of this rule requires that x^* be known at the time that the rule is invoked. As it will vary across contexts, the determination of whether $x \geq x^*$ or not must be made on a case-by-case basis. However, this does not require that all possible x^*s be known in advance. Thus, it does not imply that all x^*s could simply have been imposed by some higher authority. For example, while it is informationally too costly to regulate the speed of a motor vehicle under all possible circumstances, it is generally possible to determine *ex post* whether a particular car was driving at an efficient speed given the particular set of circumstances under which it was driving. Such an *ex post* approach to evaluating behaviour is used in other areas of law, for example in the application of negligence-based tort laws.

26. This is similar to the discontinuity created by a negligence rule. See, for example, Cooter and Ulen (1988).

27. The threshold applies to the total cost of implementing the mandate (in a least-cost way) for all state and local governments combined. In our model, we consider only a single state. The model could be extended and the threshold defined to apply to the combined cost of all states.

28. The indeterminacy of the federal government's decision when $x_o < \hat{y}$ is indicated by the shaded triangle in the lower left part of the top graph.

29. Since the threshold applies uniformly and is not tailored to the benefits or costs of meeting different levels of the mandate in any particular context, for most cases it is unlikely to correspond to the cost of the efficient level of the mandate.

References
Blume, Lawrence, Rubinfeld, Daniel L. and Shapiro, Perry (1984), 'The Taking of Land: When Should Compensation be Paid?', *Quarterly Journal of Economics*, 99, 71–92.
Cooter, Robert and Ulen, Thomas (1988), *Law and Economics*, New York: Harper-Collins.
Crandall, Robert W., Gruenspecht, Howard K., Keeler, Theodore E. and Lave, Lester B. (1986), *Regulating the Automobile*, Washington, DC: The Brookings Institution.
Dana, David A. (1995), 'The Case for Unfunded Environmental Mandates', *Southern California Law Review*, 69, 1–45.
Davis, Charles E. and Lester, James P. (1989), 'Federalism and Environmental Policy', in James P. Lester (ed.), *Environmental Politics and Policy: Theories and Evidence*, 59, 57–84.
Dinan, Terry (1994), 'A Preliminary Analysis of Unfunded Federal Mandates and the Cost of the Safe Drinking Water Act', Congressional Budget Office Staff Working Paper, Natural Resources and Commerce Division.
Freeman III, A. Myrick (1990), 'Water Pollution Policy', in Paul R. Portney (ed.), *Public Policies for Environmental Protection*, Washington, DC: Resources for the Future, pp.97–150.
Hosansky, David (1994), 'The Time May Be Ripe for Mandates Bill', *Congressional Quarterly/Weekly Report*, 52, 31 December, 3604–7.
Krier, James E. and Ursin, Edmund (1977), *Pollution and Policy*, Berkeley, CA: University of California Press.
Miceli, Thomas and Segerson, Kathleen (1994), 'Regulatory Takings: When Should Compensation be Paid?', *Journal of Legal Studies*, 13, 750–76.
Miceli, Thomas and Segerson, Kathleen (1996), 'Unfunded Mandates: The Impact of Asymmetric Information', Working paper, University of Connecticut.
National Journal (1995), 'Cutting the Strings', 27, 21 January, 3, 167.
Oates, Wallace E. and Schwab, Robert M. (1988), 'Economic Competition Among Jurisdictions: Efficiency-Enhancing or Distortion-Inducing?', *Journal of Public Economics*, 35, 333–54.
Oates, Wallace E. (1996), *The Economics of Environmental Regulation*, Cheltenham: Edward Elgar Publishing Ltd.
Olson, Mancur (1969), 'The Principle of "Fiscal Equivalence" The Division of Responsibilities Among Different Levels of Government', *American Economic Review*, 59, 479–87.
Peltzman, Sam and Tideman Nicholaus (1972), 'Local versus National Pollution Control: Note', *American Economic Review*, 62, 959–63.
Pfander, James E. (1996) 'Environmental Federalism in Europe and the United States: A Comparative Assessment of Regulation Through the Agency of Member States', in John B. Braden, Henk Folmer and Thomas Ulen (eds), *Environmental Policy with Political and Economic Integration*, Cheltenham: Edward Elgar Publishing Ltd, pp. 59–131.
Portney, Paul R. (1990), 'Air Pollution Policy', in Paul R. Portney (ed.), *Public Policies for Environmental Protection*, Washington, DC: Resources for the Future, pp. 27–96.
Revesz, Richard L. (1992), 'Rehabilitating Interstate Competition: Rethinking the "Race-to-the-Bottom" Rationale for Federal Environmental Regulation', *New York University Law Review*, 67, 1210–54.
Rose-Ackerman, Susan (1989), 'Dikes, Dams, and Vicious Hogs: Entitlement and Efficiency in Tort Law', *Journal of Legal Studies*, 18(1), 25–50.
Rose-Ackerman, Susan (1995), *Controlling Environmental Policy: The Limits of Public Law in Germany and the United States*, New Haven and London: Yale University Press.
Shavell, Steven (1987), *Economic Analysis of Accident Law*, Cambridge, MA: Harvard University Press.
Smets, Hilde and Van Cayseele, Patrick (1995), 'Competing Merger Policies in a Common Agency Framework', *International Review of Law and Economics*, 15, 425–41.
US House of Representatives, Committee on Rules (1995), 'Unfunded Mandate Reform Act of 1995: Report', Report 104–1, Part 1, GPO, 13 January.
US House of Representatives, Committee on Government Reform and Oversight (1995), 'Unfunded Mandate Reform Act of 1995: Report', Report 104–1, Part 2, GPO, 13 January.

4 International environmental regulation when national governments act strategically
Alistair Ulph

1. Introduction
In the debate over the Single European Market and other forms of trade liberalization such as NAFTA, there has been considerable concern expressed by environmentalists about the environmental implications of such moves. The particular aspect of interest on which this chapter will focus is that in a more competitive trading environment governments will be concerned about the competitive impact of imposing tougher environmental policies than other countries, and this may lead national governments that act non-cooperatively to relax their environmental policies, relative to the policies they would set if they acted cooperatively. This has been referred to as 'eco-dumping' or 'environmental dumping'. Note that the incentive for governments acting non-cooperatively to set too lax environmental policies is for trade reasons and not because of the usual free-rider problem that arises with transboundary pollution; thus eco-dumping can arise even if pollution damage is confined entirely to the country in which the pollution is generated, which is what will be assumed throughout this chapter. Concern about eco-dumping has led to the suggestion that if a government in one country believes it is faced with imports from another country that has lower environmental standards, then that government should be allowed to impose countervailing duties equal to the difference in costs of meeting the different environmental standards.

There has been considerable analysis of this issue (see Ulph (1994) for a survey). In terms of economic theory, the conclusion is that if markets are perfectly competitive, then there is no reason to believe there will be systematic eco-dumping by governments. In markets where there is imperfect competition though, it is possible to construct models where all governments do indeed have incentives for eco-dumping, although this conclusion is not at all robust. Note that these results are derived from models where pollution is related directly to the process of production – 'non-product production process methods (PPM's)'. Empirically, as an OECD (1995) report of a panel of experts on trade and environment has noted, there is little evidence of systematic eco-dumping, though the report notes that this is an area for further research.

For the purposes of this chapter the models used imply that, in the absence of any policy by a supra-national authority, eco-dumping, as defined here, is in fact the equilibrium outcome. The question arises as to what policy-makers should do about this. While the report referred to above reaffirms the principle of the OECD that member governments should not engage in eco-dumping, if incentives for governments to engage in such activities exist, then one may need to go beyond statements of principle to prevent eco-dumping. In the European context in particular, the implications of this for the subsidiarity principle, as far as environmental policy is concerned, is of interest here. It is widely accepted that where pollution has a transboundary element, such that there are well-known free-rider incentives for governments acting non-cooperatively to set too weak environmental policies, there is a role for the Commission to deal with such pollution problems (see, for example, CEPR 1993, Siebert 1991, Rauscher 1991, Ulph 1996a). But if countries relax their environmental policies to try to gain strategic trade advantages, there may be a role for the Commission to modify the policies of national governments even if pollution is entirely domestic.

Even if it is accepted that there is a role for the Commission to prevent eco-dumping, there remains the question of the form that intervention by the Commission might take. Much of the theoretical work on this topic has not progressed beyond simply deriving the cooperative and non-cooperative outcomes and showing that they are different.[1] The implication is that the Commission should just implement the cooperative solution.

But the policy debate on these matters follows rather different lines. It is frequently suggested that any incentives for downward competition in environmental policy should be eliminated by harmonizing environmental policies across countries. For example, in the agreement between the EU and Poland, Article 80 refers to harmonization of environmental regulations (Rauscher 1994). But it is well known that harmonization may not be desirable if there are significant asymmetries between countries (Rauscher 1994, Ulph 1996a). Thus, the OECD report already referred to states that 'Harmonization of non-product related PPM-related requirements may be less desirable or feasible in the case of local environmental problems. Because environmental conditions and preferences differ widely among countries, environmental process-related requirements for local problems may be best tailored to local circumstances.' But they then confuse the issue by saying 'However, some convergence of these non-product related PPM-related requirements and standards ... might be beneficial' (OECD report, page 30, paragraph 82). The alternative suggestion is that rather than harmonizing environmental policies, the Commission should simply set 'minimum standards' for environmental policies, with the hope that there will be a form of 'ratchet effect', whereby if some countries are forced to raise their environmental standards in order to meet the minimum standard, then all other countries will respond by raising their environmental standards.

However, there has been little formal analysis of policies such as harmonization or minimum standards. In a model where environmental policy (which takes the form of environmental standards) may induce relocation of firms from countries with tough policies to countries with weaker policies, Kanbur et al. (1994) have shown that environmental dumping will indeed take place in this model. But they went on to show that if countries are sufficiently different (in terms of size), then harmonization of environmental policies may not secure a Pareto-improvement over the non-cooperative outcome, whereas a policy of minimum standards could bring about such an improvement.

This chapter will present a rather different model of imperfect competition in which there is no possibility of relocation by producers. The model will be a simple variant of the Brander-Spencer (1985) model (see Barrett 1994, Ulph 1996b). Governments may use either environmental standards or environmental taxes as their policy instruments. The only asymmetry allowed in the model is for countries to have different environmental damage costs. The first result will be a replication of the finding of Kanbur et al. (1994) that if countries have sufficiently different damage costs then harmonization will not yield a Pareto-improvement over the non-cooperative outcome. However, the second result of this chapter is that when governments use environmental standards, minimum standards will not secure a Pareto-improvement over the non-cooperative outcome either, which is contrary to the Kanbur et al. finding. On the other hand, if governments use emission taxes then setting minimum environmental taxes can secure Pareto-improvements, albeit modest ones. The difference in results is due to the slopes of the government reaction functions. With emission taxes, an increase in the emission tax by one country to meet the minimum level of emission tax leads to an increase in emission taxes by other countries, so that a ratchet effect occurs; however, with emission standards, a toughening of standards by a high-pollution country leads to a relaxation of emission standards by countries with lower emissions.

This still leaves unresolved the question as to why a body like the Commission would use such simple instruments as uniform or minimum environmental standards or taxes. Why does it not simply impose a cooperative solution which Pareto-dominates the non-cooperative outcome and which would involve setting different emission standards or taxes for countries that are not identical? One possible explanation is that the Commission does not have sufficient information about the characteristics of member states, such as environmental damage costs, to compute the cooperative solution. The 1995 OECD report notes this problem, though in the context of an argument against the use of countervailing duties. There it is argued that it would be very difficult to tell whether lower environmental standards in one country were due to differences in local conditions or to an attempt by the government of that country to accord a competitive advantage to its firms. But if the Commission lacks information about the true damage costs to member states then this needs to be modelled directly. Thus what is needed is an analysis of a cooperative solution with asymmetric information in which the Commission has to provide incentives for countries to correctly reveal information about their damage costs. In the rest of the chapter, the non-cooperative and cooperative solutions with asymmetric information will be analysed. Of course, the analysis of environmental regulation under asymmetric information is by no means a new topic (see, for example, the classic paper by Dasgupta et al. 1980). However, this is possibly the first application of such an analysis to the strategic trade dimension of environmental policy.[2] The cooperative policy under asymmetric information cannot be easily characterized in terms of harmonization or minimum standards. Arguably, though, there is a sense in which asymmetric information, while not justifying complete harmonization of environmental policies, does warrant environmental standards in different countries being more similar than would be the case under full information.

In the next section of this chapter the basic model will be set out and the cooperative and non-cooperative solutions under full information will be derived for the cases where governments use emission standards and where they use emission taxes. In the third section the use of harmonization and minimum standards will be analysed, again under full information and for both policy instruments. Finally, the non-cooperative and cooperative solutions with asymmetric information will be considered, again for the cases of both sets of policy instruments.

2. Non-cooperative and cooperative equilibria with full information

The basic model
The model is a special case of the models in Barrett (1994) and Ulph (1996b), in which special functional forms have been used. Most of the results of this chapter hold for more general functional forms, but it is useful in making comparisons between equilibria with full information and asymmetric information to use special functional forms to allow closed form solutions for emission standards or taxes.

There are two identical firms, each located in a separate country, producing a homogeneous good with output levels x and y respectively. In what follows, the firm and country producing output x (think of it as the home country and the other as the foreign country) will be the primary focus, with the description of the other firm and country following by symmetry. There are no costs of production, and output is sold only to a third group of countries, with inverse demand function $p = A - x - y$. Product market competition is of the Cournot variety. Each unit of output produces a unit of pollution. However, there is a technology for abating pollution so that net emissions are $e = x - a$ where a is the level of abatement and costs of abatement are $0.5a^2$. Net emissions of pollution affect only the country in which they are emitted. The only element of asymmetry between the two countries allowed is that they may differ in their damage costs.[3] Thus, if ε denotes the level of net emissions in the foreign country, then damage costs in the home and foreign country are respectively $0.5de^2$ and $0.5\delta\varepsilon^2$.

The government in each country can affect the level of pollution by means of either an emission standard (an upper limit on pollution emitted by its domestic firm) or an emission tax. The emission standard and emission tax in the home (foreign) country are denoted by e and t (ε and τ). Government welfare is profits plus tax revenue (if any) minus damage costs. The move structure is that of a two-stage game: in the first stage the governments set their policy instruments (these can be set either cooperatively or non-cooperatively); and in the second stage the firms take these policy instruments as given and choose output levels in a Cournot game. In the rest of this section the cooperative and non-cooperative equilibria when the governments use emission standards and emission taxes will be set out.

Emission standards
1. Second-stage game   The firm in the home country takes as given the emission standard, e, and the output of the other firm, y, and chooses x to maximize $\pi(x, y) \equiv (A - x - y)x - 0.5(x - e)^2$. Solving the first-order conditions yields the equilibrium output levels:

$$X(e, \varepsilon) \equiv \frac{(2A + 3e - \varepsilon)}{8} \quad Y(e, \varepsilon) \equiv \frac{(2A + 3\varepsilon - e)}{8} \tag{1}$$

Not surprisingly, the domestic firm's output is an increasing (decreasing) function of the emission standard set by the home (foreign) country, so that raising the emission standard (relaxing environmental policy) increases the output of the domestic firm and reduces the output of the foreign firm.

2. First-stage game   Consider again the home country. The home government's welfare function is:

$$V(e, \varepsilon, d) \equiv \pi[X(e, \varepsilon), Y(e, \varepsilon)] - 0.5\, de^2$$

which, from (1), becomes:

$$V(e, \varepsilon, d) = \frac{3(2A - \varepsilon)^2 + 18e(2A - \varepsilon) - (37 + 64d)e^2}{128} \qquad (2)$$

The foreign country has welfare function $V(\varepsilon, e, \delta)$. Two ways of determining equilibrium emission standards are considered.

Non-cooperative equilibrium
The home country takes as given the emission standard of the foreign country, ε, and chooses e to maximize (2). The first-order condition can be rearranged to give the home country reaction function: $e = R(\varepsilon) \equiv (18A - 9\varepsilon)/(37 + 64d)$. The reaction function is linear, downward sloping, with slope less than 1 in absolute value. In e, ε space, the iso-welfare contour is upward sloping for $e < R(\varepsilon)$, vertical at $e = R(\varepsilon)$, and downward sloping for $e > R(\varepsilon)$ (see Figure 4.1). It is also clear that an increase in d shifts down the home country's reaction function.

There will be a similar reaction function for the foreign country, and solving the pair of first-order conditions yields the unique set of Nash non-cooperative emission standards:

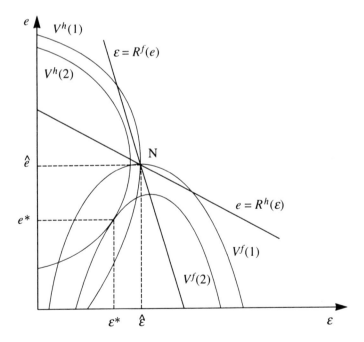

Figure 4.1: Cooperative and non-cooperative equilibria – emission standards

$$\hat{e}(d,\delta) \equiv \frac{18A(28+64\delta)}{1288+2368(d+\delta)+4096d\delta}$$

$$\hat{\varepsilon}(d,\delta) \equiv \frac{18A(28+64d)}{1288+2368(d+\delta)+4096d\delta} \tag{3}$$

It is easily demonstrated that $\hat{e}_d < 0$, $\hat{e}_\delta > 0$ and similarly for the foreign country emissions, so that an increase in the damage cost parameter of the home country, d, will result in lower home country emissions but higher foreign country emissions. In particular, it should be clear that starting from a position where $d = \delta$, and hence where non-cooperative emissions are equal in the two countries, an increase in d reduces emissions in the country with the higher damages and increases emissions in the country with the lower damages.

Cooperative equilibrium
In this case, emission standards in the home and foreign country are chosen to maximize $V(e, \varepsilon, d) + \omega V(\varepsilon, e, \delta)$ where $\omega > 0$ is a welfare weight attached to welfare in country 2. The reason for introducing the welfare weight is to ensure that the solution of the second-stage game is an equilibrium which is Pareto efficient and Pareto dominates the non-cooperative equilibrium. Carrying out the optimization yields the cooperative equilibrium emission standards:

$$e^*(d,\delta,\omega) \equiv \frac{12A\left[(3-\omega)(74\omega+128\delta\omega-6)-18(3\omega-1)(1+\omega)\right]}{\left\{(74\omega+128\delta\omega-6)(74+128d-6\omega)-\left[18(1+\omega)\right]^2\right\}}$$

$$\varepsilon^*(d,\delta,\omega) \equiv \frac{12A\left[(3\omega-1)(74+128d-6\omega)-18(3-\omega)(1+\omega)\right]}{\left\{(74\omega+128\delta\omega-6)(74+128d-6\omega)-\left[18(1+\omega)\right]^2\right\}} \tag{4}$$

For the case where $\omega = 1$, (4) can be simplified to:

$$e^*(d,\delta,1) = \frac{12A(16+64\delta)}{\left[832+2176(d+\delta)+4096d\delta\right]}$$

$$\varepsilon^*(d,\delta,1) = \frac{12A(16+64d)}{\left[832+2176(d+\delta)+4096d\delta\right]} \tag{5}$$

It is readily seen that $e^*(d, \delta, 1) < \hat{e}(d, \delta)$, $\varepsilon^*(d, \delta, 1) < \hat{\varepsilon}(d, \delta)$, i.e., the cooperative equilibrium involves lower emissions for both countries than does the non-cooperative equilibrium (see Figure 4.1). As with the non-cooperative case, if damage costs are different in the two countries, emissions will be lower in the country with the higher damage costs.

Emission taxes
1. Second-stage game   The firm in the home country takes as given the emission tax rate, t, and the output of the other firm, y, and chooses its output, x, and its abatement level, a, to maximize $\Pi(x, y) \equiv (A - x - y)x - t(x - a) - 0.5a^2$. The solution involves the home firm setting abatement level $a = t$, and the equilibrium levels of output are given by:

$$X(t, \tau) \equiv \frac{(A - 2t + \tau)}{3}, Y(t, \tau) \equiv \frac{(A - 2\tau + t)}{3} \qquad (6)$$

Thus, an increase in the home country's emission tax will reduce the domestic firm's output and increase the foreign firm's output, so that, as with standards, a relaxation of the home country's environmental policy (reduction in emission tax) will increase the home firm's output and decrease the foreign firm's output.[4]

2. First-stage game   The home country government's welfare function is:

$$W(t, \tau, d) \equiv \Pi [X(t, \tau), Y(t, \tau)] + t[X(t, \tau) - t] - 0.5[X(t, \tau) - t]^2$$

which, on inserting (6), becomes:

$$W(t, \tau, d) = \frac{\left[(2 - d)(A + \tau)^2 + (10d - 2)(A + \tau)t - (13 + 25d)t^2 \right]}{18} \qquad (7)$$

The foreign country will have a corresponding welfare function $W(\tau, t, \delta)$.

Non-cooperative equilibrium
Each country takes as given the emission tax of the other country and chooses its own emission tax to maximize welfare, which yields a pair of reaction functions:

$$
\begin{aligned}
t = \phi(A + \tau) \quad & \phi \equiv \left[\frac{(5d - 1)}{(13 + 25d)} \right] \quad \phi < 0.2 \\[2mm]
t = \psi(A + t) \quad & \psi \equiv \left[\frac{(5\delta - 1)}{(13 + 25\delta)} \right] \quad \psi < 0.2
\end{aligned}
\qquad (8)
$$

It will be assumed that d and δ are greater than 0.2, such that ϕ and ψ are positive (the possibility of the countries setting negative emission taxes arises because

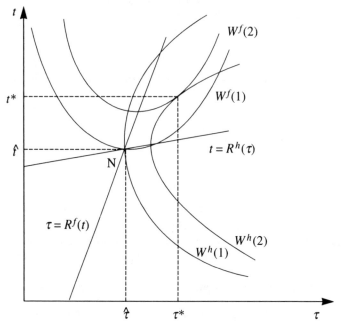

Figure 4.2:   Cooperative and non-cooperative equilibria – emission taxes

if environmental damages were very low, the optimal policy for the governments would be to set an export or production subsidy). From (8) it can be seen that reaction functions are upward-sloping, with a slope of less than 1. From (7) it is readily shown that, for $d < 2.0$, in t, τ space, the home country's iso-welfare contour is downward-sloping for $t < \phi(A + \tau)$, vertical for $t = \phi(A + \tau)$ and upward-sloping for $t > \phi(A + \tau)$ (see Figure 4.2). It is also evident that an increase in d increases ϕ, so that an increase in damage costs results in the home country setting a higher emission tax (i.e., the home country reaction function shifts upwards). To ensure that emission taxes are positive and that iso-welfare contours have the appropriate shape, it will be assumed that $0.2 < d, \delta < 2.0$.

Solving the reaction functions in (8) yields the non-cooperative equilibrium emission taxes:

$$\hat{t}(d,\delta) = \hat{t}(\phi,\psi) = \frac{\left[\phi(1+\psi)A\right]}{(1-\phi\psi)}$$

$$\hat{\tau}(d,\delta) = \hat{\tau}(\phi,\psi) = \frac{\left[\psi(1+\phi)A\right]}{(1-\phi\psi)}$$

(9)

It is easy to see that $\hat{\imath}_d = \hat{\imath}_\phi > 0$, $\hat{\imath}_\delta = \hat{\imath}_\psi > 0$, $\hat{\tau}_d = \hat{\tau}_\phi > 0$, $\hat{\tau}_\delta = \hat{\tau}_\psi > 0$, such that an increase in, for instance, home country damage costs increases both home and foreign country emission taxes, as would be expected from the properties of the reaction functions set out above. It is also clear, from (9), that if damage costs differ in the two countries, then the non-cooperative emission tax will be higher in the country with the higher damage costs.

Cooperative equilibrium

Emission taxes in the home and foreign country are chosen to maximize $W(t, \tau, d) + \omega W(\tau, t, \delta)$ which yields emission taxes:

$$t^*(d,\delta,\omega) = \frac{A\left\{\left[(5d-1)+\omega(2-\delta)\right]\left[(13+25\delta)\omega-(2-d)\right]+\left[(2-d)+\omega(5\delta-1)\right]\left[(5d-1)+\omega(5\delta-1)\right]\right\}}{\left\{\left[(13+25\delta)\omega-(2-d)\right]\left[(13+25d)-\omega(2-\delta)\right]-\left[(5d-1)+\omega(5\delta-1)\right]^2\right\}}$$

$$\tau^*(d,\delta,\omega) = \frac{A\left\{\left[\omega(5\delta-1)+(2-d)\right]\left[(13+25d)-\omega(2-\delta)\right]+\left[\omega(2-\delta)+(5d-1)\right]\left[(5d-1)+\omega(5\delta-1)\right]\right\}}{\left\{\left[(13+25\delta)\omega-(2-d)\right]\left[(13+25d)-\omega(2-\delta)\right]-\left[(5d-1)+\omega(5\delta-1)\right]^2\right\}}$$

For the case where $\omega = 1$, the cooperative emission taxes become:

$$\begin{aligned}
t^*(d,\delta,1) &= \frac{\left[A(1+7d+\delta+16d\delta)\right]}{(13+34d+34\delta+64d\delta)} \\
\tau^*(d,\delta,1) &= \frac{\left[A(1+7\delta+d+16d\delta)\right]}{(13+34d+34\delta+64d\delta)}
\end{aligned} \tag{10}$$

Some rather tedious algebra confirms that $t^*(d, \delta, 1) > \hat{\imath}(d, \delta)$, $\tau^*(d, \delta, 1) > \hat{\tau}(d, \delta)$ such that the cooperative equilibrium requires both countries to set higher emission taxes (tougher environmental policies) than they would in the non-cooperative equilibrium. As with the non-cooperative case, it is clear that if one country has higher damage costs than the other, then the cooperative emission tax (with $\omega = 1$) in that country will be higher than in the other country.

This completes the analysis of the non-cooperative and cooperative equilibria in the case of full information. There is one final point to note. The analysis has been worked out for the case where there is Cournot competition between the two firms at the second-stage game. For the purposes of this chapter, nothing of substance would change if Bertrand competition had been assumed. What is crucial is the nature of the welfare functions for the two countries when standards and taxes are used. It would still be the case that regardless of the policy instrument used, the non-cooperative equilibrium involves both countries setting less stringent environmental policies than they would if they cooperated. Moreover, the slopes of the reaction functions and iso-welfare contours for emission standards and taxes would be exactly the same as in Figures 4.1 and 4.2 respectively. Of course, as Barrett (1994) and Ulph (1996b, 1996c) have noted, there is one important difference between the Cournot and Bertrand cases. In the Cournot case, environmental policy in the non-cooperative case will be more lax than in the non-strategic case where governments use the 'naive first-best' rule of setting emission taxes equal to marginal damage costs. Conversely, in the Bertrand case environmental policy will be tougher in the non-cooperative case than in the non-strategic case. But in this chapter it is the comparisons between the cooperative and non-cooperative outcomes that are of interest rather than the comparison between the strategic and non-strategic outcomes.

3. Harmonization and minimum standards

In this section it will be assumed that if there exists some supra-national environmental authority such as the European Commission, or a federal government in a federal–state constitutional structure, then that authority seeks to improve upon the non-cooperative outcomes derived in the last section, but cannot simply impose the cooperative solution on the two parties. In this section there will be no attempt to justify why the Commission or a federal government cannot impose the cooperative solution; an obvious reason is lack of information, but this will be discussed in the next section. For simplicity, the supra-national or federal authority will be referred to as 'the Commission', while recognizing that the analysis is not confined to that specific European example.[5] Two mechanisms that the Commission may use to improve upon the non-cooperative outcome will be explored: environmental policy harmonization and minimum standards. It will be demonstrated that if countries are sufficiently different in their damage costs, then harmonization cannot effect a Pareto-improvement over the non-cooperative outcome regardless of whether emission taxes or emission standards are used. If emission standards are used, then the use of minimum standards, to the extent that this does not imply harmonization, can never effect a Pareto-improvement over the non-cooperative outcome; whereas if emission taxes are used, then minimum standards can effect a small Pareto-improvement.

Harmonization

The case where both governments use emission standards as their policy instrument will be considered first. To begin, the argument will be presented by means of a simple diagram, and then the formal analysis will be introduced. Suppose that the damage-cost parameter for the foreign country was fixed at, say, $\delta = 1$, and that the Commission requires both governments to set an emission standard of E. The first question is what is the value of E, denoted by

E^*, which yields the foreign government the highest level of welfare? This is shown in Figure 4.3. There will be a value of the home country damage-cost parameter, d^*, say, such that non-cooperative equilibrium, point N in Figure 4.3, yields the foreign country the same level of welfare as this best-harmonized policy. Since point N must involve the foreign country having higher emissions than the home country, from the analysis of the previous section it must be the case that $d^* > 1$. But if the home country has a damage cost parameter $d > d^*$, this implies a downward shift in the home country's reaction function, R^h, and this will move point N down the foreign country's reaction function and so increase the welfare of the foreign country. But this means there is no harmonized policy which Pareto-dominates the non-cooperative equilibrium when $d > d^*$. Thus, d^* denotes the maximum degree of asymmetry between the two countries beyond which harmonization will fail to yield a Pareto-improvement over the non-cooperative outcome.

The diagrammatic argument just presented can be expressed formally as follows. Define $\bar{V}(E, \delta) \equiv V(E, E, \delta)$ as the welfare of a country with damage cost parameter δ under a harmonized policy. Maximization with respect to E yields the value of the harmonized emission level, $E^*(\delta) = (3A)/(13 + 16\delta)$ which gives the foreign country the highest welfare level under the harmonized policy,

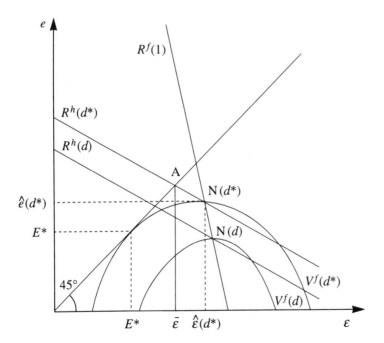

Figure 4.3: Harmonization and minimum standards – emission standards

with $\bar{V}^*(\delta) \equiv [A^2(2496 + 5568\delta + 3072\delta^2)]/[128(169 + 416\delta + 256\delta^2)]$ being the corresponding level of welfare. Now assume that in the foreign country $\delta = 1$, so that the corresponding level of maximum harmonized welfare for the foreign country is $\bar{V}^*(1) = (11136A^2)/(128 \times 841)$.

Consider the non-cooperative equilibrium. Define $\hat{V}^h(d) \equiv V[\hat{e}(d, 1), \hat{e}(d, 1), d]$ and $\hat{V}^f(d) \equiv V[\hat{e}(d, 1), \hat{e}(d, 1)]$ as the non-cooperative welfare levels of the home and foreign countries when the home country has damage cost parameter d and the foreign country has damage cost parameter 1. From the properties of the welfare function and the non-cooperative equilibrium it is evident that $\{[d\hat{V}^h(d)]/dd\} < 0$, $\{[d\hat{V}^f(d)]/dd\} > 0$, i.e., an increase in the damage-cost parameter of the home country reduces the non-cooperative welfare level of the home country and increases the non-cooperative welfare level of the foreign country. Explicit evaluation yields the following:

$$\hat{V}^f(d) = \frac{\left[A^2\left(1900416 + 8687616d + 9928704d^2\right)\right]}{\left[128\left(208849 + 738512d + 652864d^2\right)\right]}$$

Define d^* as the value of d for which $\hat{V}^f(d^*) \equiv \bar{V}^*(1)$. Then direct calculation gives $d^* = 1.3493$. Recalling that $\delta = 1$, this demonstrates that if the home country has a damage-cost parameter which is greater than the foreign country's parameter by more than 35 per cent, then there is no harmonized policy that can make the foreign country better off than the non-cooperative equilibrium.

Exactly the same analysis can be made for the case where both countries use emission taxes (see Figure 4.4) resulting in the same conclusion, except that the critical value for d is $d^* = 1.5122$.

Thus, if countries differ in their damage cost parameters by more than approximately 50 per cent, harmonization cannot yield a Pareto-improvement over the non-cooperative equilibrium, regardless of which policy instrument is used. In both cases it is the country with the lower damage costs that can be made worse off by harmonization. The reason is intuitively obvious. Start from a Nash equilibrium, keep the total level of output constant but move towards harmonization; the home country experiences an increase in output and pollution, while the foreign country faces a reduction in output and pollution. By construction of the Nash equilibrium, the *direct* effect on home country profits and hence welfare from an increase in its output equals the loss of welfare from the additional pollution, and similarly for the foreign country. The home country, though, derives an *indirect* gain in profits from the contraction of output of its rival, while the foreign country experiences an indirect loss of profit from the expansion of output by its rival. Thus, the foreign country has more to lose from harmonization than does the home country.

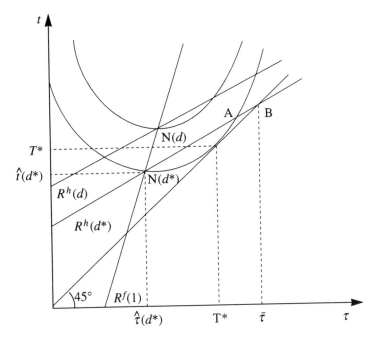

Figure 4.4:   Harmonization and minimum standards – emission taxes

Minimum standards and minimum emission taxes
It is fairly obvious that if the asymmetries between countries are too large, then a policy of harmonizing environmental policies is unlikely to yield a Pareto-improvement over the non-cooperative equilibrium. However, it is frequently thought that using minimum standards will obviate this problem since only the countries that fall below the minimum standard will be required to tighten their standards, while other countries can choose to set standards above the minimum. The hope is that these latter countries will respond to the raising of standards in the former group of countries by also tightening their environmental standards – a form of ratchet effect. As noted in the introduction, Kanbur et al. (1994) provide an example where such a minimum standards policy will work. This section will demonstrate that when governments use emission standards as their policy instrument (the case considered by Kanbur et al.) then, to the extent that minimum standards yield an outcome different from harmonization, the use of minimum standards will make the country with lower damage costs (higher emissions) worse off than in the non-cooperative equilibrium, even if countries differ only slightly in their damage costs. Conversely, when emission taxes are the chosen policy instrument, then the use of minimum standards can achieve a Pareto-improvement.

1. Emission standards   Again it will be simplest to begin with a diagrammatic exposition. Consider Figure 4.3 where the home country has higher damage costs than the foreign country, such that at the non-cooperative equilibrium, point N, the foreign country has higher emissions than the home country. A policy of minimum standards in this context would require the Commission to set an upper limit on the emission standard each government can impose on its domestic firm. There are then three cases: (a) if the upper limit exceeds $\hat{\varepsilon}$, then both countries will set their emission standards below the upper limit , and the equilibrium will just be the existing non-cooperative equilibrium; (b) if the upper limit lies in the interval $(\bar{\varepsilon}, \hat{\varepsilon})$, then the foreign country will need to reduce its emission standard to the upper limit set by the Commission, whereas the home country will not be affected by the upper limit and will be free to make its best response to the (imposed) emission standard of the foreign country; thus, the equilibrium will move along the segment AN of the home country's reaction function; and (c) if the upper limit lies below $\bar{\varepsilon}$, then both countries will be constrained to set their emission standards equal to the upper limit and the equilibrium will move down the 45° line from point A to the origin; in other words, a minimum-standards policy is now equivalent to a harmonization policy.

To distinguish minimum standards from harmonization only the second of these three cases is of interest. It is immediately clear from the diagram that when the equilibrium lies in the range AN this must make the foreign country worse off than at point N, for the reduction in output by the foreign firm is accompanied by an *increase* in emissions and output by the home firm. Both these moves make the foreign country worse off. The result is different from that of Kanbur et al. because in this model the government reaction functions have different slopes from those in Kanbur et al., whose reaction functions had properties similar to those of our emission tax case. In particular, note that the minimum-standards policy fails because it does not have the 'ratchet effect' of inducing the country that sets environmental standards that are tougher than the minimum to tighten its environmental standards in response to the tightening of environmental standards in the other country; when the foreign country tightens environmental policy, the home country relaxes its policy. Starting from the Nash equilibrium, a small reduction in the emission standard of the foreign country, keeping the emission standard of the home country fixed, will leave the foreign country neither better nor worse off (the marginal loss of profits is matched by the marginal reduction in damage costs). The fact that this is accompanied by an increase in emission standard by the home country makes the foreign country worse off.

Formalizing the argument, suppose that the Commission requires both governments to set an emission standard no higher than $\theta\hat{e}(d, \delta)$, where $\theta \leq 1$, and that θ is such that $e(\theta) \equiv \{[18A - \theta\hat{e}(d, \delta)]/(37 + 64d)\} < \theta\hat{e}(d,\delta)$, i.e., the home country's best response to the upper limit still means that it sets a lower emission standard than the upper-limit emission standard imposed on the foreign country. Define $V^f(\theta) \equiv V(\theta \hat{e}(d, \delta), e(\theta), \delta)$ as the level of welfare of the foreign country for different values of θ. Then $dV^f(\theta)/d\theta = (\partial V/\partial \varepsilon)\hat{e} + (\partial V/\partial e).e'(\theta)$. The second term is always positive, while for $\theta \le 1$ the first term is non-negative. Thus the foreign country's welfare strictly increases in θ in the range $\theta \le 1$, and so any imposition of a minimum standard which affects only the high-emission country must make that country worse off.

2. Emission taxes   As above, we begin with a simple diagrammatic argument (see Figure 4.4). Minimum standards now implies setting a minimum level of emission tax. Figure 4.4 shows a case where damage costs are higher in the home than in the foreign country. Thus, at the non-cooperative equilibrium, N, the foreign country sets a lower emission tax than the home country. Again there are three cases: (a) if the Commission sets its minimum emission tax below $\hat{\tau}$, this constraint will not affect either government; (b) if the minimum tax lies in the interval $(\hat{\tau}, \bar{\tau})$, then the constraint will affect the foreign government but not the home country; the home country will set its emission tax as a best response to the foreign government's (imposed) emission tax, and the equilibrium will lie on the home country's reaction function in the range NB; and (c) if the minimum tax imposed by the Commission is above $\bar{\tau}$, then the constraint affects both countries and the equilibrium will simply lie on the 45° line above point B.

Once more, the only case that is of interest and is distinct from the harmonization policy is the second case. Note that as long as the equilibrium lies in the range NA then the minimum-standards policy makes both countries better off. The reason is simple. Starting from the Nash equilibrium, an increase in the emission tax by the foreign country, keeping constant the tax in the home country, will, to the first order, leave the foreign firm no better or worse off (the reduction in profits exactly matches the reduction in pollution damage). The increase in the tax of the home country, though, makes the foreign country better off.

More formally, suppose the Commission requires both countries to set emission taxes at least as great as $\theta \hat{\tau}(d, \delta)$ with $\theta \ge 1$, and suppose that θ is such that the home country's best response to this lower limit is to set an emission tax at least as great as the lower limit, i.e., $t(\theta) \equiv \phi[A + \theta \hat{\tau}(d, \delta)] \ge \theta \hat{\tau}(d, \delta)$. Then define the welfare of the foreign country for any given level of θ as: $W^f(\theta) \equiv W[\theta \hat{\tau}(d, \delta), t(\theta), \delta]$. It is clear that $dW^f(\theta)/d\theta = (\partial W/\partial \tau)\hat{\tau} + (\partial W/\partial t)t'(\theta)$. The second term is strictly positive, while the first term is zero for $\theta = 1$ but negative for $\theta > 1$. Thus, a small increase in θ above 1 will allow the foreign country to be better off. To see how large θ can get without making the foreign country worse off, it is necessary to find the value of $\bar{\theta}$ such that $W^f(\bar{\theta}) = W^f(1)$. Direct evaluation for the case where $\delta = 1$ shows that the critical value is $\bar{\theta} = 1 + 27\phi/(38 - 8\phi - \phi^2)$; since $\phi \le 0.2$, this means that $\bar{\theta} \le 1.1485$. Thus it is possible to raise the emission tax of the lowest tax country by approximately 15 per cent without making that country worse off. Given the slopes of the reaction functions, that will elicit roughly a 3 per cent increase in the emission tax of the high-emission tax country. Thus, the use of minimum-emission taxes brings about a rather modest increase in emission taxes in the two countries.

To conclude this section, it has been shown that if countries are sufficiently asymmetric in their damage-cost functions, which in this example means that the high damage-cost country has costs at least 50 per cent greater than the low damage-cost country, then harmonization of environmental standards or taxes cannot yield a Pareto-improvement over the non-cooperative outcome. If governments use emission standards as policy instruments, then, for this model, minimum standards, to the extent that they are different from harmonization, make the low damage-cost country worse off than the non-cooperative equilibrium and does not achieve any tightening of standards in the high damage-cost country. On the other hand, if governments use emission taxes, then setting a minimum level of emission tax can generate an increase in emission taxes in all countries, though the extent of the increase that can be generated without making the low damage-cost country worse off is fairly modest.

4. Optimal regulation with asymmetric information

Introduction
It is reasonable to ask why one should be concerned with the issue of whether harmonization or minimum standards can deliver a Pareto-improvement over the non-cooperative outcome. Why does the Commission not just implement the cooperative solution identified in section 2? One reason might be the political issue of the relative powers to be exercised by the Commission and national governments – the 'subsidiarity' question. It is one thing to identify a *prima facie* case that there are gains to be made relative to a non-cooperative outcome, but it is another matter for the Commission to determine national environmental policies. Of course this objection could also be applied to uniform emission standards or taxes as well as to the setting of cooperative emission standards or taxes; on the other hand, the setting of minimum standards or taxes, by leaving some discretion in the hands of national governments, may be the maximum power that national governments are willing to cede to the Commission.

But this does not answer the question as to why national governments should not wish to devolve powers to the Commission if they know that this will make them all better off. The reason considered in this section is that the Commission may not know as much about the environmental damages of individual nation-states as the states themselves, and thus could not impose the full information cooperative solution identified in section 2. It could then be argued that if the Commission believes that the non-cooperative outcome results in all governments imposing too lenient environmental policies, but that it cannot determine what the 'right' policy should be for any individual country, then the only policy open to the Commission would be to attempt to tighten all environmental policies by means of minimum standards or taxes.

The assumption of asymmetric information between a central government and local governments is fairly standard in the fiscal federalism literature but may be thought to be more questionable in the environmental context where there is scope for obtaining scientific evidence about, for instance, the ability of a particular environment to assimilate a given level of pollution. Even if such information were widely available, which may be doubtful given this chapter's concern with local pollution problems, there is still the important question of whether a central authority would be able to learn the preferences of the local population for a cleaner environment. This is directly analogous to the assumption in the fiscal federalism literature that local governments have better information about local preferences for local public goods than does a central government.

However, if asymmetric information is the reason why the Commission cannot impose the full information cooperative solution identified in section 2, then the implications for policy should be deduced directly in a model of asymmetric information, and that is what is done in this section. A very simple model is developed where the Commission does not know what the environmental damage-cost parameters are for individual countries, and has to design its environmental policy so as to induce individual countries to reveal this information correctly. Of course, if the damage-cost parameter for an individual country is private information to that country, that means that both the non-cooperative and cooperative equilibria have to be reformulated to deal with this asymmetry of information. So in this section both the non-cooperative and cooperative equilibria under asymmetric information will be derived, for the cases where both governments use emission standards and emission taxes. These equilibria with asymmetric information will be compared with the corresponding equilibria with full information derived in section 2.

Asymmetric information
It is assumed that for each of the two countries, the environmental damage-cost parameter (d or δ) is private information. However, it is common knowledge to both countries and to the Commission that the damage-cost parameter can take one of only two values, high, C, or low, c, with probabilities p and $1 - p$ respectively. Thus there are three possible states of the world: both countries have high damage costs; both have low damage costs; and one has high damage costs while the other has low damage costs. In order to make the comparisons between the full and asymmetric information cases it will be useful to restate

the results for the full information equilibria derived in section 2 while using the notation developed for this section.

1. Emission standards   There are four relevant emission standards: those set by both countries in the first state, i.e., when both have high damage costs; those set by both countries in the second state, i.e., when they both have low damage costs; and those set by the high and low damage-cost countries in the third state of the world where the two countries have different damage costs. In the full information cooperative equilibria, equation (4) demonstrates that these four emission standards are, respectively:

$$e^*_{CC} \equiv e^*(C,C,1) = \frac{3A}{(13+16C)} \tag{11a}$$

$$e^*_{cc} \equiv e^*(c,c,1) = \frac{3A}{(13+16c)} \tag{11b}$$

$$e^*_{Cc} \equiv e^*(C,c,\omega) = \frac{12A\{(3-\omega)[74\omega+128c\omega-6]-18(3\omega-1)(1+\omega)\}}{[74\omega+128c\omega-6][74+128C-6\omega]-[18(1+\omega)]^2} \tag{11c}$$

$$e^*_{cC} \equiv \varepsilon^*(C,c,\omega) = \frac{12A\{(3\omega-1)[74+128C-6\omega]-18(3-\omega)(1+\omega)\}}{[74\omega+128c\omega-6][74+128C-6\omega]-[18(1+\omega0)]^2} \tag{11d}$$

It is readily shown that for $\omega = 1$,

$$e^*_{Cc} < e^*_{CC} < e^*_{cc} < e^*_{cC}; \quad 2e^*_{CC} < e^*_{Cc} + e^*_{cC} < 2e^*_{cc}$$

i.e., aggregate emissions (and hence industry output) are lowest when both countries have high damage costs, highest when both have low damage costs, and intermediate when one has high damage costs and the other has low damage costs. However, in this last case the high-damage country will produce less output than in the case where both firms have high damage costs. The reason is as follows: Start from the position where both countries have high damage-cost parameters and reduce the damage-cost parameter for one country. If the output for the high damage-cost country was kept constant, then output in the low damage-cost country would be expanded until, using the standard efficiency argument, marginal damage costs were equal in both countries. But this expansion of total output will have driven marginal profits below marginal damage costs, and so it will be necessary to reduce output in both countries.

From Section 2, equation (3), the four emission standards in the full information non-cooperative equilibrium are:

$$\hat{e}_{CC} \equiv \hat{e}(C,C) = \frac{9A}{(23+32C)} \tag{12a}$$

$$\hat{e}_{cc} \equiv \hat{e}(c,c) = \frac{9A}{(23+32c)} \tag{12b}$$

$$\hat{e}_{Cc} \equiv \hat{e}(C,c) = \frac{18A(28+64c)}{[1288+2368(c+C)+4096cC]} \tag{12c}$$

$$\hat{e}_{cC} \equiv \hat{e}(C,c) = \frac{18A(28+64C)}{[1288+2368(c+C)+4096cC]} \tag{12d}$$

As with the cooperative case, the ranking of the emissions is:

$$\hat{e}_{Cc} < \hat{e}_{CC} < \hat{e}_{cc} < \hat{e}_{cC}; \; 2\hat{e}_{CC} < \hat{e}_{Cc} + \hat{e}_{cC} < 2\hat{e}_{cc}.$$

The rationale for this ranking is the same as above.

We also know from section 2 that $e^*_{d\delta} < \hat{e}_{d\delta}, d = c, C, \delta = c, C$.

2. Emission taxes   In a similar fashion, there are four emission taxes to be determined, and in the full information cooperative case these are, respectively, from equation (10):

$$t^*_{CC} \equiv t^*(C,C,1) = \frac{[A(4C+1)]}{(13+16C)} \tag{13a}$$

$$t^*_{cc} \equiv t^*(c,c,1) = \frac{[A(4c+1)]}{(13+16c)} \tag{13b}$$

$$t^*_{Cc} \equiv t^*(C,c,\omega) = \frac{A\{[(5C-1)+\omega(2-c)][(13+25c)\omega-(2-C)]+[(2-C)+\omega(5c-1)][(5C-1)+\omega(5c-1)]\}}{\{[(13+25c)\omega-(2-C)][(13+25C)-\omega(2-c)]-[(5C-1)+\omega(5c-1)]^2\}}$$

(13c)

$$t^*_{cC} \equiv t^*(C,c,\omega) = \frac{A\{[\omega(5c-1)+(2-C)][(13+25C)-\omega(2-c)]+[\omega(2-c)+(5C-1)][(5C-1)+\omega(5c-1)]\}}{\{[(13+25c)\omega-(2-C)][(13+25C)-\omega(2-c)]-[(5C-1)+\omega(5c-1)]^2\}}$$

(13d)

For $\omega = 1$, it is readily shown that:

$$t^*_{CC} > t^*_{cC}; \quad t^*_{Cc} > t^*_{cc}; \quad t^*_{CC} > t^*_{Cc} \Leftrightarrow C > \frac{7}{8}; \quad t^*_{cC} > t^*_{cc} \Leftrightarrow c > \frac{7}{8}.$$

Finally, from (9), we have:

$$\hat{t}_{CC} \equiv \hat{t}(C,C) = \frac{A(5C-1)}{14+20C} = \frac{A\phi}{1-\phi}$$

(14a)

$$\hat{t}_{cc} \equiv \hat{t}(c,c) = \frac{A(5c-1)}{14+20c} = \frac{A\psi}{1-\psi}$$

(14b)

$$\hat{t}_{Cc} \equiv \hat{t}(C,c) = \frac{A(5C-1)(12+30c)}{(13+25c)(13+25C)-(5c-1)(5C-1)} = \frac{A\phi(1+\psi)}{1-\phi\psi}$$

(14c)

$$\hat{t}_{cC} \equiv \hat{t}(c,C) = \frac{A(5c-1)(12+30C)}{(13+25c)(13+25C)-(5c-1)(5C-1)} = \frac{A\psi(1+\phi)}{1-\phi\psi}$$

(14d)

where $\phi = \frac{(5C-1)}{(13+25C)} \quad \psi = \frac{(5c-1)}{(13+25c)}.$

It is readily shown that $\hat{t}_{cc} < \hat{t}_{cC} < \hat{t}_{Cc} < \hat{t}_{CC}.$

Asymmetric information : non-cooperative equilibria
1. Emission standards   The solution concept employed is the standard Bayesian Nash equilibrium (Fudenberg and Tirole 1991). Thus the home country will set

emission levels $\breve{e}_C$, $\breve{e}_c$ contingent on having high and low damage costs, while the foreign country will similarly set emission levels $\breve{\varepsilon}_C$, $\breve{\varepsilon}_c$.
$\breve{e}_C$ is chosen to maximize $pV(\breve{e}_C, \breve{\varepsilon}_C, C) + (1-p) V(\breve{e}_C, \breve{\varepsilon}_c, C)$ where the welfare function $V(.,.,.)$ was defined in (2). The first order condition for this maximization is:

$$36A - 18 \,[p\breve{\varepsilon}_C + (1-p)\,\breve{\varepsilon}_c] - 2(37 + 64C)\breve{e}_C = 0 \qquad (15a)$$

Similarly, the first order condition for the optimal choice of $\breve{e}_c$ is:

$$36A - 18 \,[p\breve{\varepsilon}_C + (1-p)\breve{\varepsilon}_c] - 2(37 + 64c)\breve{e}_c = 0 \qquad (15b)$$

By symmetry, (15a) and (15b) can be solved to yield the following equilibrium emission standards:

$$\breve{e}_{CC} \equiv \breve{e}_{Cc} \equiv \breve{e}_C = \frac{\left[18A(37+64c)\right]}{\left[(37+64C)(37+64c) + 9\!\left(37+64\overline{C}\right)\right]} \qquad (16a)$$

$$\breve{e}_{cC} \equiv \breve{e}_{cc} \equiv \breve{e}_c = \frac{\left[18A(37+64C)\right]}{\left[(37+64C)(37+64c) + 9\!\left(37+64\overline{C}\right)\right]} \qquad (16b)$$

where $\overline{C} \equiv pC + (1-p)c$
Comparing (16) and (12) it is clear that:

$$\hat{e}_{Cc} < \breve{e}_{Cc} = \breve{e}_{CC} < \hat{e}_{CC}; \quad \hat{e}_{cc} < \breve{e}_{cc} = \breve{e}_{cC} < \hat{e}_{cC}$$

so that the emission standards for the non-cooperative equilibrium with asymmetric information lie between the appropriate emission standards for the non-cooperative equilibrium with full information.

2. Emission taxes The details of the analysis will not be provided here since they are identical to those for emission standards. As such, the equilibrium emission taxes can be reported simply as:

$$\breve{t}_C \equiv \breve{t}_{CC} \equiv \breve{t}_{Cc} = \frac{A\phi}{\left[1 - p\phi - (1-p)\psi\right]} \qquad , \qquad (17a)$$

$$\breve{t}_c \equiv \breve{t}_{cC} \equiv \breve{t}_{cc} = \frac{A\psi}{\left[1 - p\phi - (1 - p)\psi\right]} \tag{17b}$$

It is readily shown that:

$$\hat{t}_{cC} < \breve{t}_{Cc} = \breve{t}_{CC} < \hat{t}_{CC}; \quad \breve{t}_{Cc} > \hat{t}_{Cc} \Leftrightarrow \psi < \frac{p}{1 - p}$$

$$\hat{t}_{cc} < \breve{t}_{cc} = \breve{t}_{cC} < \hat{t}_{Cc}; \quad \breve{t}_{cC} < \hat{t}_{cC} \Leftrightarrow \phi < \frac{1 - p}{p}$$

so that the non-cooperative emission taxes with asymmetric information will lie between the corresponding non-cooperative emission taxes with full information unless p is close to either zero or one.

D. Asymmetric information – cooperative equilibrium

The model in this section is a standard principal-agent model.[6] The structure of moves will be that the Commission will first ask each country to declare its damage-cost parameter. Each country will be assigned an appropriate emission standard or emission tax dependent upon which of the three possible states of the world has been declared. The aim of the Commission is to set the emission standards or emission taxes in such a way as to elicit truthful revelation. It should be clear from earlier sections that the relevant constraint for truthful revelation is to ensure that high damage-cost countries do not pretend to be low damage-cost countries in order to be allowed to set a high emission standard or low emission tax, and hence gain a larger market share. Clearly, low damage-cost countries have no incentive to pretend to be high damage-cost countries, since they would then be awarded tougher environmental policies which would reduce their market share and hence profits. Note that the possibility of the Commission using side-payments as an additional means of inducing truthful revelation is ruled out here.

1. Emission standards   If both countries declare that they have high costs they will each be assigned an emission standard e_{CC}. If both declare that they have low damage costs they will each be assigned an emission standard e_{cc}. Finally, if one country declares that it has high costs and the other low, they will be assigned emission standards e_{Cc}, e_{cC} respectively. The problem of the Commission can now be stated formally as:

$$\text{MAX } \{2p^2 V(e_{CC}, e_{CC}, C) + 2p(1 - p) \left[V(e_{Cc}, e_{cC}, C) + \omega V(e_{cC}, e_{Cc}, c)\right]$$
$$+ 2(1 - p)^2 \omega V(e_{cc}, e_{cc}, c)\} e_{CC}, e_{Cc}, e_{cC}, e_{cc}$$

s.t. $pV(e_{CC}, e_{CC}, C) + (1-p)V(e_{Cc}, e_{cC}, C)$
$\geq pV(e_{cC}, e_{Cc}, C) + (1-p)V(e_{cc}, e_{cc}, C)$

The constraint is just the requirement that a high damage-cost country is at least as well off telling the truth as lying, given that the other country tells the truth. Included in the objective function is a welfare weight ω to countries with low damage costs as in the cooperative equilibrium in section 2. This is to ensure that by appropriate choice of the welfare weight it is possible to ignore the participation constraints, i.e., it ensures that each country is strictly better off than in the non-cooperative equilibrium.

Letting λ denote the Lagrange multiplier on the incentive compatibility constraint, and using the welfare function in (2), the following set of first order conditions are obtained (assuming an interior solution):

$$(p^2 + \lambda p)[18(2A - \tilde{e}_{CC}) - 2(37 + 64C)\tilde{e}_{CC} - 6(2A - \tilde{e}_{CC}) - 18\tilde{e}_{CC}] = 0 \tag{18a}$$

$$(1-p)(p+\lambda)[18(2A - \tilde{e}_{cC}) - 2(37 + 64C)\tilde{e}_{Cc}] - p[\omega(1-p) - \lambda][6(2A - \tilde{e}_{Cc}) + 18\tilde{e}_{cC}] = 0 \tag{18b}$$

$$(1-p)(p+\lambda)[6(2A - \tilde{e}_{cC}) + 18\tilde{e}_{Cc}] - p[\omega(1-p) - \lambda][18(2A - \tilde{e}_{Cc}) - 2(37 + 64c)\tilde{e}_{cC}] = 0 \tag{18c}$$

$$(1-p)[\omega(1-p) - \lambda][12(2A - \tilde{e}_{cc}) - 18\tilde{e}_{cc}] + 2\lambda(1-p)(37 + 64C)\tilde{e}_{cc} - 2\omega(1-p)^2(37 + 64c)\tilde{e}_{cc} = 0 \tag{18d}$$

where the tilde denotes the optimal value for emission standards. (18a)–(18d) can be rearranged to solve explicitly the four emission levels as follows:

$$\tilde{e}_{CC} = \frac{3A}{(13 + 16C)} = e^*(C, C, 1) \tag{19a}$$

$$\tilde{e}_{cc} = \frac{3A}{(13 + 16\tilde{c})} = e^*(\tilde{c}, \tilde{c}, 1) \tag{19b}$$

$$\tilde{e}_{Cc} = \frac{12A[(3 - \tilde{\omega})(74\tilde{\omega} + 128\tilde{c}\tilde{\omega} - 6) - 18(3\tilde{\omega} - 1)(1 + \tilde{\omega})]}{(74\tilde{\omega} + 128\tilde{c}\tilde{\omega} - 6)(74 + 128C - 6\tilde{\omega}) - [18(1 + \tilde{\omega})]^2} = e^*(C, \tilde{c}, \tilde{\omega}) \tag{19c}$$

$$\tilde{e}_{cC} = \frac{12A\left[(3\tilde{\omega}-1)(74+128C-6\tilde{\omega})-18(3-\tilde{\omega})(1+\tilde{\omega})\right]}{(74\tilde{\omega}+128\tilde{c}\,\tilde{\omega}-6)(74+128C-6\tilde{\omega})-\left[18(1+\tilde{\omega})\right]^2} = \varepsilon^*(C,\tilde{c},1) \quad (19d)$$

where:

$$\tilde{\omega} \equiv \left[\frac{p}{p+\lambda}\right]\left[\omega-\frac{\lambda}{(1-p)}\right] \leq \omega$$

$$\tilde{c} \equiv \frac{\left[(1-p)\omega c-\lambda C\right]}{\left[(1-p)\omega-\lambda\right]} \leq c < C \qquad (20)$$

To begin, these cooperative emission standards with asymmetric information are compared with the corresponding cooperative emission standards with full information. A number of points emerge immediately. First, if $\lambda = 0$, such that the incentive compatibility constraint is satisfied as an inequality, then, from (20), $\tilde{\omega} = \omega$, $\tilde{c} = c$, and, comparing (19) and (11), the cooperative outcome with asymmetric information is the same as the cooperative outcome with full information. Obviously this is most likely to occur when there is a large difference between the costs of the two countries. When $\lambda > 0$, then the form of the emission standards in the cooperative case with asymmetric information is the same as with full information, except that $\tilde{\omega}$, $\tilde{c}$ are used in place of ω, c.

Secondly, comparing (19a) and (11a) it is seen that when both countries have high damage costs, then the full information cooperative outcome can be implemented. As demonstrated in section 2, this will be a lower level of emissions than in the non-cooperative case. This is the usual result from incentive theory: as the Commission knows that countries cannot be lying if they claim to have high damage costs, then it may as well implement the efficient (cooperative) outcome in that case.

Thirdly, comparing (19b) and (11b), and using (20), it can be seen that when both countries claim to have low damage costs they will be assigned higher emission standards with asymmetric information than in the full information cooperative case. Again, this is a standard result: the Commission wants to punish countries for falsely claiming that they have low damage costs. It does this by raising the emission standards and hence pollution levels that will be produced by low damage-cost countries. This reduces the welfare of low damage-cost countries, and in a direction that will be particularly damaging to a country that actually has high damage costs.

Comparisons of (19c) and (19d) with (11c) and (11d) is complicated by the need to solve for λ. In the next subsection, simulation results will be reported which shed light on these comparisons.

2. Emission taxes   Here too, it is not necessary to repeat the details of the analysis as they are similar to those above. Thus, the results can be summarized as follows:

$$\tilde{t}_{CC} = t^*(C, C, 1) \tag{21a}$$

$$\tilde{t}_{cc} = t^*(\tilde{c}, \tilde{c}, 1) \tag{21b}$$

$$\tilde{t}_{Cc} = t^*(C, \tilde{c}, \tilde{\omega}) \tag{21c}$$

$$\tilde{t}_{cC} = \tau^*(C, \tilde{c}, \tilde{\omega}) \tag{21d}$$

where $\tilde{c}$, $\tilde{\omega}$ were defined in (20) above, although of course the equilibrium value of λ will not be the same in the emission standard and emission tax cases.

The comparison between the asymmetric information cooperative equilibrium and the full information cooperative equilibrium is the same as for the emission standards case. In particular, assuming $\lambda > 0$, it is clear that $\tilde{t}_{CC} = t^*_{CC}, \tilde{t}_{cc} < t^*_{cc}$.

Simulation results
A number of numerical simulations have been conducted to make further comparisons between the asymmetric and full information equilibria. Parameter values $\omega = 1$, $p = 0.5$, $A = 10$, and $c = 1.0$ and a range of values for C from 1.2 to 3.6 have been used. For each set of parameter values, the four emission standards or emission taxes (subscripted cc, cC, Cc, CC respectively) have been calculated for the four cases: full information non-cooperative (FN); full information cooperative (FC); asymmetric information non-cooperative (AN); and asymmetric information cooperative (AC). Expected welfare has been calculated for a high-damage country, a low-damage country, and for the two countries taken together (note that some constants in the welfare functions have been ignored, with the result that welfare for the case of emission standards is not comparable with that for emission taxes). The calculations for emission standards are shown in Table 4.1, and for emission taxes in Table 4.2.

Four points emerge from the simulations. First, for all parameter values, the ranking of total industry emissions is the same in the cooperative asymmetric information case as in other cases, i.e., $2\tilde{e}_{CC} < \tilde{e}_{Cc} + \tilde{e}_{cC} < 2\tilde{e}_{cc}$. Similar results apply to a simple unweighted average tax for the two countries. Secondly, the ranking of individual country emission standards in the cooperative asymmetric information case can be quite different from the full information case. For values of C less than 2.8, the ranking is $\tilde{e}_{CC} < \tilde{e}_{Cc} < \tilde{e}_{cC} < \tilde{e}_{cc}$. In other words, in the case where the countries turn out to be asymmetric, the difference between the emission levels of the high- and low-damage countries is less than the difference in emissions in the cases where both countries have either high or low damage costs. Of course this is inefficient, but it is part of the need to provide incentives for countries not to claim to be low damage-cost countries when they are not. On the other hand, for high values of C the ranking of individual country cooperative emission standards with asymmetric information is like that for the full information case. However, the ranking of emission taxes in the co operative asymmetric information case is the same as in all other cases, namely: $\tilde{t}_{cc} < \tilde{t}_{cC} < \tilde{t}_{Cc} < \tilde{t}_{CC}$.

Table 4.1: Simulation results – emission standards

Damage cost C	Case	Emission standards				Expected welfare		
		Cc	CC	cc	cC	High	Low	Total
	FN	1.45	1.47	1.64	1.65	1262	1295	2557
1.2	FC	0.91	0.93	1.03	1.06	1302	1334	2636
	AN	1.46	1.46	1.64	1.64	1263	1294	2557
	AC	0.98	0.93	1.04	0.98	1311	1324	2635
	FN	1.18	1.21	1.64	1.68	1233	1314	2547
1.6	FC	0.74	0.78	1.03	1.09	1270	1347	2617
	AN	1.20	1.20	1.66	1.66	1235	1311	2546
	AC	0.86	0.78	1.09	0.93	1288	1328	2616
	FN	1.00	1.03	1.64	1.69	1213	1327	2540
2.0	FC	0.62	0.67	1.03	1.11	1249	1357	2606
	AN	1.02	1.02	1.66	1.66	1216	1324	2540
	AC	0.74	0.67	1.15	0.96	1265	1338	2603
	FN	0.86	0.90	1.64	1.71	1198	1337	2535
2.4	FC	0.53	0.58	1.03	1.13	1233	1364	2597
	AN	0.88	0.88	1.67	1.67	1201	1333	2534
	AC	0.62	0.58	1.16	1.07	1242	1353	2595
	FN	0.72	0.76	1.64	1.72	1181	1348	2529
3.0	FC	0.44	0.49	1.03	1.14	1216	1371	2587
	AN	0.74	0.74	1.68	1.68	1185	1343	2528
	AC	0.45	0.49	1.05	1.15	1216	1371	2587

Table 4.2: Simulation results – emission taxes

Damage cost C	Case	Emission taxes				Expected welfare		
		cc	cC	Cc	CC	High	Low	Total
	FN	1.18	1.19	1.30	1.32	175	180	354
1.2	FC	1.72	1.73	1.80	1.80	183	188	371
	AN	1.18	1.18	1.31	1.31	175	180	354
	AC	1.72	1.76	1.77	1.80	184	186	371
	FN	1.18	1.21	1.48	1.52	171	182	354
1.6	FC	1.72	1.73	1.90	1.92	179	190	368
	AN	1.19	1.19	1.50	1.50	171	183	353
	AC	1.69	1.81	1.84	1.92	181	187	368
	FN	1.18	1.22	1.60	1.67	168	184	353
2.0	FC	1.72	1.73	1.98	2.00	176	191	366
	AN	1.20	1.20	1.63	1.63	168	185	353
	AC	1.64	1.81	1.91	2.00	178	188	366
	FN	1.18	1.23	1.69	1.77	167	186	352
2.4	FC	1.72	1.73	2.03	2.06	173	192	365
	AN	1.21	1.21	1.73	1.73	165	187	352
	AC	1.63	1.76	1.98	2.06	175	190	365
	FN	1.18	1.24	1.79	1.89	164	188	352
3.0	FC	1.72	1.73	2.08	2.13	171	193	364
	AN	1.21	1.21	1.83	1.83	163	189	352
	AC	1.71	1.73	2.08	2.13	171	193	364

The more general point, though, is that for the state of the world where the two countries have different damage costs, the emission standards and emission taxes for the two countries are more similar in the cooperative equilibrium with asymmetric information than in the cooperative equilibrium with full information. This is particularly the case for low values of C as the need to provide incentives for truth revelation are stronger here. For reasons already explained, this requires making the environmental policies of the different countries more similar. For $C > 3.0$, the incentive compatibility constraint holds as inequality, so there is no difference between the asymmetric and full information cooperative equilibria.

Finally, considering expected welfare, note first that even with a welfare weight of 1 on the low-damage country, both high- and low-damage countries are better off in the two cooperative equilibria than in the non-cooperative equilibria. Comparing the two cooperative equilibria, the costs of asymmetric information are borne entirely by the low damage-cost (high emission) countries. This follows from the need to provide incentives not to pretend to be a low damage-cost country.

In this section, the cooperative and non-cooperative equilibria under asymmetric information have been derived. What does this imply about policy for the Commission? As noted above, for those cases where countries turn out to have different damage costs, then for moderate differences in damage costs between the two countries the emission standards and emission taxes for the two countries are much closer together in the asymmetric information case than in the symmetric information case. In this sense the policy looks somewhat like harmonization, although it must be stressed that full harmonization is not desirable. On the other hand, when the two countries have the same damage costs, then with asymmetric information policy-makers should require the low-damage (high emissions) countries to set higher emission standards and lower emission taxes, whereas the high damage-cost countries should implement the full information outcome. For these cases the policy implication is that with asymmetric information there should be an even wider disparity between the emission standards and emission taxes of high- and low-damage countries. Far from toughening policy in the most polluting countries, policy should be relaxed. Of course this is based on a comparison between the cooperative equilibria under full and asymmetric information. Relative to the non-cooperative equilibria, environmental policies should be toughened.

Conclusions

This chapter has analysed how a body such as the Commission might try to modify the environmental policies of national governments in order to overcome the incentives for environmental dumping. Consistent with earlier literature, it has been demonstrated that if the Commission has full information about damage costs, then harmonization of environmental policies will not achieve a Pareto-improvement over the non-cooperative outcome if countries have more than quite modest differences in their environmental-damage costs. Contrary to earlier results, it has been established that minimum standards will also fail in the model presented here if governments use environmental standards as their policy instruments, but may work if they use environmental taxes. In conjunction with the results of Kanbur et al. (1994), this shows that the workability of minimum standards depends upon the precise specification of the model of imperfect competition and on the choice of policy instruments. Finally, optimal policies were derived when the Commission lacks information about the damage costs of individual countries. It was shown that such asymmetries may warrant setting less differentiated policies across countries than would be the case with full information.

There are a number of obvious extensions that need to be made. First, it would be desirable to extend the basic model to admit other asymmetries between firms and countries and also to allow for domestic consumers. Secondly, it would be desirable to allow a more general specification of the policy options open to the Commission (for example, non-linear forms of taxation), and also to allow for the possibility of income transfers. Finally, and more generally speaking, it is important to consider other possible policy-formulation constraints facing the Commission, in addition to that of asymmetric information, in order to create a richer vision of how policy choices are actually made.

Acknowledgements

I am grateful to Pierre Pestieau, an anonymous referee and the editors and other participants in the Symposium on Economic Aspects of Environmental Policy for comments on an earlier version of this chapter. Remaining errors are my own.

Notes

1. The same is broadly true of the closely related literature on fiscal federalism where there is tax competition between countries or between states within a federation – see Mintz and Tulkens (1986), Oates and Schwab (1988) and Wildasin (1991). But for a treatment of tax competition that has some similarities to the approach used in this chapter see Cremer et al. (1994).
2. As mentioned in the previous note, Cremer et al. (1994) provide a treatment of tax competition under asymmetric information.
3. For a model which allows for other asymmetries between producers and countries, but does not address the policy issues covered in this chapter, see Katsoulacos et al. (1995).
4. For a discussion of why the magnitude of the response of output to a change in emission tax is greater than the response to a change in emission standard see Ulph (1996b).
5. It is also recognized that the Commission is mainly an administrative body, with executive powers lying in the hands of the Council of Ministers. The use of the term 'the Commission' is simply a shorthand.
6. For a closely related model see Roberts (1985), which considers the problem of a cartel allocating production quotas to firms when the cartel does not know the costs of the firms that make up the cartel.

References

Barrett, S. (1994), 'Strategic Environmental Policy and International Trade', *Journal of Public Economics*, 54(3), 325–38.

Brander, J. and Spencer, B. (1985), 'Export Subsidies and International Market Share Rivalry', *Journal of International Economics*, 18, 83–100.

CEPR (1993), *Making Sense of Subsidiarity*, Monitoring European Integration Report 4, London.

Cremer, H., Marchand, M. and Pestieau, P. (1994), 'Interregional Redistribution through Tax Surcharge', *CORE Discussion Paper*, 9469.

Dasgupta, P., Hammond, P. and Maskin, E. (1980), 'On Imperfect Information and Optimal Pollution Control', *Review of Economic Studies*, 47, 857–60.

Fudenburg, D. and Tirole, J. (1991), *Game Theory*, Cambridge, MA.: MIT Press.

Kanbur, R., Keen, M. and van Wijnbergen, S. (1994), 'Industrial Competitiveness, Environmental Regulation and Direct Foreign Investment', in I. Goldin and A. Winters (eds), *The Economics of Sustainable Development*, Paris: OECD, pp. 289–302.

Katsoulacos, Y., Ulph, D. and Xepapadeas, A. (1995), 'Asymmetric Oligopolies and Environmental Policy', mimeo, University College London.

Mintz, J. and Tulkens, H. (1986), 'Commodity Tax Competition Between Member States of a Federation: Equilibrium and Effficiency', *Journal of Public Economics*, 29, 133–72.

Oates, W. and Schwab, R. (1988), 'Economic Competition Among Jurisdictions: Efficiency Enhancing or Distortion Inducing?' *Journal of Public Economics*, 35, 333–54.

OECD (1995), *Report on Trade and Environment to the OECD Council at Ministerial Level*, Report of the Trade and Environmental Policy Committees, Paris: OECD.

Rauscher, M. (1991), 'National Environmental Policies and the Effects of Economic Integration', *European Journal of Political Economy*, 7, 313–29.

Rauscher, M. (1994), 'Trade Law and Environmental Issues in Central and East European Countries', *CEPR Discussion Paper*, 1045.

Roberts, K. (1985), 'Cartel Behaviour and Adverse Selection', in P. Geroski, L. Phlips and A. Ulph (eds), *Oligopoly, Competition and Welfare*, Oxford: Blackwell, pp. 33–45.

Siebert, H. (1991), 'Europe '92: Decentralising Environmental Policy in the Single European Market', *Environmental and Resource Economics*, 1, 271–88.

Ulph, A. (1994), to be published in C. Carraro and D. Siniscalo (eds), *Frontiers of Environmental Economics*, CUP (forthcoming).

Ulph, A. (1996a), 'Strategic Environmental Policy, International Trade and the Single European Market' , in J. Braden, H. Folmer and T. Ulen (eds), *Environmental Policy with Political and Economic Integration – The European Community and the United States*, Gloucester, England: Edward Elgar, pp. 235–56.

Ulph, A. (1996b), 'Environmental Policy and International Trade When Governments and Producers Act Strategically', *Journal of Environmental Economics and Management*, 30, (3), 265–81.

Ulph, A. (1996c), in C. Carraro and Y. Katsoulacos (eds), *Environmental Policy and Market Structure*, Dordrecht: Kluwer, pp. 99–130.

Wildasin, D. (1991), 'Some Rudimentary "Duopolity" Theory', *Regional Science and Urban Economics*, 21, 393–421.

5 Environmental tax competition – a simulation study for asymmetric countries
Klaus Conrad

1. Introduction

The results of the climate summits of the United Nations in Rio de Janeiro (1992) and Berlin (1995) have shown how difficult it is to achieve a joint implementation of a carbon dioxide reduction target. Without side-payments to opposing countries, progress in solving the problem of global warming and other environmental concerns (rare species, tropical forest, ozone layer) are hardly to be expected. Negotiating environmental regulations multilaterally is especially problematic because of differences in preferences, and in income levels or in production costs across countries. In addition, environmental considerations can be used to disguise protectionist policies. Since firms, located in their home countries, are predominantly owned by its residents, policies that increase home firms' profits at the expense of foreign firms look attractive to policy-makers. Moreover, they recognize a trade-off between costs of emission reduction and the preservation of market shares in the world market. Furthermore, emissions of sulphur and nitrogen oxides, for example, are to a large extent not deposited in the country that emits them because winds take some of the pollutants across borders. This implies that emissions in one country also damage the environment in other countries and vice versa. Transboundary externalities turn the respective decision problem into a game, the acid-rain game (Mäler 1989).

Assume that there are two countries, labelled domestic and foreign. The industry in question (e.g., steel or chemicals) is a homogeneous product duopoly. There is one producer of the good in each country, and they interact as Cournot duopolists. Intra-industry trade is explained by differences in marginal cost and in consumer preferences. If national governments levy emission taxes, this policy might change the international competitiveness of their firms. Therefore, it is reasonable to expect that governments will act strategically when setting their national environmental policy instruments. If the market equilibrium for any given set of policies is non-competitive, the mutual effect among firms can significantly alter the way in which environmental policies interact. Therefore, the model in this chapter is based on a two-stage game played by two competing firms, located in different countries, and by their rent-shifting governments. In the first stage, governments choose the level of the emission tax rate to regulate environmental quality. In the second stage, firms determine the degree of abatement of their abatement technology and choose their output levels. The second-stage equilibrium is a Nash equilibrium in outputs, taking the level of the tax rate as given by the preceding stage. Thus, the solution concept for finding a subgame-perfect equilibrium is backward induction. The analysis will lead to a pair of equilibrium tax rates which trade off the gain in reduced environmental damage with costs of output restrictions in terms of lower sales on the domestic and on the foreign market.[1]

In this chapter the full cooperative outcome and the non-cooperative Nash equilibrium for a game between two governments, using emission taxes as strategies, are derived.[2] Their countries can be different in economic terms (marginal costs, demand, environmental concern) and in ecological terms (only local pollution, pure upstream–downstream pollution, transboundary pollution, mutual transboundary pollution). The objective is to characterize the cooperative outcome and the Nash equilibrium if the countries are asymmetric in economic and ecological terms. In contrast to the symmetric case which is a common assumption for deriving results analytically, asymmetry requires simulations to investigate the types of equilibrium.

It is clear that cooperative behaviour is the best approach to mitigate the impact of emission on the environment. In this case the sum of national welfare is maximized. Cooperative outcomes are, however, vulnerable because countries have incentives to deviate in the hope that the other country will stick to its cooperative emission tax level. If both countries give in to these incentives, then often the countries are worse off than in the cooperative outcome. This situation is referred to as the prisoner's dilemma. In this situation each country has an interest in coming to a binding agreement. However, asymmetries in economic and ecological terms can result in a situation different from that of the prisoner's dilemma. In such a situation one country is better off and the other country worse off in comparison to the cooperative outcome. The advantaged government will not support a binding agreement, so side-payments are absolutely necessary for the stability of a cooperative outcome. As, in reality, side-payments are rare or are hardly to be expected, it can be concluded that binding agreements will not occur in these situations. The objective of this chapter therefore, is to look for such non-prisoner's dilemma Nash equilibria in order to characterize constellations where binding agreements without side-payments cannot be expected.

Before the analysis begins, a short survey of the literature is appropriate. The papers by Barrett (1994), Conrad (1993, 1996a, 1996b), Kennedy (1994) and Ulph (1992) deal with industrial policy and international strategic interactions. The papers by Barrett and Conrad are similar in spirit. They both deal with a homogeneous duopoly where production is for a third-country-market. Barrett considers environmental standards, Conrad a system of taxes and subsidies depending on marginal damage, market structure and conduct. In Ulph, production is also for a third market but the governments do not act strategically in terms of a two-stage game played by firms and governments. By making the assumption that all consumption is elsewhere, one neglects an additional way in which environmentally disguised interventionist trade or industrial policy might yield welfare gains beyond reduction in environmental damage. In Conrad (1996a, 1996b), the focus is therefore on establishing appropriate environmental-policy instruments in the presence of negative externalities, imperfect competition, non-constant returns to scale, domestic consumption and intra-industry trade. Strategic incentives to distort pollution taxes in free-trading economies are also considered in Kennedy (1994). In both papers, rent-capture effects and pollution-shifting effects will tend to distort negatively the equilibrium tax rate from its efficient Pigouvian level. The specific results on the structure of optimal policies with various instruments are likely to be very sensitive to market structure. Conrad (1996b) shows the robustness of the results by deriving the structure of optimal emission taxes if there is Bertrand price competition instead of Cournot quantity competition.

This chapter is organized as follows. The behaviour of governments is determined through backward induction. Therefore, in section 2 the international duopolists choose the optimal abatement given the tax rates, and make output decisions for given abatement levels. In section 3, the governments make the first move by committing themselves to an emission tax rate, taking the decisions of the duopolists into consideration.[3] This outcome is compared with the pair of emission-tax rates resulting from cooperative welfare maximization. In section 4, specific functional forms are chosen for the cost, demand and damage functions in order to make the analysis tractable. In section 5, pure local pollution is assumed and emission tax rates and welfare are compared under cooperation and in the non-cooperative equilibrium, simulating asymmetries in economic parameters. A similar analysis is carried out in section 6 but here there is also asymmetry in transboundary pollution. If side-payments are not at issue, the interest lies in finding non-prisoner's dilemma situations. These equilibria are an indicator that binding agreements will fail to materialize.

2. Decisions of the firms: optimal levels of abatement and production

The domestic variables will be denoted by lower-case letters, and the corresponding foreign variables by upper-case letters. To begin, the last stage will be analysed first, that is, the choice of output for the domestic as well as for the foreign market. The domestic firm produces output x for the domestic market and output x_F for the foreign market at costs $c(x + x_F, q(t))$, where $q(t)$ is the price of the polluting input (say coal), depending on the emission tax rate t. All other input prices are constant and have been omitted as arguments in the cost function. The input price $q(t)$ consists of the basic price, the cost of abatement and the costs from taxing non-abated emissions:

$$q(t) = q_0 + ca \cdot a \cdot e + t(1 - a) \cdot e \tag{1}$$

q_0 is the basic price of the input, $ca = ca(a)$ is the unit cost of abatement which depends on the degree of the abatement activity a $(0 < a < 1)$, and e is an emission coefficient of the input (e.g., tons of SO_2 per ton of input).[4] $ca' > 0$ and $ca'' > 0$ are assumed. With r for revenue, profit π of the domestic firm is:

$$\pi(x, x_E, X, X_E; t) = r(x, x_E, X, X_E) - c[x + x_E, q(t)] \tag{2}$$

Revenue r is the sum of revenue in the domestic market and of revenue in the foreign market:

$$r(x, x_E, X, X_E) = p(x + X_E)x + P(X + x_E)x_E \tag{3}$$

$x + X_E$ is total sales in the domestic country's market and $p(x + X_E)$ is the inverse domestic demand function. $X + x_E$ is total sales in the foreign country's market and $P(X + x_E)$ is the inverse foreign demand function. Similarly, profit Π of the foreign firm is given by:

$$\Pi(X, X_E, x, x_E; T) = R(X, X_E, x, x_E) - C[X + X_E, Q(T)] \tag{4}$$

where[4]

$$Q(T) = Q_0 + CA \cdot A \cdot e + T(1 - A) \cdot e \tag{5}$$

The Nash equilibrium in the four outputs is characterized by the first-order conditions:

$$\pi_x = p + xp' - c_{\bar{x}} = 0 \tag{6}$$

$$\pi_{x_E} = P + x_E P' - c_{\bar{x}} = 0 \tag{7}$$

$$\Pi_X = P + XP' - C_{\bar{x}} = 0 \tag{8}$$

$$\Pi_{X_E} = p + X_E p' - C_{\bar{x}} = 0 \tag{9}$$

Where $\bar{x} = x + x_E$ and $\bar{X} = X + X_E$.[5]

The solutions of (6) to (9) depend on domestic and foreign emission taxes t and T and can be written as:

$$x = x(t, T), x_E = x_E(t, T); X = X(t, T), X_E = X_E(t, T) \tag{10}$$

Outputs depend on marginal costs which in turn depend on the price of the pollution-intensive input. This price in turn depends on the degree of abatement a and on the tax rate t (A and T for the foreign firm respectively).

The degree of abatement $a(t)$ is a function of t and its level is chosen prior to production. In order to determine $a(t)$, the firm maximizes profit with respect to $a(t)$. This is the equivalent of minimizing the unit cost q of the pollution-intensive input in (1) with respect to a, given t: $\min_a q(a; t)$

The first-order condition is:

$$\frac{dq}{da} = cd' \cdot a + ca - t = 0 \tag{11}$$

i.e., the marginal cost of abatement is equal to the tax rate.[6] Similarly, for the foreign firm:

$$\frac{dQ}{dA} = CA' \cdot A + CA - T = 0 \tag{12}$$

The abatement parameters a and A, determined from (11) and (12), enter the subsequent output game as given parameters.

If in the first stage of the game the national governments change t, or T respectively, then the reaction functions $x = f(X, X_E, t)$ and $x_E = g(X, X_E, t)$, derived from (6) and (7), and $X = F(x, x_E, T)$, $X_E = G(x, x_E, T)$,derived from (8) and (9), will shift, and outputs in (10) and hence foreign-market shares will change. If the domestic government raises the emission tax rate t, then the domestic firm will produce and export less and the foreign firm will gain market shares. An algebraic analysis requires total differentiation of (6) to (9) with respect to x, x_E, X, X_E, t and T. Using Shephard's lemma (i.e., $c_q(x + x_E, q) = v$ where v is the quantity of the pollution-intensive input), the following is obtained:[7]

$$\frac{dx}{dt} < 0, \frac{dx_E}{dt} < 0, \frac{dX}{dt} > 0, \frac{dX_E}{dt} > 0 \tag{13}$$

$$\frac{dx}{dT} > 0, \frac{dx_E}{dT} > 0, \frac{dX}{dT} < 0, \frac{dX_E}{dT} < 0 \tag{14}$$

A firm's Nash equilibrium levels of output for the domestic and for the foreign market decrease in the domestic tax and increase in the foreign tax. To simplify the computations the demand functions are assumed to be linear, which implies:

$$\frac{dx_E}{dt} = \frac{p'}{P}\frac{dx}{dt}, \quad \frac{dX_E}{dt} = \frac{P}{p'}\frac{dX}{dt} \tag{15}$$

$$\frac{dx_E}{dT} = \frac{p'}{P}\frac{dx}{dT}, \quad \frac{dX_E}{dT} = \frac{P}{p'}\frac{dX}{dT}$$

It is easily shown that the supply of goods on both markets declines in the tax rate, i.e.,

$$\left(\frac{d}{dt}\right)(x + X_E) < 0, \quad \left(\frac{d}{dt}\right)(X + x_E) < 0 \tag{16}$$

and similarly for T. Thus the governments know that environmental taxes will raise prices in both markets.

In the next section the governments are introduced. Their goal is to maximize national welfare, being aware of the effect of emission taxes on the supply of goods on domestic and foreign markets, and hence on the terms of trade. The goal is to establish an effective environmental policy paired with high consumer and producer surplus and rent-shifting in foreign trade.

3. Decisions of the governments: an optimal emission tax to maximize national welfare

Now the first stage of the game will be analysed. First, the situation under non-cooperative behaviour will be characterized. Then the optimality conditions for the cooperative outcome will be derived.

Taxing a pollutant under non-cooperative behaviour
The domestic government maximizes the sum of home consumer surplus, profit of the domestic firm and the revenue (or minus the cost) of any policies carried out minus damage from emissions, given its expectation about the emission tax rate of the foreign country. Transboundary pollution implies that non-abated foreign emissions also have an impact on national damage and on marginal damage. The convex damage function from total pollution u is $d(u)$ where total pollution depends on the level of the pollution-intensive inputs, on the degree of abatement, and on the shares of domestic pollution leaving the

country and on the shares of foreign pollution entering the country ($0 \leq s \leq 1$, $0 \leq S \leq 1$). Hence, total pollution is $u = (1 - s) \cdot (1 - a)\, e \cdot v + S(1 - A)e \cdot V$, where v and V are the quantities of the polluting inputs. The objective function is:

$$\max_t\, w(t; T) = \int_0^{x+X_E} p(\xi)d\xi - p(x + X_E)(x + X_E) \tag{17}$$

$$+ \pi(x, x_E; X, X_E, t) + t(1 - a)e \cdot v - d(u)$$

Similarly, the objective function of the foreign government is:

$$\max_T\, W(T; t) = \int_0^{X+x_E} P(\xi)d\xi - P(X + x_E)(X + x_E) \tag{18}$$

$$+ \Pi(X, X_E; x, x_E, T) + T(1 - A)e \cdot V - D(U)$$

where $U = (1 - S)(1 - A)\, e\, V + s(1 - a)e\, v$ is the foreign ambient emission level.

Taxes affect the degree of abatement (see (11) and (12)) but not the resolution of the output game given abatement levels, which is represented by (10).[8] The first-order condition for (17) is an implicit reaction function of the domestic government.[9] This function can be rewritten in terms of an optimal tax $\hat{t}$ on a transboundary pollutant which depends on marginal damage, market structure and conduct:

$$\hat{t} = (1 - s) \cdot md \left\{ 1 + \cfrac{1}{(1-s)md \cdot (1-a)ev_{\bar{x}}\,\dfrac{dx}{dt} - ev\,\dfrac{da}{dt}} \left[\frac{p}{\eta_p}\left(\frac{x}{x + X_E}\,\frac{dx}{dt} \right) \right. \right.$$

$$\left. \left. + \frac{X_E}{x + X_E}\,\frac{d(x + X_E)}{dt} \right) - \frac{P}{\eta_p}\,\frac{x_E}{X + x_E}\,\frac{dX}{dt} + S \cdot md \cdot (1 - A)eV_{\bar{x}}\,\frac{d\bar{X}}{dt} \right] \right\} \tag{19}$$

where $md = d'(u)$, respectively, $MD = D'(U)$ is the marginal damage of the domestic (foreign) country, $\eta_p = (d(x + X_E)/(dp)(p/x + X_E) < 0$ is the domestic price elasticity of demand, and $\eta_p = (d(X + x_E)/(dP)(P/X + x_E) < 0$ is the foreign price elasticity. The economic interpretation of the optimal tax rate is fortunately easier than (19) appears to be. It is equal to marginal damage multiplied by a factor (1 + four strategic terms):

$$\hat{t} = (1-s) \cdot md \left\{ 1 + \frac{1}{\text{domestic externality effect}} \right. $$

$$\left. \left[\begin{array}{c} \text{dead weight} \\ \text{loss effect} \end{array} + \begin{array}{c} \text{import} \\ \text{effect} \end{array} + \begin{array}{c} \text{export} \\ \text{effect} \end{array} + \begin{array}{c} \text{transboundary} \\ \text{externality effect} \end{array} \right] \right\}$$

Since $dx/dt < 0$, $d(x + X_E)/dt < 0$, $dX/dt > 0$, and $d\bar{X}/dt > 0$, all four terms in the squared bracket are positive. Divided by a negative term, since $d\bar{x}/dt < 0$ and $da/dt > 0$, four terms will be subtracted from unity. This implies that there are four economic aspects which motivate the government to set the tax rate below marginal damage. Since a higher tax rate set by one government will reduce the availability of goods in both countries, prices will increase. Therefore, the government is concerned about: (1) the loss in consumer surplus due to the reduced availability of goods on the domestic market. It is labelled the dead-weight-loss-effect; it shows that the government is motivated to set the tax rate below marginal damage in order to correct the high prices under monopolistic domestic supply. Secondly, the government seeks to shift rents from the foreign to the domestic firm (2) in the domestic market (second term), and (3) in the foreign market (third term). The second term is labelled the import-effect; it represents the loss in market power on the domestic market due to import pressure from higher domestic emission taxation. The third term is labelled the export-effect; it shows the reduced competitiveness of the domestic firm in the foreign market due to a higher production level of the foreign firms thanks to the domestic emission tax. Furthermore, (4) the government is concerned about more pollution by the foreign country offsetting its own efforts to reduce it (fourth term). It is labelled the transboundary externality effect. Since under an emission tax, output $\bar{X} = X + X_E$ of the foreign country increases, it will produce $(1 - A)eV_{\bar{X}}$ additional units of emissions which cause $md \cdot (1 - A)eV_{\bar{X}}$ additional damage. This, however, is not the effect that the national government had in mind when imposing an emission tax. All four aspects imply that restricting output in the Pigouvian sense (by $t = md$) is not optimal for an open economy with transnational pollution. If the magnitude of these four aspects is very high, there will in the limit be no emission tax at all.

Finally, the sum of all four rent-capturing effects is divided by a domestic externality effect which reflects the effectiveness of environmental policy on the quality of the domestic environment. First, a tax increases the degree of abatement a and hence reduces domestic pollution. Then a tax reduces total production $\bar{x}$, hence less is needed from the polluting factor ($v_{\bar{x}}$), therefore less will be emitted and this reduces damage. If a lower production level reduces the demand for the pollution-intensive input significantly ($v_{\bar{x}}$ is large), abating emissions by reducing output is very effective and marginal damage taxation is a powerful tool. If this effect is small ($v_{\tilde{x}}$ is small), then more should be subtracted for strategic reasons from unity because the rent-capturing effects are more important than the environmental concern. They could even dominate this concern by turning t into a negative tax rate, i.e., a subsidy. Incidentally, it should be observed that even under perfect competition in both markets ($\eta = -\infty$), the transboundary pollution-effect recommends taxation below marginal damage.

The foreign government can act in a similar way by imposing an emission tax T, allowing that the other country is passive. A non-cooperative Nash equilibrium in emission taxes occurs if each government is assumed to choose its tax level given the tax level of the other government. The optimal values of the tax rates in equilibrium are the solution of the two implicit reaction functions $\partial w/\partial t = 0$ and $\partial W/\partial T = 0$.[10] Since the tax rate of the foreign government affects welfare of the other government only indirectly through its impact on output levels, the solution implies marginal damage taxation with four rent-seeking deductions. To see the difference in the tax rule if the government does not behave strategically, the objective function (17) is differentiated with respect to t but it is assumed that the quantities are not functions of t and T. The first-order condition is:

$$-c_q\left[\frac{\partial q}{\partial a}\frac{da}{dt} + \frac{\partial q}{\partial t}\right] + (1-a)ev - t \cdot e \cdot v\frac{da}{dt}$$

$$-(1-s)\cdot md\cdot\left(-ev\frac{da}{dt}\right) = 0$$

Using (11) and $c_q = v$, as expected, the Pigouvian tax rule $t = (1-s)\,md$ results.

Optimal emission taxes under cooperative behaviour
When side-payments are possible and are conditioned on not deviating from the agreement, the best the governments can jointly do is to maximize international welfare with respect to t and T, consisting of the sum of consumers' and producers' surplus and total tax revenue minus total damage from global pollution:

$$\max_{t,T} TW(t,T) = \int_0^{x+X_E} p(\xi)d\xi - c[x + x_E, q(t)] + t(1-a)ev - d(u)$$

$$+ \int_0^{X+x_E} P(\xi)d\xi - C[X + X_E, Q(T)] + T(1-A)eV - D(U) \quad (20)$$

with $D(U)$ as the damage function of the foreign country. Since revenue from export is outlay for import by the other country, these trade values cancel out. The first-order conditions have to be solved:

$$\frac{\partial TW}{\partial t} = 0 \text{ and } \frac{\partial TW}{\partial T} = 0 \tag{21}$$

simultaneously for t and T, i.e., the following two equations in t^c and T^c:

$$t^c = m\bar{d} + \frac{1}{(1-a)ev_{\bar{x}}\dfrac{d\bar{x}}{dt} - ev\dfrac{da}{dt}}\left[\frac{p}{\eta_p}\frac{\bar{x}}{x+X_E}\frac{dx}{dt} + \frac{P}{\eta_P}\frac{\bar{X}}{X+x_E}\frac{dX}{dt}\right.$$

$$\left. -(1-A)eV_{\bar{X}}\frac{d\bar{X}}{dt}\left(T^c - M\bar{D}\right)\right] \tag{22}$$

$$T^c = M\bar{D} + \frac{1}{(1-A)eV_{\bar{X}}\dfrac{d\bar{X}}{dT} - eV\dfrac{dA}{dT}}\left[\frac{P}{\eta_P}\frac{\bar{X}}{X+x_E}\frac{dX}{dT} + \frac{p}{\eta_p}\frac{\bar{x}}{x+X_E}\frac{dx}{dT}\right.$$

$$\left. -(1-a)ev_{\bar{x}}\frac{d\bar{x}}{dT}\left(t^c - m\bar{d}\right)\right]$$

where $m\bar{d} = (1-s)\,md + s \cdot MD$ and $M\bar{D} = S \cdot md + (1-S) \cdot MD$. If (22) (or (21)) are solved for the cooperative tax rates, a value for each is obtained depending on the exogenous parameters in the model. Written as in (22), the structure of the tax rates is recognized. Compared to the non-cooperative case, the tax rates now reflect marginal damage in both countries and an adjustment term. It is possible to write (22) in an implicit version with the tax rates t^c and T^c, appearing in (22) explicitly, on the left-hand side. These forms lead to the conclusion that the cooperative tax rates are below the weighted marginal damages. The reason for the downward adjustment of the Pigouvian tax is again to reduce the welfare loss to consumers resulting from lower levels of production.

4. Specification of the model

In order to get qualitative results on the changes in tax rates, production and intra-industry trade under asymmetry in economic conditions, specifications of the functions have to be chosen. For the domestic country, the demand function is:

$$p(x + X_E) = - \alpha_D(x + X_E) + \beta_D$$

the cost function is:

$$c(x + x_E, q(a; t)) = \gamma_D \cdot q(a; t) \cdot (x + x_E)$$

the abatement cost function is:

$$ca(a) = f_D [(1 - a)^{-1} - 1]$$

and the damage function is:

$$d(u) = u_o \cdot u^{\mu_D}, \mu_D > 1$$

The same functional forms will be chosen for the foreign country. The subscript for the parameters is F instead of D, and u_o is the same for both countries. With these specifications, the first-order conditions (6)–(9) for the Nash equilibrium in the quantities x, x_E, X, and X_E can be solved as functions of t and T. These quantities enter the implicit reaction functions $\hat{t}$ (in (19)) and $\hat{T}$, which can be solved to obtain the Nash-equilibrium tax rates. Marginal damage for the domestic country is:

$$md = u_o \cdot \mu_D \cdot [(1 - s) \cdot (1 - a) e \cdot v + S \cdot (1 - A) e \cdot V]^{\mu_D-1}$$

where $v = c_q$, $V = C_Q$, and a and A follow from (11) and (12), respectively. There was, incidentally, no chance to find an explicit solution; that is, a system of six equations had to be solved numerically for the unknown variables x, x_E, X, X_E, t and T. After the solution had been found, welfare was calculated according to (17) and (18).

To find the solution of the cooperative outcome, the values t^C and T^C are determined from (21). Quantities and tax rates are then used to calculate national welfare from (17) and (18), respectively.[11] The chosen parameters for a symmetric solution are:[12]

$$\alpha_D = \alpha_F = 0.5; \beta_D = \beta_F = 100; \gamma_D = \gamma_F = 1\ 5; e = 20;$$
$$q_o = Q_o = 3; f_D = f_F = 10; \mu_D = \mu_F = 1.2; u_o = 0.2.$$

5. Environmental policy under different cost and demand conditions - the case of a local pollutant

First, the trade-off between economic costs in terms of costs of abatement and lower production levels, and the protection of the environment have been modelled. Transboundary pollution is excluded for the moment, i.e.,$(s; S) = (0;$

0), such that only the transboundary flow of goods is the cause of strategic behaviour. When side-payments are possible, there could be a cooperative outcome. The tax rates would still be below marginal damage but the market-share rivalry could be settled. Since no binding agreements are possible, both countries will typically end in a Nash equilibrium where the sum of welfare is not maximized. One of the objectives is to determine whether in each asymmetric situation both countries are worse off in comparison to the cooperative outcome. In such a prisoner's dilemma situation each country has an interest in making a binding agreement. When only one country is worse off (non-prisoner's dilemma situation), binding agreements under the corresponding asymmetric situation are not expected if side-payments are not at issue.

First, the set of possible strategies has been enlarged by two more, namely, by $t = 0$ and/or $T = 0$, and by $t = (1 - s) \cdot md$ and/or $T = (1 - S) \cdot MD$. Since these are special cases of the non-cooperative tax rates $\hat{t}$ and $\hat{T}$, they will not become dominant strategies. The payoff matrix in Table 5.1 gives the values of the welfare functions under a combination of pairs from the four different tax rates.

Table 5.1: Payoff matrix under four tax rates

	$T = 0$		$T = T^P$ Pigou		$T = \hat{T}$ non-coop.		$T = T^C$ coop.	
$t = 0$	4130	4130	4356	3694	4104	4232	4109	4227
$t = t^P$ Pigou	3694	4356	3904	3904	3642	4504	3642	4505
$t = \hat{t}$ non-coop.	4232	4104	4503	3642	**4213**	**4213**	4219	4209
$t = t^C$ coop.	4227	4109	4505	3642	4209	4219	4215	4215

Notes
'*P*' denotes the Pigouvian tax rate equal to marginal damage from non-transboundary pollution.
^ denotes the non-cooperative tax rate.
'*c*' denotes the cooperative tax rates.
Their values are given in Table 5.2.

Since symmetry has been assumed, the value of export is equal to the value of import if both governments employ the same tax rule. As no transboundary pollution was also assumed, solutions under the same tax rule do not differ by country. Starting from the cooperative solution $(t^C, T^C) = (0.37, 0.37)$ with the highest welfare, the standard prisoner's dilemma situation with lower strategic tax rates $(\hat{t}, \hat{T}) = (0.31, 0.31)$ is clearly the solution of the game. If both governments choose the higher Pigouvian tax rate equal to 1.13 in order to internalize the negative externality, then welfare is lower than in a case of no tax $(t = T = 0)$. Under imperfect competition there is a trade-off between environmental concern and consumer surplus. If the weight u_o in the damage function had been increased, then welfare under a Pigou tax would have been higher than under a case of no taxation.

Table 5.2: Tax rates under different tax policies

	$T = 0$		$T = T^P$ Pigou		$T = \hat{T}$ non-coop.		$T = T^C$ coop.	
$t = 0$	0.00	0	0.00	1.02	0.00	0.31	0.00	0.37
$t = t^P$ Pigou	1.02	0	1.13	1.13	1.06	0.33	1.06	0.37
$t = \hat{t}$ non-coop.	0.31	0	0.33	1.06	**0.31**	**0.31**	0.31	0.37
$t = t^C$ coop.	0.37	0	0.37	1.06	0.37	0.31	0.37	0.37

Table 5.3: Environmental policy – the case of a local pollutant (s = S = 0)

$u_o = 0.2$	symmetric	$\beta_F + 10\%$	$\mu_F + 1\%$	$\alpha_F + 10\%$	$\gamma_F + 10\%$
$\hat{w}$	4213	4427	4234	4204	4241
w^c	4215	4442	4273	4198	4289
$\hat{W}$	4213	5254	3885	3897	3770
W^c	4215	5246	3862	3908	3743
$\hat{t}$	0.31	0.29	0.31	0.27	0.316
t^c	0.37	0.34	0.28	0.36	0.266
$\hat{T}$	0.31	0.24	0.46	0.32	0.43
T^c	0.37	0.34	0.61	0.36	0.59
$\hat{\pi}$	3304	3600	3635	3341	3698
π^c	3162	3636	4137	3045	4375
$\hat{\Pi}$	3304	4023	2663	3027	2552
Π^c	3162	3636	2048	3045	1836
$\hat{x}$	57.5	56.6	60.3	59.2	60.8
x^c	56.2	56.9	64.3	56.2	66.1
$\hat{x}_E$	57.5	63.2	60.3	53.8	60.8
$x_E{}^c$	56.2	63.5	64.3	51.3	66.1
$\hat{X}$	57.5	66.7	51.6	51.2	50.5
X^c	56.2	63.5	45.3	51.3	42.9
$\hat{X}_E$	57.5	60.0	51.6	56.3	50.5
$X_E{}^c$	56.2	56.9	45.3	56.5	42.9
max $w + W$	8430	9688	8135	8107	8033

In Table 5.3, values for some variables of the model are presented in column one. They can be used to evaluate the strategies under asymmetric constellations.

Such cases are presented in columns two to five. A shift of the foreign demand function is indicated by $\beta_F + 10$ per cent (i.e., 110 instead of 100). The payoff matrix and the matrix for the tax rates for the two dominant strategies are shown in Table 5.4.

Table 5.4: Payoff matrix under a shift in foreign demand

$\beta_F + 10\%$	$\hat{T}$		T^C		$\hat{T}$		T^C	
$\hat{t}$	**4427**	**5254**	4444	5243	**0.29**	**0.24**	0.3	0.34
t^C	4425	5256	4443	5246	0.34	0.24	0.34	0.34

The equilibrium tax rates are $(\hat{t}, \hat{T}) = (0.29, 0.24)$. The payoff in the equilibrium does not indicate a prisoner's dilemma situation because the payoff for the foreign country is 8 units higher than the payoff in the cooperative solution. If the domestic government were to offer an amount of at least 8 to the foreign country for not deviating from the cooperative solution, then domestic welfare would be 4435 ($= 4443 - 8$) and higher than 4427, the value in equilibrium. Hence, only a side-payment could convince the foreign government to accept a cooperative outcome.

The case of a greater environmental concern in the foreign country can be generated by increasing the convexity of the damage function, i.e., by simulating a situation $\mu_F + 1$ per cent (see column 3). The payoff matrix and the matrix of the tax rates are shown in Table 5.5.

Table 5.5: Payoff matrix under a greater environmental concern

$\mu_F + 1\%$	$\hat{T}$		T^C		$\hat{T}$		T^C	
$\hat{t}$	**4234**	**3885**	4274	3860	**0.31**	**0.46**	0.32	0.61
t^C	4233	3887	4273	3862	0.28	0.46	0.28	0.61

The equilibrium tax rates are $(\hat{t}, \hat{T}) = (0.31, 0.46)$ with the cooperative rates at $(t^C, T^C) = (0.28, 0.61)$. Again, the foreign country can improve its welfare by 23 in the equilibrium situation. A side-payment of at least 23 could stabilize a binding agreement. From the third column in Table 5.3, it is evident that a cooperative solution implies a shift of production to the country where environmental concern is less pronounced. This can be achieved by a low tax in the domestic country ($t^C = 0.28$) and a high tax rate in the foreign country ($T^C = 0.61$). But decreasing the tax and raising production for the domestic and the foreign market improves profits of the foreign firm by more than 600 and entails a welfare gain of 23 for the foreign country.

Next, the case where the demand curve is steeper in the foreign country (α_F + 10 per cent) is considered. Since $\eta_{x,p} = 1 - \beta/\alpha x$, this implies that foreign demand is less price elastic than domestic demand at any quantity. The payoff matrix is set out in Table 5.6.

Table 5.6: Payoff matrix under less price-elastic foreign demand

$\alpha_F + 10\%$	$\hat{T}$		T^C		$\hat{T}$		T^C	
$\hat{\imath}$	**4204**	**3897**	4206	3896	**0.27**	**0.32**	0.27	0.36
t^C	4196	3910	4199	3908	0.36	0.32	0.36	0.36

Now the equilibrium tax rates are $(\hat{\imath}, \hat{T}) = (0.27, 0.32)$. In the cooperative case the tax rates are equal to (0.36), and output and profits are the same but more goods will be supplied at the more price-elastic domestic market (see the fourth column in Table 5.3; $x + X_E > X + x_E$). Given its more elastic demand, the domestic government raises local profits and consumers' surplus by lowering the tax and hence the marginal cost. Domestic supply and domestic production is higher in equilibrium for the country with the more elastic demand. This time, incidentally, welfare is higher not for the foreign but for the domestic country in the non-cooperative equilibrium.

Finally, the situation of a cost disadvantage of the foreign firm has been simulated (γ_F + 10 per cent) (Table 5.7). Obviously, the government with a marginal cost disadvantage is not happy with the allocation of resources under a cooperative outcome. It would not experience a prisoner's dilemma situation in the non-cooperative equilibrium.

Table 5.7: Payoff matrix under a foreign cost disadvantage

$\gamma_F + 10\%$	$\hat{T}$		T^c		$\hat{T}$		T^c	
$\hat{\imath}$	**4240**	**3770**	4292	3738	**0.31**	**0.43**	0.32	0.59
t^c	4237	3776	4289	3743	0.26	0.43	0.26	0.59

Although the repercussions of transboundary pollution have been excluded, it has already been shown that considerations about domestic supply, foreign trade and local pollution are the reasons for deviating from a cooperative outcome. Only the symmetric case is characterized by a prisoner's dilemma situation. Since asymmetry prevails in the real world, the importance of side-payments is already recognized. The prospect of a prisoner's dilemma situation need not help stabilize a cooperative outcome.

6. Environmental policy under different cost and demand conditions – the case of transboundary pollution

Transboundary pollution can be symmetric, *e.g.*,$(s, S) = (0.1; 0.1)$, or asymmetric, e.g., $(s, S) = (0.1; 0)$. In the first case, 10 per cent of emission crosses the border and 10 per cent of foreign emission will be added to the domestic ambient pollution level. The second case, which is the upstream–downstream country situation, will be the focus here. First, however, the results of the simulation $(s, S) = (0.1; 0.1)$ under symmetry in economic parameters will be presented. At first sight, this simulation appears unnecessary because transboundary emissions cancel each other out (Table 5.8).

Table 5.8: Payoff matrix under symmetry in transboundary emissions

$s = 0.1$ $S = 0.1$	$\hat{T}$		T^c		$\hat{T}$		T^c	
$\hat{t}$	4169	4169	4296	4089	0.1	0.1	0.09	0.37
t^c	4089	4296	4215	4215	0.37	0.09	0.37	0.37

Therefore, and as expected, the tax rates and welfare in the cooperative state are the same as those obtained when pollution was local. But the incentives to deviate are higher if one country's emission from production crosses the border. By lowering its tax, the country then produces more, which means more emission crosses the border. Since part of the damage is abroad, the Pigouvian component in the tax becomes smaller. Thus, it can be concluded that the more intensive the transboundary emission relation, the higher is the incentive to deviate from the cooperative outcome and the worse are the welfare figures in the prisoner's dilemma situation.

Next, an upstream–downstream case is generated by setting $s = 0.1$ and $S = 0$. Here, ten per cent of domestic pollution will cross the border, whereas the domestic country will not be afflicted by foreign pollution. The questions to be answered are: will total welfare be lower if this type of transfrontier pollution is introduced? Will cooperation imply that production takes place mainly in the downstream country? Who should levy a higher emission tax in the cooperative outcome? Are the non-cooperative tax rates in the transfrontier case lower or higher than in the local pollution case?[13] First, a symmetric solution with equal parameters in the cost, demand and damage functions is calculated. The payoff matrix is shown in Table 5.9.

As can be seen from the first column in Table 5.10, the cooperative case is characterized by equal supply in either country $(x^C + X^C_E = X^C + x^C_E)$ and hence by a uniform price. Production, however, is higher in the upstream country $(\bar{x}^C > \bar{X}^C)$. This kind of allocation provides for the best distribution of waste, given the convexity of the damage function and the convex combination of marginal damages as part of the cooperative tax rates. If the downstream country were to produce more under a cooperative solution, its marginal damage would be too high given the transboundary pollution from the upstream country in addition to its local pollution, which stays within the country.

Table 5.9: Payoff matrix under transboundary emissions

$s = 0.1$ $S = 0$	$\hat{T}$		T^C		$\hat{T}$		T^C	
$\hat{t}$	**4645**	**3748**	4692	3718	**0.141**	**0.270**	0.144	0.44
t^C	4614	3797	4661	3766	0.31	0.271	0.31	0.44

Table 5.10: Environmental policy – the upstream—downstream case ($s = 0.1; S = 0$)

$u_o = 0.2$	symmetric	$\beta_F + 10\%$	$\mu_F + 1\%$	$\alpha_F + 10\%$	$\gamma_F + 10\%$
$\hat{w}$	4645	4878	4686	4629	4696
w^c	4661	4928	4803	4623	4845
$\hat{W}$	3748	4766	3380	3441	3313
W^c	3766	4756	3312	3481	3220
$\hat{t}$	0.14	0.12	0.14	0.10	0.14
t^c	0.31	0.27	0.22	0.30	0.18
$\hat{T}$	0.27	0.19	0.42	0.28	0.40
T^c	0.44	0.40	0.69	0.42	0.67
$\hat{\pi}$	4017	4347	4396	4050	4472
π^c	3598	4113	4677	3462	5085
$\hat{\Pi}$	3108	3810	2479	2833	2364
Π^c	2747	3182	1659	2648	1407
$\hat{x}$	63.4	62.5	66.3	65.1	66.9
x^c	60.0	60.7	68.4	60.2	71.3
$\hat{x}_E$	63.4	69.2	66.3	59.2	66.9
$X_E{}^c$	60.0	67.4	68.4	54.8	71.3
$\hat{X}$	55.8	65.0	49.8	49.5	48.6
X^c	52.4	59.6	40.7	47.9	37.5
$\hat{X}_E$	55.8	58.3	49.8	54.5	48.6
$X_E{}^c$	52.4	53.0	40.7	52.7	37.5
max $w^c + W^c$	8427	9685	8115	8104	8065

Total welfare under cooperation was 8430 in the local pollution case and is now 8427 (4661 + 3766). Hence, the existence of a transboundary externality reduces welfare. It is a stronger externality than the pure local externality. The reduction is even more significant for the non-cooperative solution. The sum of national welfare drops from 8426 to 8393. The governments end up in a prisoner's dilemma situation with emission tax rates lower than in the local pollution case. However, it is interesting to note that symmetric transboundary pollution is not a cause for having a lower cooperative welfare, whereas asymmetric transboundary pollution is.

Table 5.11: Asymmetric economic conditions – the upstream–downstream case (s = 0,1; S = 0)

$\beta_F + 10\%$	$\hat{T}$		T^c		$\hat{T}$		T^c	
$\hat{\imath}$	4878	**4766**	4952	4719	0.12	0.2	0.13	0.41
t^c	4854	4804	4928	4757	0.28	0.2	0.28	0.41
$\beta_D + 10\%$								
$\hat{\imath}$	**5741**	3903	5778	3880	0.07	0.26	0.07	0.41
t^c	5693	3978	5730	3954	0.28	0.26	0.28	0.41
$\mu_F + 1\%$								
$\hat{\imath}$	4686	**3380**	4810	3301	0.14	0.42	0.15	0.70
t^c	4679	3391	4803	3312	0.22	0.42	0.22	0.70
$\mu_D + 1\%$								
$\hat{\imath}$	**4313**	3786	4320	3782	0.28	0.27	0.28	0.34
t^c	4238	3903	4246	3898	0.54	0.27	0.54	0.34
$\alpha_F + 10\%$								
$\hat{\imath}$	**4629**	3441	4661	3421	0.10	0.28	0.10	0.43
t^c	4590	3502	4623	3481	0.30	0.28	0.30	0.43
$\alpha_D + 10\%$								
$\hat{\imath}$	4294	**3776**	4354	3738	0.15	0.23	0.15	0.43
t^c	4272	3809	4333	3771	0.30	0.23	0.30	0.43
$\gamma_F + 10\%$								
$\hat{\imath}$	4696	**3314**	4846	3218	0.14	0.4	0.15	0.67
t^c	4695	3315	4845	3220	0.18	0.4	0.18	0.67
$\gamma_D + 10\%$								
$\hat{\imath}$	**4193**	3752	4195	3750	0.26	0.26	0.26	0.31
t^c	4089	3915	4092	3913	0.55	0.26	0.55	0.31

In Table 5.10, the simulation results under transboundary pollution are presented with asymmetries in the same parameters as modelled in Table 5.3.

In addition to changing the parameters of the foreign downstream country, the parameters of the domestic upstream country have also been changed by the same percentage figures. Payoff matrices and tax rates for all cases have been summarized in Table 5.11. Comparing total welfare in the non-cooperative equilibrium and in the cooperative outcome for all cases presented in Tables 5.3 and 5.10, transboundary externality always reduces the sum of national welfare. A general conclusion from Table 5.11 is that tax rates are lower in the strategic equilibrium than in the cooperative case. This was not always the case when asymmetries with local pollution were simulated (see Table 5.3). By virtue of being an upstream country, emission tax rates can be lowered. Secondly, there is no prisoner's dilemma situation except in the symmetric case. Thirdly, the advantage of being an upstream country, expressed by higher welfare figures in the symmetric case, can be reduced or even reversed by differences in economic conditions. If the foreign downstream country market is bigger (β_F + 10 per cent), the welfare figures approach each other. The first row in Table 5.11 represents a situation where even the upstream country should offer side-payments of at least 9 to the downstream country for not deviating from the cooperative outcome. However, under a double advantage (being upstream and having a bigger market (β_D + 10 per cent)), the upstream country wants to see side-payments. Otherwise, it would levy only a quarter of the cooperative tax rate. A similar situation emerges in the case of a more environmentally concerned downstream country (μ_F + 1 per cent). Under this double disadvantage one expects an individual benefit from a cooperation. However, as this implies a high emission tax ($T^c = 0.7$), welfare is higher under the low tax of the non-cooperative equilibrium. Moreover, by simulating a difference in the slope of the demand function (α_F, α_D), it is evident that the interest in the cooperative outcome with binding agreements switches from yes to no. It can also be seen that differences in the slope are not reflected in the cooperative tax rates; they are the same in either case (the same holds for β). Finally, if marginal cost differs, then the country with the higher marginal cost is better off in the equilibrium (the γ_D, γ_F cases). Under a cooperative outcome the country with higher marginal cost has to restrict its output. In the non-cooperative equilibrium, however, it produces more and its firm's profit compensates for more environmental damage.

The difference in the economic performance when pollution is local (Table 5.3) and when pollution is transboundary results from the fact that the domestic government representing an upstream country lowers its strategic emission tax by about 50 per cent in all cases considered here. The differences are evaluated in terms of the change in the volume of trade. Table 5.12 demonstrates that the domestic country is a net exporter if the foreign market is bigger, if there is more environmental concern and if foreign marginal costs are higher. If the slope of the foreign demand function is steeper, it is a net importer. Under transboundary pollution ($s = 0.1$), the upstream country has a comparative advantage and improves the real balance of trade in all cases. The tax competition resulting in lower tax rates in the transboundary pollution case also reduces prices. Prices under cooperative tax rates, omitted in Table 5.13, are always higher by about 3 per cent.

Table 5.12: The upstream–downstream case and the net volume of trade

	symmetric	$\beta_F + 10\%$	$\mu_F + 1\%$	$\alpha_F + 10\%$	$\gamma_F + 10\%$
		$s = 0$	$S = 0$		
$x_E^c - X_E^c$	0	+6.6	+6.3	−5.2	23.2
$\hat{x}_E - \hat{X}_E$	0	+3.2	+8.7	−2.5	10.3
		$s = 0.1$	$S = 0$		
$x_E^c - X_E^c$	+7.6	+14.4	+ 27.7	+1.9	+33.8
$\hat{x}_E - \hat{X}_E$	+7.6	+10.9	+16.5	+4.7	+18.3

Table 5.13: The upstream–downstream case and the price level

	symmetric	$\beta_F + 10\%$	$\mu_F + 1\%$	$\alpha_F + 10\%$	$\gamma_F + 10\%$
		$s = 0$	$S = 0$		
p	42.5	41.7	44	42.3	44.3
P	42.5	45	44	42.3	44.3
		$s = 0.1$	$S = 0$		
p	40.4	39.6	42	40.2	42.3
P	40.4	42.9	42	40.2	42.3

Finally, a situation of transboundary pollution has been generated by setting $s = 0.2$ and $S = 0.1$. Twenty per cent of pollution in the domestic country crosses the border and 10 per cent comes from the foreign country. Compared to $(s, S) = (0.1; 0)$, one might expect the same environmental policy from both governments but this is not the case. If 20 per cent crosses the border and 10 per cent enters from abroad, the level of pollution is 90 per cent under symmetric economic conditions as in the case of $(s, S) = (0.1; 0)$. Similarly, the foreign country receives 20 per cent and 10 per cent leaves its border. Therefore a level of 110 per cent is equivalent to the case $(s, S) = (0.1; 0)$. This reasoning, however, is not sound since the strategic behaviour is different if production abroad affects domestic pollution. If one suffers from 20 per cent pollution from production in the neighbouring country, then why not produce more at home and invest in abatement measures? Therefore, production in equilibrium is higher by 15 per cent in the downstream country if the situation is $(s, S) = (0.2; 0.1)$ instead of $(0.1; 0)$.

If the outcome of this case is compared with the case $(s, S) = (0.1; 0)$ (see Table 5.14), it is clear that cooperative tax rates and total welfare do not differ much with respect to transboundary pollution. But under tax competition both governments cut tax rates now by more than 30 per cent in order to increase production in the home market and to raise firms' profits. The consequence of a more intensive transboundary externality is that in the corresponding prisoner's dilemma situations, the sum of welfare decreases by 0.006 per cent in the (0.1; 0) case, by 4.8 per cent in the (0.2; 0.1) case and by 13.5 per cent in the (0.3; 0.2) case.

If $(s, S) = (0.2; 0.1)$ is increased to $(0.3; 0.2)$, an even more intensive tax competition is evidenced. The downstream country is the main loser if (s, S) increases as the upstream country follows a 'beggar-thy-neighbour policy'. Why be concerned with environmental protection if one's own pollution crosses the border and one cannot avoid pollution entering from abroad? In any case, each simulation (symmetric in the economic parameters) is characterized by a prisoner's dilemma. This is not always the case as the next simulation will show.

Finally, a situation of significant transboundary pollution is presented by setting $s = 0.4$ and $S = 0.1$. Although firms make a profit, the welfare of the downstream country is negative due to damage valuation (last row in Table 5.14). A cooperative outcome is very important for the downstream country. It would lose 1432 in the Nash equilibrium $(-682 + 2114)$, but has only to pay at least 72 to the upstream country with which it maintains a cooperative agreement $(3000-2928)$. Here, symmetry in economic conditions does not imply a prisoner's dilemma. As for the location of production, it is low in the downstream country under the cooperative outcome but doubles in equilibrium.

Production in the upstream country is more than three times larger than production in the downstream country and also doubles in equilibrium. With respect to abatement efforts, the rates of abatement (see (11) and (12)) can be calculated given the tax rates. Under the cooperative solution, the rate of abatement of the upstream country is 8 per cent and that of the downstream country is 10 per cent. In equilibrium, the rate of abatement of the upstream country decreases to 3 per cent.

Table 5.14:   *The intensity of transboundary pollution and its effect on the tax competition* ($u_o = 0.3$)

$s = 0.1$ $S = 0.$	$\hat{T}$		T^c		$\hat{T}$		T^c	
$\hat{\imath}$	3264	2282	3306	2254	0.76	0.92	0.77	1.09
t^c	3224	2343	3268	2315	0.96	0.93	0.96	1.09
$s = 0.2$ $S = 0.1$	$\hat{T}$		T^c		$\hat{T}$		T^c	
$\hat{\imath}$	3260	2053	3606	1836	0.46	0.63	0.47	1.1
t^c	3012	2444	3361	2222	0.95	0.63	0.95	1.1
$s = 0.3$ $S = 0.2$	$\hat{T}$		T^c		$\hat{T}$		T^c	
$\hat{\imath}$	3146	1683	4135	1088	0.15	0.33	0.13	1.11
t^c	2503	2749	3467	2115	0.95	0.3	0.95	1.11
$s = 0.4$ $S = 0.1$ $u_o = 0.5$	$\hat{T}$		T^c		$\hat{T}$		T^c	
$\hat{\imath}$	**3000**	−2114	4259	−2823	0.72	1.45	0.73	2.3
t^c	1621	126	2928	−682	1.9	1.4	1.9	2.3

Conclusions

In this chapter, two competing firms operating on the domestic and on the foreign market, and two environmental authorities using taxes strategically to maximize national welfare, have been modelled. The objective has been to calculate Nash equilibria for the two-stage game under different parameter constellations. Each change of a parameter represented a different situation on the demand, cost or environmental side. This provided the opportunity to study the properties of equilibria present in the asymmetric firm and environmental model. The question of interest is whether one party will gain in the non-cooperative tax competition. If one country is better off in the Nash equilibrium in comparison to the cooperative solution, this country will prevent a binding agreement when side-payments are not at issue. If a prisoner's dilemma situation with both parties ending up in a worse position is the prevailing outcome, then a binding agreement will increase their national welfare.

In Table 5.15, the answers to this question have been summarized. Under the standard assumption in the literature of symmetry, the prisoner's dilemma was observed in all but one case. Except for that case, binding agreements are advantageous for both governments. If transboundary pollution is important ((s, S) = (0.4; 0.1)), then the upstream country will not agree to a cooperative allocation without side-payments, even if the countries are identical in economic terms. The required side-payments for a cooperation increase drastically in these situations. Under asymmetry, one country is better off and the other worse off in a non-cooperative equilibrium. These non-prisoner's dilemma situations make it rather difficult to convince the government, representing the better-off country, of the need to cooperate. It may even occur that a downstream country shows no interest in cooperation. This is the case if its consumers are more price elastic. There is a trade-off between environmental quality improvement by lower production and a loss in consumer surplus by higher prices. In the non-prisoner's dilemma situation tax competition reduces marginal cost. The downstream country, having the more elastic demand curve, gains consumer surplus, which compensates for more emission from higher production.

Table 5.15: Who gains in a non-cooperative environmental tax competition?

$s = 0, S = 0$ or $S = 0.1, S = 0$	symmetry	$\beta_F > \beta_D$ market size	$\mu_F > \mu_D$ damage	$\alpha_F > \alpha_D$ elasticity	$\gamma_F > \gamma_D$ marg. cost
Prisoner's dilemma	X				
Domestic country gains				X	
Foreign country gains		X	X		X
$s = 0. 1; S = 0$	symmetry	$\beta_F < \beta_D$	$\mu_F < \mu_D$	$\alpha_F < \alpha_D$	$\gamma_F < \gamma_D$
Prisoner's dilemma	X				
Domestic upstream country gains		X	X		X
Foreign downstream country gains				X	

	$(s, S)=(0.2;0.1)$ symmetry	$(s, S)=(0.3;0.2)$ symmetry	$(s, S)=(0.4;0.1)$ symmetry
Prisoner's dilemma	X	X	
Domestic upstream country gains			X

It has also been demonstrated that changing the situation from local to transboundary pollution reduces total welfare. A symmetric transboundary pollution does not change total welfare in the cooperative outcome, whereas an upstream–downstream situation is a negative externality which reduces total welfare even in the cooperative outcome. As welfare decreases in the prisoner's dilemma situation with the intensity of the transboundary externality, the benefits of cooperation increase, which stresses the need for cooperation on emission policies.

Given these results of different properties in the equilibria under strategic environmental tax competition, which depend on differences in demand, in supply, on local and transboundary pollution and on environmental concern, one should not expect international agreements on taxes on air pollutants in the near future if governments do not talk about side-payments.

Acknowledgements

I wish to thank Stefan Schmidt for able research assistance and Ulrike Schimmel, Ulrich Schwalbe, Helmut Seitz and Wolfram Wißler for helpful discussions. The paper was prepared for the International Symposium on 'Economic Aspects of Environmental Policy Making in a Federation', KU Leuven, 14–16 June 1995. I am grateful to Henry Tulkens for his remarks as a discussant of this paper and to an anonymous referee for helpful suggestions.

Notes

1. The methodological background of this chapter is the strategic industrial policy developed by Brander and Spencer (1983, 1985) and extended by Eaton and Grossman (1986). With respect to negative externalities, trade policy and (emission) tax competition, it parallels the work by Markusen (1975), Krutilla (1991) and Mintz and Tulkens (1986).
2. This analysis is restricted to the use of taxes as instruments while taxes might not be the preferred instrument for both governments (e.g., subsidies).
3. This is the same model as developed in Conrad (1996a).
4. The emission coefficient e of the input is assumed to be the same in the two countries.
5. The second-order conditions and the condition for uniqueness and global stability of the equilibrium are assumed to hold.
6. The second-order condition is satisfied since $ca_{aa} > 0$ by assumption.
7. An Appendix containing the mathematical details will be sent by the author on request.
8. It is assumed that the marginal cost of public funds equals unity, i.e., there is substitution possible between tax revenue and other surplus possibilities at a rate of 1 to 1.
9. See Conrad (1996a) for mathematical details.
10. To ensure the existence of a non-cooperative fiscal equilibrium, the subclass of conceivable reaction functions is considered, i.e., both reaction functions are nonincreasing (see Mintz and Tulkens 1986, p. 154)
11. An Appendix showing the equations of the model for the Nash-quantities, for abatement, for the strategic tax rates and for the cooperative tax rates as well as for welfare under the specifications chosen will be provided on request.
12. The magnitudes of the parameters are not based on a case study. These are chosen arbitrarily and did not produce corner solutions.
13. As suggested by the referee, there is another cooperative solution concept that could be of interest: if participation constraints are added, this means that the welfare of each of the countries is higher than in the non-cooperative solution. This approach could generate solutions with still different tax rates than the cooperative solution with side-payments.

References

Barrett, S. (1994), 'Strategic Environmental Policy and International Trade', *Journal of Public Economics*, **54**, 325–38.

Brander, J.A. and Spencer, B.J. (1983), 'Strategic Commitment with R&D: The Symmetric Case', *Bell Journal of Economics*, **14**, 225–35.

Brander, J.A. and B.J. Spencer (1985), 'Export Subsidies and International Market Share Rivalry', *Journal of International Economics*, **18**, 83–100.

Conrad, K. (1993), 'Taxes and Subsidies for Pollution Intensive Industries as Trade Policy', *Journal of Environmental Economics and Management*, **25**, 121–35.

Conrad, K. (1996a), 'Optimal Environmental Policy for Oligopolistic Industries under Intra-Industry Trade', in C. Carraro, Y. Katsoulacos and A. Xepapadeas (eds), *Environmental Policy and Market Structure*, Dordrecht: Kluwer, pp. 65–83.

Conrad, K. (1996b), 'Choosing Emission Taxes under International Price Competition', in C. Carraro, Y. Katsoulacos and A. Xepapadeas (eds), *Environmental Policy and Market Structure*, Dordrecht: Kluwer, pp. 85–98.

Eaton, J. and Grossman, G.M. (1986), 'Optimal Trade and Industrial Policy under Oligopoly', *Quarterly Journal of Economics*, **100**, 383–406.

Kennedy, P. (1994), 'Equilibrium Pollution Taxes in Open Economies with Imperfect Competition', *Journal of Environmental Economics and Management*, **27**, 49–63.

Krutilla, K. (1991), 'Environmental Regulation in an Open Economy', *Journal of Environmental Economics and Management*, **20**, 127–42.

Mäler, K.-G. (1989), 'The Acid Rain Game', in H. Folmer and E. van Ierland (eds), *Valuation Methods and Policy Making in Environmental Economics*, Amsterdam: Elsevier Science Publishers, pp. 122–41.

Markusen, J.R. (1975), 'International Externalities and Optimal Tax Structure', *Journal of International Economics*, **5**, 15–29.

Mintz, J. and Tulkens, M. (1986), 'Commodity Tax Competition Between Member States of a Federation: Equilibrium and Efficiency', *Journal of Public Economics*, **29**, 133–72.

Ulph, A. (1992), 'The Choice of Environmental Policy Instruments and Strategic International Trade', in R. Pethig (ed.), *Conflicts and Cooperation in Managing Environmental Resources*, Berlin: Springer, pp. 111–29.

6 The welfare economics of environmental regulatory authority: two parables on state vs federal control

Perry Shapiro and Jeff Petchey

Introduction

There are two parables with a common moral: interstate externalities are neither necessary nor sufficient to justify federal intervention in environmental regulation. The first parable demonstrates that the federal government might have a role in protecting the welfare of groups not represented in the public decision process. Even if there are no interstate air pollution spillovers, the existence of a mobile factor of production creates a potential for welfare-improving intervention by central government. The second parable demonstrates that a cluster of conditions must be present to justify the assignment of regulatory responsibility to the federal government. If neighbouring states have sufficient trust in one another's morality, are fully informed about one another's policies, or the rewards for cooperation are sufficiently high, they can achieve efficient air-quality standards in a common air basin. There is no need for the central government to be involved in the policy process.

Shapiro (1993) started an enquiry into the welfare economics of environmental regulatory authority. The enquiry grew out of a dissatisfaction with the standard models on the regulation of intra- and interstate environmental quality. Without going into detail, the commonly held idea is that if there are no interstate spillovers, regulatory authority should reside with the individual states, and if there are externalities that transcend state borders, the federal government should be responsible.

These conclusions are consistent with a model in which states have well-defined preference functions, and a decision calculus that is the same as for an individual. When there are no interstate externalities, it is efficient for states to regulate themselves. If there are externalities, each state will over-pollute, because states will ignore the damage done to their neighbours by their own actions. This, then, is justification for the central government to take control because it will, again acting as a welfare opitimizer, account for all the potential damage. This is sometimes referred to as 'internalizing the externalities'.

There are bothersome features of these models. First, they attribute to the states well-defined preference functions. This is an assumption that requires statewide homogeneous preferences, or governments that are omniscient Pigouvian welfare maximizers. Secondly, these models usually assume a costless federal government that is all-knowing and benevolent. There is little discussion about the problems caused by heterogeneous preference and imperfectly informed self-serving costly governments.

Shapiro (1993) examines the efficient allocation of environmental regulatory authority in a pluralistic society. Citizen preferences are not the same and state decisions are based on majority rule, rather than Pigouvian welfare maximization. The federal government is Pigouvian, but is not fully informed about individual preferences. These conditions minimally relax the assumptions of the standard model, but the conclusions are much altered. Specifically, there is not a clear-cut dominance of federal over state control of interstate externalities. Within the context of the model, states are allowed to engage in treaties between themselves without the interference of a higher level of government.

This chapter continues the enquiry with two different stories, parables, about the nature of the environmental regulatory problem. The first parable is about control of air-quality standards in two states in which the pollution effects are purely local – there are no interstate spillovers. The problem becomes an interstate one, however, by the presence of a mobile factor of production. The state decisions are made by a fixed, immobile factor (the landed oligarchy of the title) to maximize its own welfare. The mobile factor responds to changes in the environmental quality, and interstate wage differentials are adjusted so that the welfare of the mobile factor is the same in both states. The parable highlights an important part that the federal government can play in environmental regulation even though the pollution problem is purely local. The states can collude to the detriment of the mobile factor. Federal regulation can act as a protection for the welfare of a group that is not represented in state public decision-making.

The second parable postulates a problem of interstate spillovers, but asks when it is really necessary for the federal government to intervene. While both states recognize that interstate cooperation is beneficial, the cooperation can be achieved without federal control. Each state can engage in treaties to regulate its own production of pollution for the common good. It will be demonstrated that if the regulatory actions of each state are observable by the other, treaties between them can be self-enforcing, i.e., there would be no need for the federal government to become involved. If there is some uncertainty as to the actions of the neighbouring state, the conclusion might be different. In that case federal intervention might be desirable to prevent an accidental misinterpretation of the actions of one state by another. The desirability of federal control depends on the level of trust between the states, the reward for adhering to the treaty, as well as the additional cost incurred by the employment of federal powers.

Parable 1: landed oligarchy and immiseration of the masses

Direct externalities are but one way in which the actions of one state may affect the welfare of another. It is clear if two states share an air basin, for instance, that their welfare can be improved if they cooperate in the setting of local emission standards. It is commonly argued that the presence of such externalities is a justification, indeed a mandate, for federal, rather than local, regulatory authority. We have argued (Shapiro 1993) that this is not necessarily the case: achieving efficient pollution standards demands interstate coordination, but that requires cooperation between the states, not necessarily federal intervention.

There is another case, recently explored by Wildasin (1991) and Oates and Schwab (1988), in which interstate welfare dependence is not caused by a direct externality, but by factor migration between states. Wildasin has examined this in the case of interconnected labour markets while Oates and Schwab consider the case of mobile capital. In both these cases, the public-policy choices have direct local effects only, there are no interstate spillovers. Nonetheless, the policy choice of one state can affect the other by causing the migration of either capital or labour, thus affecting local income and tax bases. When there are these sorts of interstate effects, the case for and against federal intervention is complicated. The presence of both mobile and immobile factors of production in, say, two states, creates at least three different preference groups.[1] If the immobile factor is considered to be the state, state policy-formation will not incorporate the welfare of the mobile group. Even when states cooperate, they may do so to enhance their own welfare, but may not consider the well-being of the under-represented mobile factor. Indeed, as shown below, interstate cooperation may be equivalent to collusion by the immobile factors to improve their position at the cost of the mobile ones. Federal government intervention may be justified by the need to have the welfare of the migrating group represented in the choice of policy outcomes. However, it will be demonstrated that if the federal government is constrained by realistic informational limitations they may be unable to do as well as the states themselves.

The model used is a simple one. There are two states in a federation denoted by $i = 1, 2$. In each there are two groups of citizens. The first is mobile and with identical preferences in both states. They have preferences over a private good, x_i, the consumption of which may vary across states, and environmental quality, a_i, which is also location specific. Mobile residents make no contribution to the maintenance of the local environment and spend all of their income on the private good.

There are k_1 and k_2 immobile residents in each state. Within each state all members of the immobile group have the same preference, but there may be interstate differences. The maintenance of the environment, the provision of a_i, is paid for by the immobile group, and, as such, the immobile ones set the environmental standards. Since there is no distinction between the preferences of the immobile factor and the welfare that is maximized to determine state policy, for expositional convenience the immobile group in each state will be referred to as the state.

The utility function of a representative mobile resident is continuous and twice differentiable. It has the form u_i (x_i, a_i) where a small u is used to denote preferences of the mobile group. The mobile migrate freely between states to equate per capita utilities. In other words, the bundle of private and public goods offered in state 1 must give mobile residents the same utility as a bundle offered in state 2. Thus, in equilibrium there is the constraint:

$$u_1 (x_1, a_1) - u_2 (x_2, a_2) = 0 \qquad (1.1)$$

The federation has a total population of mobile residents equal to N which is also labour supply. Each mobile resident supplies one unit of labour. In equilibrium, where (1.1) holds, n_1 mobile residents locate in region 1 and n_2 locate in region 2 so that $N - n_1 - n_2 = 0$.

The output, y_i, of state i is a function of its fixed labour resource k_i, its employment of the mobile factor and its choice of environmental quality a_i:

$$y_i = F_i(k_i, n_i, a_i)$$

Since its immobile resource is fixed, the production function can be written:

$$y_i = f_i(n_i, a_i) \qquad (1.2)$$

with

$$\frac{\partial f_i(n_i, a_i)}{\partial n_i} > 0, \quad \frac{\partial^2 f_i(n_i, a_i)}{\partial n_i^2} \le 0, \quad \frac{\partial f_i(n_i, a_i)}{\partial a_i} < 0, \quad \frac{\partial^2 f_i(n_i, a_i)}{\partial a_i^2} \le 0 \text{ and } \frac{\partial^2 f_i(n_i, a_i)}{\partial a_i \partial n_i} = 0$$

$$(1.3)$$

The output, y_i, of state i depends on the level of employment of the mobile factor and its choice of air quality. The properties of the production function derivatives imply that air-quality choices have output costs.[2]

The wage received by the mobile factor in state i is $w_i = \partial f_i (n_i, a_i)/\partial n_i$. From (1.3) the wage paid in a state is inversely related to the number of mobile factors it can attract. The income, or rent, for the immobile factor is $I_i = f_i(n_i, a_i) - w_i n_i$. This income is an increasing function of the level of n_i. By the application of the equilibrium condition (1.1), this income is also a declining function of $a_{j\neq i}$, the level of air quality chosen by the neighbouring state. This can be seen by defining state income as function of state air-quality decisions:

$$I_i(a_i, a_j) = f_i(n_i, a_i) - w_i n_i \backslash w_i = \partial f_i(n_i, a_i) / \partial n_i \text{ and}$$
$$u_i(x_i, a_i) = u_j (x_j, a_j), x_i = w_i, x_j = w_j$$

Lemma 1: $I_i(a_i, a_j) > I_i(a_i, a_j')$ if $a_j' > a_j$.

Proof: Suppose from an equilibrium allocation of air quality, state j increases its air standard to $a'_j > a_j$. With no change in the wage rates of the two states, $u(x_i, a_i) < u(x_j, a_j)$ and the mobile factor would migrate from i to j. The maintenance of the migration equilibrium conditions requires the wage in state i to rise relative to that in state j.

The change in the relative wage cannot be accomplished by either an increase in the wages in both states or a decrease in both. If both were to increase, the demand for the mobile factor would decrease in both states ($n_1 + n_2 < N$). Similarly, if both were to decrease, the demand for the mobile factor would exceed its supply ($n_1 + n_2 > N$). Therefore either w_i must rise or w_j must fall.

If w_i rises, the marginal product of the mobile factor in i must rise as well. By (1.3) n_i must fall as well. The result is a decline in I_i.

From (1.3) w_j can decline only with an increase in n_j. The result is a decrease in both n_i and I_i.//

The public-policy outcome when states do not cooperate and act only in their own interest will now be compared with those arising from cooperation between states. In the non-cooperative case individual state choices are affected by what they believe (conjecture) are the responses to their own policies by others and the effect this will have on their own welfare. In the model of public policy with migration, there are two important aspects of a choice in air-quality standards. The first is the direct effect of the environmental quality on the utility of the state's immobile residents; and the second is the effect on the local labour supply of a change in a particular air-quality standard. The first effect is known, the second is, in general, not known. As is common it is assumed that each state conjectures the effect of its own policies on its labour supply. From the equilibrium condition, one state's outcome depends on the policy of the other and the ultimate labour response depends on the policy choices of both states. The possible conjectures will be restricted to those that are more or less rational and continuous. Each state believes that an increase in the air-quality standard will lead to increased income. The operating mechanism they perceive may be simple or complex, for instance, they may know the preference functions of the mobile factor and, from that knowledge, work out correctly the labour response to policy or they may simply conjecture that improved environmental quality will attract labour. Similarly, a state may know the response of the other state to its own policies or it may not, but it does assume that an increase in its own standards will *not* be met by a decrease in its neighbours. A state's conjectural income $\tilde{I}$ is considered to be a continuous and monotonically decreasing function of its neighbour's policy choices, namely, $\tilde{I}_i(a_i, a_j) \leq \tilde{I}_i(a_i, a'_j)$, if and only if $a_j \geq a'_j$.

The feasible set of air-quality standards are also defined as:

$$A = \{a_1, a_2 \mid I_i(a_i, a_j) \geq 0, a_i \geq 0, i = 1 \text{ and } 2\}$$

If the preferences of the mobile factor are continuous in a, then A is a bounded convex set.

For all air-quality standards in the feasible set, define the income-constrained utility function of each state as

$$V_i(a_i, a_j) = U_i[I_i(a_i, a_j), a_i]. \tag{1.4}$$

It can now be shown that the higher the environmental standards of one state, the worse off is the other.

Lemma 2: For any a_i, $V_i(a_i, a_j) \geq V_i(a_i, a'_j)$ for $a_j \leq a'_j$ and equality if and only if $a_j = a'_j$.

Proof: The proof is immediate from Lemma 1. As $I_i(a_i, a_j) > I_i(a_i, a'_j)$ for $a_j < a'_j$, for any level of a chosen by i, there will be a corresponding smaller amount of the private good consumed when j has chosen a'_j than when it chooses a_j.//

It is clear that one state's choice affects the other's, by way of its effect on the location of the mobile factor of production. There are many different ways in which one state can account for its effect on the other and thus its effect on the other's decisions, as discussed above. The equilibrium from this interaction will depend on what states believe about how their own welfare is affected by their choices. In order to model this, the state conjectural income constrained utility function is introduced, defined as:

$$\tilde{V}_i(a_i, a_j) = U_i(\tilde{I}_i(a_i, a_j), a_i) \tag{1.5}$$

State i's reaction function is then:

$$\tilde{a}_i = \tilde{a}_i(a_j) = \arg\max_{a_i} \tilde{V}_i(a_1, a_2) \tag{1.6}$$

A non-cooperative equilibrium (NCE) is defined as the pair of quality standards that equates the values of the reaction functions and demand functions in the two states. That is, the policies a^*_1 and a^*_2 are NCE if and only if:

$$\tilde{a}_1(a^*_2) - a^*_1 = 0 \tag{1.7}$$

and

$$\tilde{a}_2(a^*_1) - a^*_2 = 0, \, a^*_1, a^*_2 \in A. \tag{1.8}$$

While it is not the main focus of this chapter, at this point it is natural to be concerned with the existence of a non-cooperative equilibrium. The equilibrium may not exist but a set of sufficient conditions to insure its existence can be provided. For this purpose, take the inverse of equation (1.2) to define the level of air quality as a function of output and employment

$$a_i = f_i^{-1}(y_i, n_i) \equiv g_i(y_i, n_i) \tag{1.9}$$

and let $\bar{a}_i \equiv g_i \, (0, 0)$ be the maximum level of air quality a state could enjoy, achieved if it employed no labour and consumed no private goods. Let:

$$\tilde{a}_1(\tilde{a}_2(a_1)) - a_1 = \Phi_1(a_1)$$

be the excess demand for air quality in state 1. A similar function could be defined for state 2.

Theorem 1 (Existence):   If $\Phi_1(0) > 0$ and $\Phi_1(\bar{a}_1) < 0$ a NCE exists.

Proof: The existence of an a^*_1 such that $\Phi_1(a^*_1) = 0$ is assured by the continuity. Since $\tilde{a}_2(a^*_1)$ is the optimal choice for state 2 given a^*_1, $\Phi_2[\tilde{a}_2(a^*_1)]$ $= 0$ as well. //

The NCE, in which the states act independently will be contrasted to a cooperative allocation, in which they coordinate their policies if they can improve their own welfare. It will be shown that interstate cooperation can improve the position of the states (the fixed factors) but it reduces the welfare of the mobile factor. In order to do this, the potential set of utilities of the states is defined as the set Z:

$$Z = [V_1(a_1, a_2), V_2(a_1, a_2) \, / \, a_1, a_2 \in A].$$

The cooperative equilibrium must be efficient (for the fixed factors) in the sense that it internalizes the migration externality, and Pareto-improving from the point of view of the fixed factors. With this definition of Z, the two state efficiency locus (contract curve) can be defined as

$$E = [a_1, a_2 \mid V_i(a_1, a_2) \geq V_i(a'_1, a'_2) \text{ and}$$
$$V_j(a_1, a_2) \geq \overline{V}_j, a_1, a_2, a'_1, a'_2 \in A, \forall \overline{V}_j \in Z]$$

The cooperative equilibrium is not only efficient; it must meet a participation constraint as well. It must be rational for each state to join in a cooperative arrangement with the other – each state must be no worse off cooperating than they are in the NCE. The set of potential cooperative outcomes are policy allocations that are both efficient and meet the participation constraint. The set of fixed factor efficient allocations (FEA) is defined:

$$FEA = [a_1, a_2 \mid V_i(a_1, a_2) \geq V_i(a^*_1, a^*_2), a_1, a_2 \in E, i = 1, 2]$$

An allocation in the FEA is Pareto-improving for the two states.

It will now be shown that cooperation between the states will lower the level of environmental standards in both states. The resulting welfare effects are that the immobile factors (the states) are better off with cooperation, but the mobile factor is worse off.

Lemma 3:   All public-policy allocations that are Pareto-improving for the two states must have lower environmental standards in both states than those achieved without cooperation: $(a_1, a_2) < (a^*_1, a^*_2)$ for $(a_1, a_2) \in FEA$.

Proof: The NCE is individually rational in that it maximizes the welfare of each state conditional on the choice of the other. Therefore, from Lemma 2, the utility of one state can only be improved if the other state reduces its air-quality standards. Suppose then that State 1 were to reduce its standards. This will increase utility in State 2. Since State 1 was optimizing, conditional on State 2's original choice, its utility will fall unless State 2 also reduces its standards, that is, a reduction in standards by one state without a reduction in standards of the other cannot be an FEA. Therefore, allocations in the FEA will involve lower air-quality standards in both states relative to the NCE. //

Lemma 3 apparently contradicts the commonly held idea that interstate competition leads to a degradation in environmental regulation. The phenomenon, labelled 'race to the bottom', is a manifestation of state competition for industries in which environmental regulation reduces the return on capital.[3] Environmental standards are reduced to a level lower than they would have been in the absence of competition. These arguments ignore the possibility that a state's competitive advantage may be enhanced by improvements in its environmental quality. That possibility forms the basis of Lemma 3. If states compete with one another by improving their environment, interstate competition will lead to stricter regulation than would be the case if they did not compete. Competition induces a 'race to the top'.

It will now be shown that interstate cooperation makes the mobile factor worse off than it was in the NCE.

Theorem 2 (Immiseration):   Allocations in the FEA yield lower utility for the mobile factor relative to what it is in the NCE.

Proof: Suppose the welfare of the mobile factor does not decline in the movement from a NCE to an FEA. But by Lemma 3, the level of air quality declines in both states. Therefore, for the utility of the mobile factor to remain unchanged, the wage of the mobile factor must increase to compensate for the diminution of environmental quality. But an increase in the wage rate would reduce the demand for the mobile factor below N. This cannot be an equilibrium. //

These results contrast with existing results from non-cooperative and cooperative models used in the federalism literature. It is generally argued that cooperation is unambiguously Pareto-improving. This conclusion has been used to characterize the superiority of coordinated over competitive outcomes, leading to the view that 'cooperative federalism' Pareto-dominates 'competitive federalism'. Breton (1987) has criticized this view because it implicitly assumes that the preferences of all citizens are taken into account by state governments. He argues that, to the contrary, states act in their own interests rather than in the interests of citizens and that, in such a world, collusion between states is against citizens' interests. Indeed, Breton develops a theory of 'competitive federalism' which argues that citizens' interests are better served by competitive outcomes as such outcomes constrain the power of governments to act against the individual interest.

The results here (the Immiseration Theorem in particular) support and formalize Breton's arguments. It has been shown that if there is a group of mobile citizens whose preferences are not represented, then collusion between states makes them worse off. As will be shown below, for this group competitive federalism is preferred to cooperative or collusive federalism. This result of course has strong parallels with the theory of the firm where collusion between firms hiring mobile workers can make the latter worse off. Naturally, the collusive outcome is preferred by the states as it enables them to extract cooperative surplus from the mobile factor.

An example and extension

Here an example is constructed with a simple quadratic production function and Cobb Douglas preference functions with equal parameters on private consumption and environmental quality. It is assumed that the production function of state 1 is $y_1 = (N - n_2) - b_1 (N - n_2)^2$ and state 2 is $y_2 = n_2 - b_2 n_2^2$. The wage rate (marginal product) in state 1 is $w_1 = 1 - 2b_1 (N - n_2)$. Similarly, state 2's wage rate, or marginal product, is $w_2 = 1 - 2b_2 n_2$.

The above wages are the only source of income for the mobile group. Thus, the budget constraint for a representative mobile individual is $x_i = w_i = 1 - 2b_i n_i$ (recall that mobile individuals make no contribution to the maintenance of environmental quality) and all income is spent on the private good. This function satisfies the technology conditions imposed above in that the marginal product in region i is a *decreasing* function of mobile population in region i. The preference function of the mobile factor is $u_i = x_i a_i$.

The state, or immobile factor, income is $I_i = b_i n_i^2$. The state divides its income between the consumption of the private good, denoted X_i, and the choice of the environmental standard, a_i, which it sets and for which it is the exclusive contributor. For the simplicity of this example, it is assumed that environmental quality can be induced at a constant price, 1, per unit. This is, of course, a particularly simplistic and unrealistic choice. The state income constraint is $X_i + a_i = I_i$ and the preference function of the immobile factor is $U_i = X_i a_i$.

The non-cooperative equilibrium (NCE)

A non-cooperative outcome (NCE) will now be characterized where states take account of the migration responses to choices of a. It is assumed that states have zero conjectures with regard to the other state's choice of a, but accurate conjectures with regard to the effect of their choice of a on regional population. Therefore, state i solves (with Cobb Douglas preferences):

$$\text{Max } X_i \cdot a_i \qquad (1.10)$$
$$a_i$$

$$\text{Sto: } X_i + a_i - b_i n_i^2 = 0$$

Solving yields the first-order conditions:

$$b_1 n_1^2 + 2b_1 n_1 a_1 \frac{\partial n_1}{\partial a_1} - 2a_1 = 0$$

$$b_2 n_2^2 + 2b_2 n_2 a_2 \frac{\partial n_2}{\partial q_2} - 2a_2 = 0 \qquad (1.11)$$

where

$$\frac{\partial n_1}{\partial a_1} = \frac{1 - 2b_1 n_1}{2(b_1 a_1 + b_2 a_2)}$$

$$\frac{\partial n_2}{\partial a_2} = \frac{1 - 2b_2 n_2}{2(b_1 a_1 + b_2 a_2)} \qquad\qquad (1.12)[4]$$

The reaction functions (1.11) for states 1 and 2 can be solved simultaneously (numerically) with the migration condition and $N - n_1 - n_2 = 0$, to find non-cooperative solutions for the provision of air quality, regional populations and per capita utilities for the immobile and mobile factors.

Note that in choosing a_i state i will draw mobile labour into state i at the expense of state j (see Lemma 1). This is the nature of the externality underlying the non-cooperative equilibrium. Observe also that an equilibrium established by the solution to (1.11) and (1.12) will yield an inefficient mobile population distribution where $mp_i = w_i \neq mp_j = w_j$. This can be seen directly from the migration equilibrium condition where if $a_1 \neq a_2$ (as will be so in the general case where $b_1 \neq b_2$), then marginal products or wage rates will not be equated across states. The differential choices of a_i across states creates a location-specific externality which distorts migration decisions. Thus, there are two sources of distortion in the model: over-provision and an inefficient distribution of the mobile factor (which results from differential policies, not from the over-provision).

Fixed factor efficient allocation (FEA)
As was shown above, the two states can improve their welfare by coordinating their decisions. In so doing they can extract surplus from the mobile labour which is unrepresented in local collective choice decisions.

As argued, any cooperative solution involves two participation constraints: the fixed factor in state 1 has to be at least as well off in a treaty as in the non-cooperative outcome; and similarly for the fixed factor in state 2, the cooperative quality standards must be a fixed factor efficient equilibrium. This requires that the cooperative allocations must result in welfare outcomes along a contract curve between the two fixed factors. All points on this curve are Pareto-improving from the point of view of the fixed factors. The actual outcome depends on the bargaining strength of the two states.

The model will now be solved for the cooperative case to demonstrate the Immiseration Theorem. In this regard, state 1 in a cooperative agreement would solve:

$$\text{Max } X_1 a_1 + \lambda \, (X_2 a_2 - \bar{U}_2)$$
$$\substack{a_1}$$

$$\text{Sto: } X_1 + a_1 - b_1 n_1^2 = 0 \quad \text{(state 1 resource constraint)} \quad (1.13)$$
$$X_2 + a_2 - b_2 n_2^2 = 0 \quad \text{(state 2 resource constraint)}$$
$$w_1 a_1 - w_2 a_2 = 0 \quad \text{(migration constraint)}$$

(1.13) maximizes the utility of the fixed factor in state 1 while keeping utility of the fixed factor in state 2 at its NCE level. In solving (1.13) a_1 is rewritten in terms of a_2 and obtains two first-order conditions:

$$\frac{w_2}{w_2}\left(b_1 n_1^2 - 2a_2\right) = 0$$

$$-2b_1 n_1 a_2 \left(\frac{w_2}{w_1}\right) - \frac{2b_1 n_1}{w_1}\left(b_2 + \frac{w_2}{w_1}\right) + 4a_2^2\left(\frac{a_2}{w_1^2}\right)\left(2b_2 + \frac{2b_1 w_2}{w_1}\right) + \lambda b_2 a_2 = 0$$

$$(1.14)$$

Solving a similar problem for state 2 (while holding state 1 at its NCE utility level) allows cooperative solutions to be generated for levels of provision, regional populations, and per capita utilities for both the mobile and immobile factors at the two end points of the contract curve. Taking a convex combination of these points yields a contract curve itself and generates allocations in the FEA.

Numerical solutions for the NCE and FEA allocations
Row 1 of Table 6.1 presents numerical solutions for utilities and regional populations for the NCE. Row 2 shows utilities and regional populations in the treaty where state 2 is held to its non-cooperative utilities and the cooperative surplus accrues to the immobile factor in state 1. The final row shows outcomes when state 1 is held to its non-cooperative utility and the immobile factor of state 2 receives all the cooperative surplus. The rows in between characterize outcomes where both immobile factors are better off. Thus, columns 1 and 2 characterize allocations in the FEA. Column 3 shows how utility for the mobile factor varies in the FEA and the first cell in this column shows the utility received by the mobile factor in the non-cooperative outcome.

The main result here is that the treaty is Pareto-improving for the immobile factors (relative to the non-cooperative outcome) but always makes the mobile factor worse off than in the non-cooperative outcome. This was shown formally in the Theorems above. Thus, the treaty is not Pareto-improving overall and indeed the mobile factor would have a clear preference for the non-cooperative outcome. Also note that the distribution of the mobile factor, as shown in column 4, between states is sub-optimal in both the non-cooperative and cooperative outcomes. This can be seen by solving for the efficient population from $mp_1 = mp_2$ to obtain:

$$n_2^e = \frac{b_1 N}{b_1 + b_2} \tag{1.15}$$

and substituting the parameter values used in the solutions in Table 6.1 to get $n_2^e = 1.7727$.

Table 6.1: Utilities for non-cooperative and cooperative outcomes[*]

	U_1	U_2	u_m	n_2
Non-cooperative (NCE)	0.0070	0.0251	0.1519	1.7616
Treaty (U_1Max and U_2 Min) FEA	0.0465	0.0251	0.0832	1.4676
	0.0455	0.0280	0.0769	1.2947
	0.0442	0.0305	0.0798	1.3219
	0.0431	0.0330	0.0833	1.3477
	0.0421	0.0355	0.0882	1.3728
Treaty (U_1 Min and U_2 Max)	0.0070	0.0373	0.0973	1.3955

Note: *Calculated for $b_1 = 0.12$, $b_2 = 0.1$ and $N = 3.25$.

Uniform federal standards
Generally, the level of provision will differ across states depending on technology. The federal government could impose a constraint on the states that, in either a non-cooperative outcome or treaty, provision be uniform (i.e., uniform standards), but that the states be left free to choose the level of provision. State i's non-cooperative problem when the federal government imposes a uniform standards constraint becomes

$$\text{Max } X_i \cdot a_i$$
$$a_i$$
$$\text{Sto: } X_i + a_i - b_i n_i^2 = 0 \tag{1.16}$$
$$a_i - a_j = 0$$

Solving yields two first-order conditions:

$$b_2 N + \left(1 - \frac{2b_1 b_2 N}{b_1 + b_2} \right) - 2a = 0$$

$$b_1 N + \left(1 - \frac{2b_2 b_1 N}{b_1 + b_2} \right) - 2a = 0 \qquad (1.17)$$

which has a solution if and only if the states are identical and $b_1 = b_2$. Thus, if the federal government imposes a uniform standards requirement when states act non-cooperatively there will only be a non-cooperative equilibrium if states are identical and in general there will be no equilibrium.

Alternatively, the federal government may impose a uniform standards requirement on the states in a treaty. Now state 1 would solve:

$$\text{Max } X_1 a_1 + \lambda (X_2 a_2 - \bar{U}_2)$$
$$a_1$$

$$
\begin{aligned}
\text{Sto: } & X_1 + a_1 - b_1 n_1^2 = 0 && \text{(state 1 resource constraint)} \\
& X_2 + a_2 - b_2 n_2^2 = 0 && \text{(state 1 resource constraint)} && (1.18) \\
& w_1 a_1 - w_2 a_2 = 0 && \text{(migration constraint)} \\
& a_1 - a_2 = 0 && \text{(equal standards constraint)}
\end{aligned}
$$

and similarly for state 2. The solution yields first-order conditions which can be solved numerically for utilities, levels of provision and regional populations in a treaty with uniform standards. Solutions are presented in Table 6.2.

Table 6.2: Treaty with federally mandated uniform standards[*]

U_1	U_2	u_m	n_2
0.0014	0.0148	0.1655	1.7727

Note: *Calculated for $b_1 = 0.12$, $b_2 = 0.1$ and $N = 3.25$

Comparing the results in Table 6.2 with those in Table 6.1, it is clear that the mobile group prefers the treaty with uniform standards to either the non-cooperative outcome or the treaty where the levels of provision differ across states. Hence, federal intervention has benefited the mobile group and this is their preferred outcome. It is also evident from column 4 of Table 6.2 that uniform federal standards establish an efficient distribution of the mobile factor. This is due to the fact that equal levels of provision imply equality of marginal products by the mobile factor in equilibrium. Thus, federal intervention to impose uniform standards across states benefits the mobile factor and is efficient.

However, the immobile factor is made worse off by the imposition of uniform standards and thus federal uniform standards are not Pareto-improving relative to the unconstrained treaty. Indeed, both states would prefer the non-cooperative outcome to the treaty with uniform standards of a. Another interesting result here is that if the federal government wants uniform standards of a across states, then it must allow the states to cooperate in a treaty. This is because, as shown above, there will in general be no non-cooperative equilibrium when there are federally imposed uniform standards.

Parable 2: distrust and federal authority

The aim of this example is to explore the need for central government intervention. For that reason the example is kept at its simplest. There are two stages or decision points – thought of as two succeeding years. In the first year the states will decide whether or not to form a cooperative agreement with the externality causing neighbour. If a treaty is formed, both states abide by the agreement in the first year and then, depending on the observed outcome, they decide whether or not to continue to abide by it in the second year. The expected payoff in the second year depends upon whether or not they do abide by the terms of the treaty. The game between the two states is set up in such a way that it is in both their interests to adhere to the terms of the agreement.

The parable is this. Two states share a common air basin, and in the process of producing their GDP they also produce air pollutants. The quantity that is generated by each state $i = 1, 2$ is denoted by a_i. Each of the states also consumes, breathes, pollutants, the quantity of which is the sum of what they produce and some amount that is positively related to their neighbour's production. The total quantity consumed in state i is denoted by A_i:

$$A_i = a_i + (a_j + \theta_i) \tag{2.1}$$

where θ_i is a random variable with expected value 0. It is distributed independently of either a_i or a_j. It is assumed that a state knows the quantity of pollutants it produces itself, and how much it consumes. From this it can get an unbiased estimate of its neighbour's production as the difference between what it consumes and what it produces.[5]

Each state is assumed to have well-defined preferences over both the produced good and environmental quality, which is degraded not only by its own production but by the economic activity of its neighbour as well. The structure of this model is similar to the commonly used one of interstate externalities. There are, however, two less common features. The first is the explicit one of the addition of a random variable to the externality. The important consequence is that one state may be uncertain about the actions of its neighbours.[6] The second uncommon feature, which will not be explicitly modelled but assumed, concerns the structure of the welfare outcomes of state decisions. With the exception of the random variable, the externalities of equation (2.1) have the structure of a voluntary contribution model, which produces a prisoner's dilemma problem. Within these models it is always to the advantage of one participant to increase its pollution contribution were the other state to reduce its contribution.[7] Here the possibility of a different set of payoffs is allowed for, namely, ones in which the states may be better off reducing their production of pollutants if their neighbour does so as well.

Rather than specify production and preference functions (as is commonly done), the example will be simplified by assuming there are two target levels of pollution production for each state. For clarity, quantities will be assigned to them. There is the non-cooperative equilibrium level $a^0_i = 2$ and the efficient level $a^*_i = 1$ The expected payoffs to the participants depend on the actions of its neighbour. They are the same for both states, but as will be shown the need for federal intervention may depend on whether or not the payoffs are common knowledge. These payoffs are as shown in Table 6.3.

Table 6.3: Payoffs

		State 1	
a		1	2
State 2	1	R(1, 1)	R(2, 1)
	2	R(1, 2)	R(2, 2)

The relationship between these payoffs is important in determining the need for federal intervention. There are various, well-studied configurations. A possible one is:

$$R(1, 1) > R(2, 1) > R(1, 2) > R(2, 2) \qquad (2.2)$$

In this case there is no need for a treaty, let alone federal intervention. Both sides are compelled to the right thing: (1, 1) is the unique Nash equilibrium. It is difficult to imagine an economically interesting example of this payoff structure, as it represents an ideal world among the most ethically motivated. Another possibility is the commonly studied prisoner's dilemma where each state has an incentive not to cooperate, as in Parable 1:

$$R(2, 1) > R(1, 1) > R(2, 2) > R(1, 2) \qquad (2.3)$$

Because there is a unique Nash and dominant strategy equilibrium $(2, 2)$, it is unlikely that interstate cooperation would be successful in inducing the Pareto-efficient outcome $(1, 1)$ without federal intervention.[8]

A final configuration is particularly interesting:

$$R(1, 1) > R(2, 1) > R(2, 2) > R(1, 2) \tag{2.4}$$

The Pareto-efficient outcome is best for both, if it can be induced. Indeed, it should be sustainable if both states can perfectly observe the other's actions. But there are two Nash equilibria: an efficient one $(1, 1)$ and an inefficient one $(2, 2)$.

This payoff structure can arise in an economically reasonable way as suggested in the following hypothetical case: Suppose that the neighbouring states are small relative to the world market and they produce goods that are substitutes. In other words, the neighbours are competitors in international trade. In order to achieve an efficient air-quality standard, they must both reduce production. Each state is better off reducing its own production if its neighbour does so as well. But, if the neighbour does not reduce its production, its consumed level of air pollution, A_i, will remain unacceptably large even though it might reduce its own production to its economic disadvantage.

At the first stage, each state decides whether or not to engage in a treaty or cooperative agreement with the other. If a state enters into a treaty, it will abide by the agreement, namely, to set $a = 1$.[9] The decision to enter into a treaty and abide by its conditions depends on the level of trust, denoted by the symbol τ, that one state has in the other. τ is formally defined as the (subjective) probability one state assigns to the possibility that the other adheres to the terms of a treaty. A high degree of trust, in the context of these examples, means a large value of τ. While both states have the same payoff structure, neither knows the payoff structure of the other state. Therefore, neither can know with certainty what the response will be to either of its possible choices.

Interstate cooperation would be sought only if the two states were in an inefficient $(2,2)$ equilibrium. If one state entered into the treaty, the expected value of its sincere participation must exceed that derived from the inefficient outcome and that derived from participating in the treaty and choosing the antisocial act. The conditions for sincere participation are:

$$\tau R(1, 1) + (1 - \tau)R(1, 2) > R(2, 2) \tag{2.5a}$$

and

$$\tau R(1, 1) + (1 - \tau)R(1, 2) > \tau R(2, 1) + (1 - \tau)R(2, 2) \tag{2.5b}$$

In the case of the prisoner's dilemma, (2.5a) may hold if τ, the level of trust, is sufficiently large, but neighbourly trust can never be large enough to satisfy (2.5b). The lesson here is well known. In this two-stage decision process, successful cooperation between states is not possible without some form of coercion: states must be compelled by other means to undertake and adhere to a mutually advantageous treaty.

There are then two extremes. If the payoff structure is as it is in (2.2), there is no place for central control, and if it is as in (2.3), it is impossible to achieve an efficient policy without the federal intervention. Case (2.4) creates more possible answers, and it is that one that needs to be analysed in more detail.

The interesting possibility arises when τ is sufficiently large for both states to undertake a sincere treaty, one to which they will both adhere in the first period. In the second period they observe the actions of the treaty partner and decide on that basis whether or not to honour the commitment negotiated in the original compact. Each state will estimate the air-pollution production of the other by using the relationship in (2.1) and, on the basis of its estimate, will decide whether or not it is in its best interest to continue honouring the treaty.

Each state knows how much air pollution it has produced, a_i, and how much it consumes, A_i. On this basis it computes an unbiased estimate of the air-pollution production of its neighbour:[10]

$$\hat{a}_j = A_i - a_i = a_j + \theta_i. \tag{2.6}$$

It is assumed that each state knows the distribution of the random variable, but not necessarily its true value. For the second-stage decision it reassesses its trust in the neighbour by using Bayes Theorem to update the subjective probability that the neighbour adheres to the treaty.

Suppose θ_i is a discrete random variable, with a known distribution. A state, therefore, knows the probability, $P(\hat{a}_j | a_j = 1$ or $2)$ of $\hat{a}_j$, conditional on the choice made by the other state. It computes the subjective probability of treaty compliance as:

$$\Pr\left(a_j = 1 | \hat{a}_j\right) = \frac{P\left(\hat{a}_j | a_j = 1\right)\tau}{P\left(\hat{a}_j\right)} \tag{2.7}$$

where $P(\hat{a}_j) = P(\hat{a}_j | a_j = 1)\tau + P(\hat{a}_j | a_j = 2)(1 - \tau)$. Based on its estimation and updating, it computes the expected value of the two decisions open to it: it can continue to comply and choose $a = 1$, or it can decide to violate the treaty and choose $a = 2$. The expected value of compliance, given the observed $\hat{a}$ is:

$$EV(a = 1 \mid \hat{a}) = \Pr(a_j = 1 \mid \hat{a}_j) \, R(1, 1) + [1 - \Pr(a_j = 1 \mid \hat{a}_j)] R(1, 2) \qquad (2.8a)$$

and the expected value of treaty violation is:

$$EV(a = 2 \mid \hat{a}) = \Pr(a_j = 1 \mid \hat{a}_j) \, R(2, 1) + [1 - \Pr(a_j = 1 \mid \hat{a}_j)] R(2, 2). \qquad (2.8b)$$

There is a simple decision rule: adhere to the conditions of the treaty in the second period if and only if $EV(a = 1 \mid \hat{a}) \geq EV(a = 2 \mid \hat{a})$. As the efficient outcome is one in which both parties choose $a = 1$, it can now be asked what the value of central government intervention or a regulatory policy would be.

Ignoring obvious questions raised by the limits to information possessed by the central government and the reality of modelling it as an omniscient social-welfare maximizer, for simplicity let the federal government be omniscient and benevolent. While the good offices of the centre might be available to secure mutual compliance to the efficient outcome, it will require resources to govern. For ease, let the cost of central government be *CG* per state.

The first thing to notice about (2.8a) and (2.8b) is that if each state can observe the other's choice, $\theta = 0$, there is no need for the federal government to get involved. By choosing to engage in the treaty, the states will comply with it in the first stage. Compliance in the first stage will be observed correctly by the neighbour and, as the payoff from mutual compliance is higher than any other, both will honour the treaty in the second stage whether or not there is a federal government mandate. In fact, given that the federal government is resource-using, it would be inefficient for it to be involved. Federal involvement in this case would yield no benefit and would incur the cost of central administration.

Imperfect information appears to be a necessary, though not sufficient, condition for federal intervention. One might suspect that if there were a high degree of trust between the two states, optimality could be achieved without the intervention of a higher level of government. From equations (2.7) and (2.8ab), it can be seen that the higher is τ, the higher will be the subjective conditional probability of neighbour compliance. The higher this probability, the larger is the expected value of own compliance (choosing an $a = 1$) compared with the expected value of own non-compliance (choosing an $a = 2$). It is a striking, but not surprising, conclusion that central authority is important in maintaining interstate cooperation when the states distrust each other.[11]

Distrustfulness and confusion are important elements in a compelling case for federal authority. In fact Publius, the corporate pseudonym of the authors of the *Federalist Papers* (1982), recognized this more than two centuries ago. They wrote that:

> ... instead of their being 'joined in affection and free from all apprehension of different interest', envy and jealousy would soon extinguish confidence and affection,

and the partial interests of each confederacy, instead of the general interest of all America, would be the only object of their policy and pursuits. Hence, like most other *bordering* nations, they would always be either involved in disputes and war, or live in the constant apprehension of them. (p.19)

As noted, even the presence of these two elements does not necessitate the intervention of central government. Suppose that τ is large enough to satisfy the conditions in (2.5ab) for a treaty, but not so large as to prevent states reassessing their commitment to uphold the conditions of an interstate compact. Let θ be a random variable that can take on one of three values: -1, 0 or 1. Consider two possible distributions of θ: a uniform distribution, $f(\theta)$, in which all of the possible values have probability $1/3$; and a triangular distribution, $g(\theta)$, in which the 0 value is four times more likely than either of the two non-zero values. The estimated $\hat{a}$'s can take on four possible values -0, 1 and 2 if the neighbouring state chooses $a = 1$, and 1, 2 and 3 if it chooses $a = 2$. The distributions of θ and $\hat{a}$ are given in Table 6.4.

Table 6.4:   Distributions and probabilities

Uniform distribution					Triangular distribution			
θ	-1	0	1			1	0	-1	θ
$f(\theta)$	$1/3$	$1/3$	$1/3$			$1/6$	$2/3$	$1/6$	$g(\theta)$
$\hat{a}$	0	1	2	3	3	2	1	0	$\hat{a}$
$P(\hat{a} \mid a = 1)$	$1/3$	$1/3$	$1/3$	0	0	$1/6$	$2/3$	$1/6$	$Pa(\hat{a} \mid = 1)$
$P(\hat{a} \mid a = 2)$	0	$1/3$	$1/3$	$1/3$	$1/6$	$2/3$	$1/6$	0	$P(\hat{a} \mid a = 2)$

While neither state knows whether or not its neighbour is complying with the treaty, both will do so during the initial stage. Therefore there are three possible estimated $\hat{a}$ values, 0, 1 or 2. If it is 0, it is certain that the neighbour is complying, and naturally the response will be to continue to comply. But if the random variable takes on the values 1 or 2, there is a chance that the estimated $\hat{a}$ will lead to the erroneous conclusion of neighbour non-compliance. The chance of this depends on the distribution of the random variable. If it has a uniform distribution, the estimated $\hat{a}$ gives new information only if it is 0, but both neighbour compliance and non-compliance are equally likely if $\hat{a}$ is either 1 or 2. Examining (2.7) for particular values of $\hat{a}$ shows:

$$\Pr(a_j = 1 \mid \hat{a}_j = 0) = 1$$
$$\Pr(a_j = 1 \mid \hat{a}_j = 1) = \tau \qquad (2.9)$$
$$\Pr(a_j = 1 \mid \hat{a}_j = 2) = \tau$$

If the level of trust were high enough to enter into the treaty initially, then there is no chance that neighbour compliance could be misinterpreted as non-compliance. In other words, if the random variable is uniformly distributed, there is no need for the intervention of higher levels of government. The states will be able to maintain an efficient outcome through a treaty unenforced by any other entity.

It appears then that something more than distrustfulness and confusion is necessary to require the intercession of the central government. If the random variable has a uniform distribution, the only observation that would induce a state to defect from the treaty is an $\hat{a} = 3$, and this value is never observed if both states initially comply with the cooperative agreement. A case for federal intervention can be made, however, if the random variable has a distribution for which its values have different probabilities, as, for example, the triangular distribution given in Table 6.4.

$$Pr\left(a_j = 1 \mid \hat{a}_j = 0\right) = 1$$

$$Pr\left(a_j = 1 \mid \hat{a}_j = 1\right) = \frac{4\tau}{(1+3\tau)} > \tau$$

$$Pr\left(a_j = 1 \mid \hat{a}_j = 2\right) = \frac{\tau}{(4-3\tau)} < \tau \qquad (2.10)$$

If τ is large enough for compliance in the first stage, a state would be induced to violate the treaty only if it observed $\hat{a} = 2$, and then only if the payoffs for cooperation were not large relative to the ones for non-cooperation. For a state to decide to violate the treaty if $\hat{a} = 2$, the expected value of doing so must exceed the expected value of adhering to the cooperative agreement:

$$\frac{\tau}{4-3\tau}\left[R(1,1) - R(2,1)\right] + \frac{4(1-\tau)}{4-3\tau}\left[R(1,2) - R(2,2)\right] < 0 \qquad (2.11)$$

Since $R(1, 1) > R(2, 1)$, for sufficiently large τ the inequality will not hold. Similarly, if $R(1, 1)$ is very much larger than $R(2, 1)$, relative to the difference between $R(2, 2)$ and $R(1, 2)$, the inequality will hold only if the states are very distrustful of each other.

Without federal intervention there are four possible outcomes for the second stage. The first is that both $\hat{a}$'s are less than 2 and both states decide to honour the treaty. The second is that $\hat{a}_1 < 2$ and $\hat{a}_2 = 2$ and state 1 continues to honour the treaty, but state 2 defects. The third is that $\hat{a}_1 = 2$ and $\hat{a}_2 < 2$ and state 1 defects while state 2 cooperates. Finally, the fourth is that both $\hat{a}_1 = 2$ and $\hat{a}_2 = 2$ and the terms of the treaty are abandoned by both states. The first outcome occurs with probability 25/36, the second and third with equal probability of 5/36, and the final one with probability 1/36. In this simple example the criterion for giving the regulatory authority to the central government is:

$$\frac{25}{36} R(1,1) + \frac{5}{6} R(2,1) + \frac{5}{6} R(1,2) + \frac{1}{6} R(2,2) < R(1,1) - CG. \quad (2.12)$$

The right-hand side of the inequality is the net return to each state from using a central authority and the left-hand side is the expected return of an interstate compact without the use of a federal regulatory authority. Clearly the greater the cost of federal control, the less the likelihood that it would be efficient to use it. In particular, in this example, if the federal cost exceeds the return to mutual cooperation by more than one sixth of $R(1, 1)$, federal control will never be optimum.

Therefore there seems to be scope for central government intervention only if there is a cluster of factors. First, there must be uncertainty about the policies undertaken by the treaty partner. Secondly, the estimates of the partner's policies must be able to reveal something new about the probability of default (for example, a non-uniform distribution of θ_i). Thirdly, the rewards for adhering to the agreement cannot be too large relative to the benefits of defection (Telser 1980), and finally, the level of trust between the two treaty partners must not be too high. Without this cluster, interstate cooperation can guarantee efficient policies without help from the federal government as interstate treaties would be self-enforcing. However, even if all these conditions are met, there may still be no place for the exertion of central authority, unless its net expected value is greater than its cost.

Conclusions

Parables are stories with morals and there is a moral to these parables as well. Namely, interstate externalities are neither necessary nor sufficient to justify federal intervention in environmental regulation. The first parable demonstrates that the federal government might have a role in protecting the welfare of groups not represented in the public decision process. Even if there are no interstate air-pollution spillovers, the existence of a mobile factor of production creates a potential for welfare-improving intervention by the central government. The second parable demonstrates that a cluster of conditions must be present to justify the assignment of regulatory responsibility to the federal government. If neighbouring states have sufficient trust in one another's morality, are fully informed about one another's policies, or the rewards for cooperation are sufficiently high, they can achieve efficient air-quality standards in a common air basin. There is no need for the central government to be involved in the policy process.

Appendix 1

The derivation of the adjustment equations (1.12) requires that states have information on the migration effects of their choice of a. For this to occur, a state must know the form of the migration condition. Substituting $x_i = w_i = 1 - 2b_i n_i$ into the migration constraint can be written as (with Cobb Douglas preferences):

$$(1 - 2b_1 n_1^2).\, a_1 - (1 - 2b_2 n_2^2).a_2 = 0 \tag{A}$$

States must also know how the variables respond to changes in a. Consider state 1 for example. It will need to know how regional populations vary with changes in a_1. In particular, state 1 must know $\partial n_2/\partial a_1$. Assuming it knows $\partial n_1/\partial a_1$ and that $N - n_1 - n_2 = 0$, then it will also know that $\partial n_1/\partial a_1 = -\partial n_2/\partial a_1$ (for a two-state model in any case). Note that state 1 does not need to know how a_2 responds to changes in a_1 because state 1 holds zero conjectures with respect to state 2's choice of a. However, state 1 does need to know the b parameters (the technology). It seems reasonable to suppose that it would know b_1 but it must also discover b_2. Because states are assumed to know the form of the migration condition, (A) can be rewritten as:

$$b_2 = \frac{1}{2n_2} - \frac{a_1}{2n_2 a_2}\left(1 - 2b_1 n_1\right) \tag{B}$$

Since b_2 is a function of things that state 1 knows, it could 'learn' state 2's technology in one period. The same reasoning applies to state 2.

Appendix 2: supplement to proof of Lemma 1

Let $f_{in}(n_i, a_i) = \partial f_i(n_i, a_i)/\partial n_i$. Since mobile-factor payments are equated to the marginal product, the labour demand function is $n_i = f_{in}^{-1}(w_i, a_i) = h_i(w_i, a_i)$. Employing the common notation that a function subscripted by one of its arguments means the partial derivative of the function with respect to the argument, the conditions (1.3) imply $h_{iw} < 0$ and $h_{ia} = 0$.

There are two equilibrium conditions. The first is the full employment of the mobile factor:

$$h_1(w_1, a_1) + h_2(w_2, a_2) = N$$

and the second is the equal utility of the mobile factor:

$$u_1(w_1, a_1) - u_2(w_2, a_2) = 0$$

Consider a change in the air-quality standards of state 1 and no change for state 2. Define $w_{ia} \equiv \partial w_i / \partial a_1$ and differentiate the two equlibrium conditions:

$$h_{1w}w_{1a} + h_{2w}w_{2a} = 0$$
$$u_{1w}w_{1a} - u_{2w}w_{2a} + u_{1a} = 0$$

Solving these two equations:

$$w_{1a} = -\frac{h_{2w}u_{1a}}{u_{1w}h_{2w} + u_{2w}h_{1w}} < 0 \quad \text{and} \quad w_{2a} = \frac{h_{1w}u_{2a}}{u_{1w}h_{2w} + u_{2w}h_{1w}} > 0$$

Notes

1. We explored the welfare analysis of regulatory authority in which there were direct externalities and where the citizens of states had heterogeneous preferences. We concluded that if the informational limitation of the federal government were recognized, the central government would be unable to achieve standards that obviously dominate those negotiated through interstate treaties. Shapiro (1993) and Petchey and Shapiro (1994).
2. For the example given below, a simple, albeit unrealistic, specification is chosen in which air quality has a constant cost, no matter the level of output.
3. See Revesy (1992) for a detailed exposition of the arguments.
4. The derivation of these equations is given in Appendix 1.
5. This formulation also includes the case in which each state knows exactly what the other has produced. In that case $\theta_i = 0$.
6. See preceding note.
7. A free-rider problem.
8. This game has been much studied in the context of infinitely repeated games and the conclusions are different.
9. A state might sign a treaty with no thought of compliance – as a means of deceiving an opponent – in order to enjoy greater rewards for antisocial actions.
10. Unbiased is assured, because $E(\theta_i) = 0$.
11. France and Germany may be better able to support a mutual defence arrangement when the authority resides with NATO than if it were exclusively in the hands of their own armed forces.

References

Breton, A. (1987), 'Towards a Theory of Competitive Federalism', A.Breton, G. Galiotte, P. Solmon and R.Wintrobe (eds), Villa Colombella Papers on Federalism, *European Journal of Political Economy, Special Issue*, 3 (1,2), 263–329.

Oates, W.E. and Schwab, R.M. (1988), 'Economic Competition Among Jurisdictions: Efficiency Enhancing or Distortion Inducing?', *Journal of Public Economics*, 35, 333–54.

Petchey, J. and Shapiro, P. (1994), 'One People One Destiny: The Concentration of Power and Conflict of Interest in Australian Federalism', paper presented at the International Seminar on Public Economics (ISPE) Conference on Fiscal Policy in Emerging Federations, Nashville, TN.

Revesy, R.L. (1992), 'Rehabilitating Interstate Competition: Rethinking the "Race-to-the-Bottom" Rationale for Federal Environmental Regulation', *New York University Law Review*, 67, 1210–53.

Shapiro, P. (1993), 'Which Level of Government Should be Responsible for Environmental Regulation? Alexander Hamilton and John C. Calhoun in the Environmental Protection Agency', paper presented at the Symposium on Environmental Policy with Economic and Political Integration: The European Community and the United States, University of Illinois, Champaign-Urbana.

Telser, L.G. (1980), 'A Theory of Self-enforcing Agreements', *Journal of Business*, 53(1), 27–44.

Wildasin, D.E. (1991), 'Income Redistribution in a Common Labour Market', *American Economic Review*, 81 (4), 759–74.

Wills, G. (ed.) (1982), *Federalist Papers*, New York: Bantam Classics.

7 Fiscal competition and cooperation in natural resource markets

Gregory S. Amacher and Richard J. Brazee

Introduction

Governments face pressures to satisfy budgets, encourage capital development and provide public goods to their resident base. Competition among governments is recognized as causing inefficiencies in the provision of local public goods. Often, the fact that one government's policy affects the ability of other governments to raise revenue and to provide public goods means an efficient level of public goods is not achieved. A feature common to many natural resource markets is that some governments control public capital stocks, while others derive tax revenue benefits from use of public capital by firms and consumers in their constituency. Coordination of policies is important in natural resource markets, as inefficiencies are realized through *in situ* changes in resource stocks, along with corresponding changes in benefits derived from uses of the resource.

An important objective is to determine how a failure in government coordination affects public-goods provision compared with perfect coordination, as well as finding interventions that move the collection of governments as close as possible to the efficient allocation. Whether this movement is attainable without some form of intervening higher government has been the subject of previous research in fiscal federalism (Gordon 1983, Beck 1978). More recently, Wildasin (1988) and Futagami (1989) studied the interaction between small numbers of governments where public goods are provided either through expenditure decisions or complementary tax decisions, and each government has incentives to provide local public goods in a way that balances only its budget. Wildasin, in particular, shows that Nash equilibria for expenditures and taxes are not equivalent in the small-numbers case. In both Wildasin's and Futagami's models, if the governments were to coordinate fully, less than the optimal amount of public good would be provided.

These models omit important characteristics of natural resource capital markets. Often, natural resource capital is used by a government to produce both private benefits from its exploitation as well as public benefits from its preservation. Another common feature in previous research is that only fiscal externalities are included. Yet, in natural resource markets, both Pigouvian and fiscal externalities occur since exploitation of a resource reduces benefits from its preservation. The government's preferences for revenue generation from consumption of the natural resource, and public-goods benefits from preservation of the resource, are important in affecting the allocation of public and private goods in equilibrium. In forest markets, for example, harvests of public forests forgo non-timber benefits for several generations. In exhaustible resource exploration and extraction, non-use resources are lost for even longer periods of time. The relative weight that governments (and their constituencies) put on these external costs is important in predicting how important not coordinating is to policy choices.

The purpose of this chapter is to investigate policy design when multiple governments cooperate to varying degrees, and when capital exists that has natural resource characteristics. As is typical in practice, a higher government that controls use of a public natural resource stock is assumed. Public capital can be either a perfect or imperfect substitute for private capital in the production of goods by firms. The higher government has incentives to provide public goods by preserving the public capital stock, as it faces a national constituency that values these public-goods benefits. It oversees lower government constituencies that consist of: (1) firms that use public capital as an input; and (2) consumers that value public-goods provisions. The higher government controls rates of consumption of the public capital. Lower governments impose tax rates on production to raise revenues. Both lower and higher governments face their respective revenue constraints.

It can be expected that there will not be full cooperation between governments when local public goods are being produced, when revenues are not shared and when constituencies are different. Thus both coordinated and strategic policy design are examined under these assumptions. How these results depend on each government's preferences for revenue and public-goods provision is also examined.

Description of the resource market

A stylized resource (i.e., factor) market where there are two levels of government which allocate public and private goods is assumed.[1] Several simplifying assumptions are made. It is assumed that each government sets its policies to allocate public goods to its constituency and to balance its budget. The higher level of government (denoted by h) owns the public capital stock. The pure existence of this public capital stock represents a socially valuable public good. However, public capital may also be consumed as an input to the production of private goods. The higher government collects revenue when public capital is sold to private firms that are within the jurisdiction of lower governments. There are $i = 1, ..., N$ lower governments that raise revenue through taxation of firms in their constituency. Lower governments do not manage or control the public capital stock, but they can tax transactions involving firms' consumption of public capital.

Lower and higher governments may have different constituencies. For convenience it is assumed that firms are all identical within a constituency. There are also consumers within each constituency. Consumers obtain public benefits from the higher government's *in situ* unconsumed capital stock. It is assumed that each lower government can be identified with one representative consumer and one representative firm.

The firm in locality i maximizes the utility of profits:[2]

$$U_i(\pi_i) \tag{1}$$

where profits equal

$$\pi_i = (p - \tau_0^i)f(k_i, L_i, \beta s_i Z) - s_i p_z \beta Z - wL_i - rk_i - T^h - T^i \tag{2}$$

In (1)–(2), π_i is profits; L_i is labour; w is the labour wage rate; τ_0^i is the tax rate administered by lower government i on production;[3] Z is the *in situ* public capital stock; β is the proportion of the *in situ* resource stock that is consumed; T^h and T^i are transfer taxes administered by the higher and lower government respectively; k_i is the firm's private capital stock; r is the cost of capital: s_i is the share of public capital inputs captured by the firm in constituency i such that $\Sigma_i s_i = 1$; p is the price of the firm's output; and p_z is the price of public capital purchased from the higher government.

Two types of substitutability between private and public capital are distinguished. When the higher government produces a finished intermediate good and sells it to the firm, then production is defined as 'separable' in the firm's profit function:[4]

$$f(k_i, L_i, \beta s_i Z) = f(k_i, L_i) + \beta s_i Z \tag{2a}$$

In the other case, public and private capital are not separable in production.[5]

In addition, there is a consumer in locality i that derives utility from unconsumed public capital:

$$\Phi_i[(1 - \beta)Z] \tag{3}$$

In equation (3), the value of the public good to the consumer in the ith constituency is defined, where $(1 - \beta)$ represents the proportion of the *in situ* public capital stock that the government sets aside for public consumption. If the benefits of unconsumed public capital only accrue to consumers outside constituency i, then $\Phi_i[(1 - \beta)Z] = 0$.

The higher form of government oversees the public capital stock, Z. This government provides unconsumed public capital to consumers in all constituencies who treat public capital as a public good and obtain utility from its existence. Total benefits derived from the public capital stock equal $\Phi_N[(1 - \beta)Z]$, where N is the number of constituencies.[6] Note that if these national public-goods benefits accrue to a consumer in constituency i, then $\Phi_i[(1 - \beta)Z]$ is some subset of $\Phi_N[(1 - \beta)Z]$ (i.e., $\Sigma_i\Phi_i(.) = \Phi_N(.)$).

The lower governments compete for the higher government's capital through their choice of tax rates. If tax rates are too high, firms will have reduced incentives to consume public capital. If only one lower government existed, then $s_i = 1$ and the firm in constituency i captures 100 per cent of public capital offered by the higher government. Competition between governments would then be exclusively intrajurisdictional.

With many lower governments, the following constraint on consumption of public capital in the ith constituency is required:

$$s_i\beta Z = \beta Z - \Sigma_{-i}s_{-i}\beta Z <=> s_i = 1 - \Sigma_{-i}s_{-i} \qquad (4)$$

where $-i$ indicates constituencies other than the ith.

The N lower governments need to balance their budgets through the taxation of inputs and outputs:

$$\tau_0^i f(k_i, L_i, \beta Z s_i) + T^i \geq R_i, i = 1, ..., N \qquad (5)$$

where R_i is a minimum revenue requirement for government i.

The higher government obtains revenue to provide the public good from selling βZ of the public capital stock to private firms. The higher government faces the following revenue constraint:

$$-A\beta Z + \Sigma_i s_i p_z \beta Z + T^h + g\Sigma_i[\tau_0^i f(k_i, L_i, \beta Z s_i)] \geq R_h \qquad (6)$$

where A is the constant marginal cost of providing Z to firms. The fourth LHS term in brackets is a measure of how much the higher government cares about revenue lower governments obtain from taxing activities related to public capital consumption. $g \varepsilon [0, 1]$ is the weight that the higher government attaches to the lower government's revenue situation. It serves here as the measure of fiscal federalism between the higher and lower governments. Fiscal federalism becomes more likely as g approaches zero.

Increases in the higher government's public capital allocation now have two effects. First there are Pigouvian externalities associated with lost public-goods benefits. These can be both local and national. Secondly, there are potential fiscal externalities associated with the interactions of the higher and lower governments in determining β and τ_0^i (intrajurisdictional competition). These fiscal externalities result from the different revenue constraints facing lower and higher governments. Moreover, the governments face potentially different constituency groups. There is no incentive for any lower government to determine its taxes such that the resulting local allocation of public goods is made with the welfare of other constituencies or other government revenue targets being considered.

Several applications in natural resource markets identify with the broad stylized features of the model in (1)–(6). Some examples are:

1. Forest markets in virtually the whole world – the higher government must determine how much of its forest to harvest. However, these forests have unique values that are lost once harvested, and this loss is balanced against the benefits from use of national forests for profit in private production of lumber. Lower governments also obtain tax revenue from either directly taxing or collecting 'payments in lieu of taxes' from public-forest harvests.
2. Mineral/oil leasing on North American public lands – the federal government controls the maximum number of leases to firms. The state governments obtain severance-tax revenue from mining output.
3. Water markets in the USA – the federal government can control flow rates of rivers where water is an input to agricultural production. States obtain tax revenue from agricultural products produced using the water, but these revenue objectives conflict with the mission of the federal government in providing for the sustained production of inflow public benefits like fishing.

There are several distinct policy scenarios that could arise from government interactions. The allocation of public capital to firms and consumers is potentially different under each policy. First, governments could coordinate perfectly in determining tax rates and public capital allocated to private production. However, this is unlikely because governments have different constituencies and revenue constraints, and because public goods may not be valued by every consumer in every constituency. A second, more likely, alternative is where governments do not coordinate and/or behave strategically when setting policies.

Since strategic policy design is probably the most likely outcome, two important questions are:

1. How is the provision of public-goods benefits from the *in situ* resource stock affected by fiscal competition between governments?
2. Under what conditions can cooperation reduce the social costs associated with fiscal federalism?

Coordinated policy design

The representative firm within each lower government's jurisdiction determines its optimal choices for s_i, L_i, and k_i to maximize (1) subject to (2). The firm has an incentive to choose its share of public capital to account for choices of other firms that compete for public capital. It is assumed that firms play a simultaneous-move Nash game in their determination of the share of public capital consumed in production. Under Nash equilibrium assumptions, for every i, $\partial s_{-i}/\partial s_i = 0$, where s_{-i} is the share of public capital consumed by firms in constituencies other than i. Initially, assuming that private production is non-separable in private and public capital, the first-order conditions for the ith firm become:

$$(\partial U/\partial \pi_i)[(p-\tau_0^i)\partial f(k_i, L_i, s_i\beta Z)/\partial L_i - w] = 0 \qquad (7a)$$

$$(\partial U/\partial \pi_i)[(p-\tau_0^i)\partial f(k_i, L_i, s_i\beta Z)/\partial k_i - r] = 0 \qquad (7b)$$

$$(\partial U/\partial \pi_i)[(p - \tau_0^i)\beta Z\partial f(L_i, k_i, s_i\beta Z)/\partial s_i - p_z\beta Z + \lambda_s] = 0 \text{ and} \qquad (7c)$$

$$-\lambda_s^i(s_i - 1 - \Sigma_{-i}s_i) = 0; \lambda_s^i \geq 0 \qquad (7d)$$

where λ_s^i is the multiplier for the constraint in (4). Conditions (7a)–(7d) can be solved for the ith firm's choice of labour, capital and share of public capital consumed as functions of prices, taxes and public capital allocations:

$$L_i^*(p, p_z, \tau_0^i, w, r, \beta, T^h, T^i), k_i^*(p, p_z, \tau_0^i, w, r, \beta, T^h, T^i),$$
$$\text{and } s_i^*(p, p_z, \tau_0^i, w, r, \beta, T^h, T^i) \qquad (8)$$

Two features of these conditions are important to this analysis. First, the comparative statics of these decisions with respect to tax rates are generally ambiguous. An exception is the case where production is *separable* in public and private capital. In this case, it can be shown that the public capital share constraint given by (4) is always binding. Also, public capital, βZ, drops out of the first-order conditions in (7a)–(7c). Thus, changes in the higher government's capital allocation have no effect on firms' decisions, i.e., $\partial L_i^*/\partial \beta = \partial k_i^*/\partial \beta = \partial s_i^*/\partial \beta = 0$. Note also that lump-sum changes in the firm's income do not affect its optimal decisions, i.e., $\partial L_i^*/\partial T^h = \partial k_i^*/\partial T^h = \partial s_i^*/\partial T^h = 0$, and $\partial L_i^*/\partial T^i = \partial k_i^*/\partial T^i = \partial s_i^*/\partial T^i = 0$.

In the case where production is *non-separable* in public and private capital, the firm's choice of labour and capital *are* affected by changes in public capital allocations, but each ith firm's share of public capital is not affected as long as the constraint in (4) is binding. When the constraint is not binding, then $s_i < 1 - \Sigma_i s_{-i}$, such that, from the Kuhn–Tucker condition, $\partial f(.)/\partial s_i < (p_z)\beta Z/(p - \tau_0^i)$

can be shown. In this case, $\partial s_i / \partial \tau_0^i$ is not necessarily equal to zero. The responsiveness of changes in s_i to changes in taxes and public capital outlays can be interpreted as the mobility of capital in and out of the lower government jurisdictions.

If the optimal choices for labour, private capital and public capital inputs are substituted into the firm's utility function, then an indirect utility function may be defined for all i:

$$V^i(\tau_0^i, p, p_z, \beta, w, r, T^h, T^i) \qquad (9)$$

(9) can be used to determine the marginal effect of a change in some policy on the welfare of the firm. This is the derivative of the indirect utility function with respect to the policy. Generally, the firm's welfare is decreasing in taxes, but increasing in public capital allocated for consumption by the higher government.

Changes in the public capital stock also affect consumers who value public goods from the unconsumed public capital resource. The change in consumer welfare is given by the derivative of the public-goods benefit function with respect to β, $\Phi_N'[(1 - \beta)Z]$ and $\Phi_i'[(1 - \beta)Z]$. Consumer welfare is decreasing in public capital consumption.

The description of the firm's problem can now be embedded into a policy-design problem facing the higher and lower governments. In the fiscal federalism problem, government coordination is guaranteed when governments share revenue constraints and face the same constituency (Gordon 1983). Under these assumptions, governments would choose β, τ_0^i, T^h, and T^i to maximize the welfare of consumers and firms subject to a joint revenue constraint:[8]

$$\text{Max } \{\Sigma_i V^i(\tau_0^i, p, p_z, \beta, w, r, T^h, T^i) + \gamma_N \Phi_N[(1 - \beta)Z]\} \qquad (10)$$

$$\text{subject to: } R^c \le R_h + \Sigma_i R_i = \{\Sigma_i[\tau_0^i f(k_i, L_i, \beta Z s_i)]$$
$$- A\beta Z + \Sigma_i s_i p_z \beta Z + \Sigma_i T^i + T^h\}$$

where R^c is the shared revenue constraint and $\Phi_N(.) = \Sigma_i \Phi_i(.)$.[9] The parameter γ_N represents the weights attached by the government to the welfare of consumers of public goods relative to the welfare of firms that consume public capital as inputs to production. These weights indicate government preferences for public-goods provision.

Policy design is analysed by examining the Kuhn–Tucker conditions associated with (10). Since T^i and T^h are equivalent in the revenue-sharing case, only T^h will be considered. The first-order conditions[10] for the government's choice of τ_0^i, β, and T^h become:[11]

$$\Sigma_i(\lambda_c - \alpha_i)f(.) = -\lambda_c\Sigma_i\{[\partial f(.)/\partial L_i][\partial L_i/\partial \tau_0^i]+[\partial f(.)/\partial k_i][\partial k_i/\partial \tau_0^i]\}\tau_0^i \quad (11a)$$

$$-\Sigma_i s_i p_z Z\alpha_i - \gamma_N\Phi_N'(.)Z - \lambda_c(p_z - A)Z + \lambda_c\Sigma_i\tau_0^i\{[\partial f(.)/\partial L_i][\partial L_i/\partial \beta]$$
$$+[\partial f(.)/\partial k_i][\partial k_i/\partial \beta]\} = 0 \quad (11b)$$

$$(\lambda_c - \alpha_i) = 0, \ V^i \quad (11c)$$

where α_i is the firm's marginal utility of income, and λ_c is the multiplier for government revenue, R^c, in equation (10). The solutions to (11a)–(11c) are denoted as τ_0^{ic}, β^c, and T^c, respectively.

In (11a)–(11c) it has been assumed that public and private production are non-separable. However, policy design will be examined under both separability and non-separability of public and private production. For convenience, it is assumed in each of these cases that the constraint on the share of public capital consumed by firms in each constituency (equation (4)) is binding.

Case 1: separable public and private production
When the production function is separable, the first two RHS terms in (2) become $\{(p - \tau_0^i)[f(k_i, l_i) + \beta s_i Z] - s_i p_z \beta Z\}$. The condition for the optimal production-tax rate, τ_0^{ic}, is a modification of the one in (11a):

$$\Sigma_i(\lambda_c - \alpha_i)f(.) = -Z\beta\Sigma_i[s_i\lambda_i - s_i\alpha_i] - \lambda_c\Sigma_i\{[\partial f(.)/\partial L_i][\partial L_i/\partial \tau_0^i]$$
$$+[\partial f(.)/\partial k_i][\partial k_i/\partial \tau_0^i]\}\tau_0^i \quad (12)$$

The first term on the RHS of (12) represents the direct revenue effect of increasing the tax on public capital consumption by firms. The second term in braces is the indirect effect of the tax on government revenue collections through equilibrium changes in firms' capital and labour use. Changes in revenue depend on the public capital consumption rate only through the direct effect, as the second RHS term is not a function of β.

If it is assumed that transfer taxes are not available to the government ($T^h = 0$), the optimal size of β in (11b) can be compared with the optimal production tax in (12). Immediately it can be seen that the public capital allocation is related to the design of production taxes in each locality. Consider the government's choice of public capital consumption. With separable production, this is a modification of equation (11b):

$$\gamma_N\Phi_N'(.)Z = \lambda_c(p_z - A)Z + \lambda_c\Sigma_i s_i\tau_0^i Z + \Sigma_i(p - \tau_0^i - p_z)\alpha_i s_i Z \quad (13)$$

In equation (13), changes in labour and private capital are absent, as β is absent from the firm's first-order conditions. Condition (13) suggests that public capital is consumed so that the marginal welfare cost of lost public-goods benefits to consumers from consuming public capital (LHS) equals the marginal revenue collected from sales of public capital to firms in each locality (first term on RHS) plus the marginal increases in production-tax revenue (second term on RHS) plus welfare effects of increased income from public capital consumption to firms (third term on RHS).

There are two results which can be obtained easily from comparing equations (12) and (13). First, condition (13) suggests that taxes and public capital allocations are interdependent. Given that $\Phi_N(.)$ is concave, more public capital is consumed when production taxes are non-negative, since τ_0^i enters as a positive term on the RHS of (13).[12] When production taxes are positive, there is less of the *in situ* resource available for public-goods production. Consumers of public-goods benefits are worse off when production taxes are positive and revenue is shared between higher and lower governments.

The second result depends on government preferences for revenue generation and public-goods provision. The government's preferences for revenue generation through the bindingness of its revenue constraint, and the government's preference for public-goods provision are measured by the weights attached to public-goods benefits in (10) (i.e., γ_N and γ_i). Since government revenue increases in public capital consumption through the term $\lambda_c \Sigma_i s_i \tau_0^i Z + \lambda_c (p_z - A)Z$ in (13), when either the lower or higher government's revenue multiplier approaches infinity, β approaches 1 in (13). This is because the RHS approaches infinity. Thus, under perfect coordination, as any government becomes increasingly revenue constrained, public capital consumption will be relied on more heavily as a source of revenue. As a result, there will be less of the *in situ* resource available for public-goods production, and fewer public-goods benefits accruing to consumers. However, as the weight any government attaches to the welfare of consumers increases, γ_N increases in (10), and public capital consumption decreases. Now the stock of the *in situ* resource available for public-goods production is larger.

These results can be summarized in the following proposition:

Proposition 1: When governments perfectly coordinate and face shared revenue constraints, public capital allocations and tax choices are related. When production tax revenue is increasing in public capital consumption, there are fewer public goods produced if any government's budget becomes increasingly constrained. Firms are better off in this case, but consumers of public goods are worse off because there is less of the in situ *resource for public-goods production.*

The above analysis assumes that only the lower government raises revenue from taxation of production through τ_0^i. The possibility that the higher government can also raise tax revenue using an individual-specific transfer tax,

T^h, will now be considered. To do this, conditions (11a) and (11c) must be examined simultaneously with the first-order condition for the transfer tax. Condition (11c) describes the government's choice of T^h under either separable or non-separable public and private production. Substituting (11c) into (11a), the LHS of (11a) becomes zero. Thus, from the RHS of (11a), the tax on public production must be strictly zero for the first-order condition to hold as a strict equality. Therefore, when revenue is shared and the government can raise all revenue using a pure transfer tax, production taxes are optimally zero. Now consider how zero production taxes affect the public capital allocation. When $\tau_0^i = 0$, the second positive term in braces on the RHS of (13) is zero. The government can no longer capture additional production-tax revenue from increases in public capital consumption. Instead, public capital is allocated according to the following condition:

$$\gamma_N\Phi_N'(.)Z = \lambda_c(p_z - A)Z + (p - p_z)\alpha_i s_i Z \tag{14}$$

Since τ_0^i is absent in (14), less revenue is raised from public capital consumption, so that less public capital is allocated to private production. This gives rise to the following proposition:

Proposition 2: When governments perfectly coordinate and a transfer tax is available, then production taxes are optimally zero, and less public capital is allocated for consumption by firms. As a result, more public goods are provided by the higher government and there are larger in situ *resource stocks. Consumers of public-goods benefits are better off.*

Case 2: non-separable public and private production
When public and private capital are non-separable, many of the results for Case 1 still hold. Condition (11b) now describes optimal public capital consumption. Both β and τ_0^i are still interdependent, and as the government's preferences for revenue generation dominate its preferences for public-goods production (i.e., as λ_c approaches infinity), public capital consumption increases as long as marginal production tax revenues are increasing in β. However, in (11b) the marginal change in production-tax revenue now depends on public capital consumption through equilibrium changes in the firm's input uses:

$$\lambda_c\Sigma_i\tau_0^i\{[\partial f(.)/\partial L_i][\partial L_i/\partial\beta]+[\partial f(.)/\partial k_i][\partial k_i/\partial\beta]\}$$

As long as this marginal revenue effect is increasing in β, Propositions 1 and 2 continue to hold.

Finally, when the assumption that the constraint on s_i is binding is relaxed, the only modification necessary to (11a)–(11c) is to include a term that represents distortions in s_i when policies change. However, as long as marginal revenue collections increase in public capital consumption, Propositions 1 and 2 will continue to hold.

With perfect coordination, the decomposition of public goods as having national and/or local characteristics is of no interest to the governments since all governments care about both local and national consumers of public capital. The interdependence of public capital consumption and production taxes provides an incentive for governments not to coordinate when they do not share revenue targets. Since each government's revenue is a function of another government's actions, and as public capital is not shared equally over lower governmental jurisdictions, there are incentives for lower governments to choose a different production tax than τ_0^{ic} in (11a) and (12). As a result, the higher government will also not choose an optimal level of public capital consumption equal to β^c. In the next section, the implications of strategic interaction on the level of the *in situ* resource available are investigated.

Strategic policy design
The revenue-sharing assumption was critical in (10) to ensure perfect coordination. In practice, revenue is not always shared among governments and greater pressures are being placed on lower governments to fund their own projects (Oates 1994). Therefore, there is little incentive for governments to jointly determine the best tax and public capital consumption policies for the combined welfare of all localities. In addition, governments are probably not very concerned about the constituencies of other governments.[14] This section explores how incentives for non-coordinated policy design affect the choices of taxes and public capital consumption compared to perfect coordination.

To impose some structure on the strategic policy-design problem, it is assumed that all lower governments must determine production taxes in a simultaneous-move game of complete and symmetric information. Each local government's policy choices represent its reaction function both to other lower governments and the higher government. Production taxes are chosen taking into account other taxes and public capital allocations. All governments must again raise a certain level of revenue. Finally, it is assumed for now that the constraint on s_i in equation (4) is binding.

A leader–follower model between governments is assumed, where the higher government moves first and selects the public capital allocation, taking as given the reaction functions of the lower governments. Assume that lump-sum taxes are not available, so that $T^h = 0$. The N lower governments separately choose tax rates τ_0^i according to:

$$\text{Max } \{ V^i(\tau_0^i, p, p_z, \beta, w, r) + \Phi_i[(1 - \beta)Z] \} \tag{15}$$

$$\text{subject to: } \tau_0^i f(k_i, L_i, \beta Z s_i) \geq R_i; \ i = 1, ..., N.$$

The solutions to (15) represent reaction functions of government i to other local governments and to the higher government. Denote this reaction function as $\tau_0^i(\beta)$.

The higher government leads by determining β, taking the lower government's reaction functions, $\tau_0^i(\beta)$, $i = 1, 2, ..., N$, as given:

$$\text{Max } \Sigma_i V^i(\tau_0^i, p, p_z, \beta, w, r) + \gamma_N \Phi_N[(1 - \beta)Z] \tag{16}$$

$$\text{subject to: } -A\beta Z + \Sigma_i s_i p_z \beta Z + T^h + \Sigma_i g[\tau_0^i(\beta)f(k_i, L_i, \beta Z s_i)] \geq R_h$$

Denote the solution to (16) as β^s.

The revenue constraints in (15) and (16) assume that public and private production are non-separable. The separable case is again obtained by rewriting the production function as equation (2a) in each revenue constraint. Two cases that depend on this separability are now examined. It is also initially assumed that the higher government does not have a transfer tax available ($T^h = 0$), and that public capital is taxable by the lower governments.

Case 1: separable public and private production
The lower government's reaction function is the first-order condition for equation (15):

$$(\lambda_i - \alpha_i)f(L_i, k_i) = (\alpha_i - \lambda_i)s_i \beta z$$
$$- \tau_0^i \lambda_i[(\partial f(.)/\partial L_i)(\partial L_i/\partial \tau_0^i) + (\partial f(.)/\partial k_i)(\partial k_i/\partial \tau_0^i)] \tag{17}$$

where λ_i is the multiplier for the lower government's revenue constraint. The reaction function is decreasing in β, $\partial \tau_0^i/\partial \beta \leq 0$, for every i, since the production function does not depend on β, and the second and third terms on the RHS of (17) are independent of β under separable production. The reaction function is also independent of tax choices of other localities as long as s_i is binding. As the higher government increases capital allocated to private firms, the lower government free-rides by reducing taxes to increase the welfare of its own residents and by collecting increased revenue from taxes on public production.

The higher government leads by taking the lower government's reaction function as given and by choosing public capital consumption according to the first-order condition of (16). However, under separable production, the lower governments also collect tax revenue from public capital sold from the higher government to the firms in each locality. Thus the revenue constraint of the higher government becomes:

$$-A\beta Z + \Sigma_i s_i p_z \beta Z + T^h + g\Sigma_i[\tau_0^i(\beta)f(k_i, L_i) + \tau_0^i(\beta)s_i \beta Z] \geq R_h \tag{18}$$

Using (18) in place of the revenue constraint in (16) and using the reaction functions determined by equation (17), the first-order condition with respect to β yields:

$$\gamma_N \Phi_N'(.)Z = \Sigma_i \alpha_i s_i (p - \tau_0^i - p_z)Z - \lambda_H AZ + \Sigma_i \lambda_H s_i p_z Z + g\lambda_H \Sigma_i [\partial \tau_0^i(\beta)/\partial\beta]$$

$$[f(L_i, k_i) + s_i \beta Z] + \Sigma g_i \lambda_H \tau_0^i(\beta)s_i Z + \Sigma_i [\partial \tau_0^i(\beta)/\partial\beta][-\alpha_i s_i \beta Z] \quad (19)$$

where λ_H is the multiplier for the higher government's revenue constraint. Condition (19) is equivalent to the condition for public capital consumption under perfect coordination except for the terms in braces on the RHS. As federalism increases and g approaches zero, condition (19) is equivalent to the perfect-coordination case except for the term in, $\Sigma_i \{ [\partial \tau_0^i(\beta)/\partial\beta][-\alpha_i s_i Z] \}$. This term is non-negative given the sign of $\partial \tau_0^i(\beta)/\partial\beta$ for all i from (17). Therefore, the RHS is larger than in the perfect-coordination case. Using the concavity of $\Phi_N(.)$, public capital consumption decreases in strategic competition, $\beta^s \le \beta^c$. Thus, the *in situ* resource stock is higher under strategic competition. From (17), lower governments must increase production taxes to compensate for lost revenues from decreased public capital consumption. Finally, since the government has only one choice variable in (18), social welfare levels must be lower when governments do not coordinate than they are when policies are chosen to maximize equation (10). This is summarized in the following proposition:

Proposition 3: When governments face separate revenue constraints and do not coordinate their policies, public capital consumption is lower and production taxes are higher compared to policy design under perfect coordination. More of the in situ *resource stock is preserved under strategic policy design. Consumers of public benefits are better off. However, firms are worse off since they face higher taxes. In general, social welfare decreases compared to that of the perfect-coordination case.*

Proposition 3 suggests a basic difference in policy design between governments that coordinate and those that do not. In the perfect-coordination case, since tax revenues were increasing in public capital consumption, β^c was higher when production taxes were employed. When governments do not coordinate, the lower governments have an incentive to free-ride off of higher government capital allocations by reducing tax rates. However, as federalism increases the higher government does not care about the revenue situation of the lower government, as revenues are not shared. Therefore, it has an incentive to decrease public capital allocations even though the production tax is strictly positive.

Finally, how the lower and higher governments' revenue preferences affect the allocation of public capital can be determined by examining how β^s and $\tau_0^i(\beta)$

depend on the bindingness of government revenue constraints, λ_i, and the size of g. As the higher government cares more about the revenue collections of the lower governments, g increases. Thus the RHS of (19) becomes more negative through the term, $g\Sigma_i\{[\partial\tau_0{}^i(\beta)/\partial\beta][\lambda_H(f(L_i, k_i) + s_i\beta Z)]\}$. Public capital consumption comes closer to the perfect-coordination level. As λ_i increases, the differences between public capital consumption under perfect coordination and strategic design lessen. This follows from (17). It can be shown that each lower government's response function, $\partial\tau_0{}^i(\beta)/\partial\beta$, decreases in absolute value. When the lower government's revenue constraint is increasingly binding, it cannot afford to decrease taxes substantially even though public capital can be taxed. Therefore, it follows that:

Proposition 4: The inefficiencies of non-coordinated policy design decrease as fiscal federalism decreases, or as the lower government becomes increasingly revenue constrained.

Case 2: non-separable public and private consumption

When public and private production are non-separable, many of the above results generally do not hold, with the exception of the importance of fiscal federalism in Proposition 4. The results in Proposition 3 are ambiguous, since the sign of $\partial\tau_0{}^i/\partial\beta$ is indeterminant and depends on substitution between public capital and private capital in firms' production functions. This is also the case when the constraint on public capital shares is not binding.

Conclusions

In this chapter it is shown that policy design and subsequent changes in the resource stock will depend on the degree to which governments cooperate and their preferences for raising revenue through exploitation of the resource stock. It is shown how non-coordinated policy design leads to inefficient changes in the *in situ* resource stock. Changes in this stock differentially affect consumers who value natural resource capital for its public-goods benefits, and firms that use public capital in the production of private goods. The model is based on a stylized framework that is consistent with many natural resource markets. One higher level of government oversees the public capital stock, while lower governments obtain revenue from taxing the activities of firms within their constituencies. Both higher and lower governments face revenue constraints that must be met through their choice of policies. However, revenue constraints and the constituencies of each government generally differ across the governments. Perfect coordination is introduced as in other fiscal federalism models, i.e., by assuming that revenue is shared among governments. Finally, perfect information is assumed, which is reasonable given that different levels of the same government are assumed to be involved.

Previous models of fiscal federalism are extended by including natural resource capital, and by examining levels of cooperation among different levels of government. It is shown that the *in situ* resource stock is larger when governments do not coordinate or behave strategically, compared to the case where they coordinate perfectly. Therefore, there is an over-provision of public goods when governments behave strategically, and consumers of public goods are better off. This occurs because the higher government allocates less of the public capital stock for consumption by private firms in any lower government's constituency. Consumers of benefits from *in situ* public capital are worse off when governments coordinate perfectly, since the *in situ* resource stock is lower. These results are magnified as the higher government cares less about lower governments' revenue collections. However, as lower governments' revenues become increasingly constrained, the inefficiencies of non-coordinated policy design lessen. This is because the lower governments are less able to free-ride off of revenues from higher government public capital allocations.

The results in this chapter are important in practice. Many mechanisms exist in natural resource markets for cooperation among governments, either through formal trade laws or through the typical legislative process. Moreover, in North America increasing pressures are being placed on lower forms of governments to fund their own projects. It has been shown what the implications of revenue constraints are if a natural resource stock can be exploited for revenue generation. It has also been shown what changes in natural resource stocks can be expected as governments move toward greater cooperation or revenue autonomy. Finally, it has also been shown that both local and global values of natural resources are important in predicting the inefficiencies inherent in strategic policy design.

An interesting extension of the model would be to examine cooperative bargaining between governments in the design of policies. This often happens in practice through the legislative process, particularly for governments at different levels. Bargaining between governments would probably lead to compromises in policies, so that the resulting resource stock would occur somewhere between the strategic and perfect coordination outcomes. The strategic outcome could be included as a threat point in the bargaining game. As the local values of public goods increased, or as governments increasingly shared revenue constraints, a cooperative bargaining equilibrium would be expected to be closer to the perfect-coordination one.

Notes

1. An earlier version of this chapter appears in Gregory Amacher's Ph.D. dissertation.
2. The factor market is studied in this chapter. Most natural resource policies specifically target intermediate inputs, and the tax revenue from these policies is substantial (Boyd and Hyde 1989). Further, the factor market is where many examples of intergovernmental cooperation arise.
3. For a firm maximizing profits the marginal utility of income is equal to 1.

4. τ_0^i represents a tax on production. When the production function is 'separable', public capital is a perfect substitute for private production. As the government cannot distinguish between private and public production in terms of the final product, the tax rate on private and public production is equivalent. Such a situation is consistent with forest and mineral markets throughout the world.

5.   In this case, the tax rate τ_0^i is applied to both of the firm's products, so that the RHS of (2) includes the term $\tau_0^i[f(k_i, L_i) + \beta s_i Z]$. This case is common in forestry markets. For example, intermediate goods such as chips for pulp, which may be resold, are often produced from public forests.

6.   Separable production is often the case in natural resource markets since resources provide raw material. Consider North American forests, where higher government forests are sold to firms, and these are perfect substitutes for the firms' own trees. A similar situation exists with mineral leasing on publicly owned land.

7.   National and local public goods are modelled to include the possibility that constituencies of the governments differ in how the public good is valued.

8.   Note that with separable public and private production, equation (5) becomes $\tau_0^i f(k_i, L_i) + \tau_0^i \beta Z s_i + T^i \geq R_i$.

9.   The joint-revenue constraint is obtained by adding equations (5) and (6), and assuming that $g = 1$ in (6). The assumption consistent with this constraint is that revenue-sharing is imposed by some law (perhaps outside the political confines of the higher and lower governments). Since revenue-sharing is often suggested as a remedy to policy-incentive problems (Starrett 1988), it is not restrictive to use this as an assumption in finding the coordination baseline policy.

10. In the model, $(1 - \beta)Z$ is a pure public good. β represents the proportion of the total capital stock the government preserves from consumption. The value of consumption of the preserved capital in each locality is $\Phi_i(.)$.

11. In (11a)–(11c), Roy's identity is used to define $\partial V^i(.)/\partial \tau_0^i$, $\partial V^i(.)/\partial \tau_0^i$, and $\partial V^i(.)/\partial \beta$ in terms of the marginal utility of income (Varian 1984).

12. The first-order conditions under perfect coordination are symmetric. Thus, the conditions for only one tax rate need be examined.

13. As β represents a transfer of income from the government to firms, dead-weight losses of such a transfer are positive, or $\lambda_c > \sum_i \alpha_i$.

14. As λ approaches infinity, τ_0^i is bounded away from zero, since an infinitely binding revenue constraint implies that taxes are non-zero.

15. This is especially true when $\Phi_i(.)$ is zero for some localities. In addition $\lambda > 0$, when $\tau_0^i > 0$.

References

Amacher, Gregory S. (1993), 'Three Essays in Natural Resource Ecocnomics: Optimal Forest Taxation, Fiscal Federalism, and Time Series Cross Section Estimation', Ph.D. dissertation, University of Michigan, Michigan: Ann Arbor.

Beck, J. (1978), 'Tax Competition, Uniform Assessment, and the Benefit Principle', *Journal of Urban Economics*, 13, 127–46.

Boyd, R. and Hyde, W. (1989), *Forestry Sector Intervention: The Impacts of Public Regulation on Social Welfare*. Ames, Iowa:Iowa State University Press.

Futagami, K. (1989), 'A Game Theoretical Approach To Reconstruction of Public Finance', *Journal of Public Economics*, 40, 135–50.

Gordon, R. (1983), 'An Optimal Taxation Approach to Fiscal Federalism', *Quarterly Journal of Economics*, 98, 567–86.

Oates, W. (1994), 'Federalism and Government Finance', in J. Quigley, and E. Smolensky (eds), *Modern Public Finance*, Cambridge, MA.: Harvard University Press, pp. 126–51.

Starrett, D. (1988), *Foundations of Public Economics*, Cambridge: Cambridge University Press.

Varian, H. (1984), *Microeconomic Analysis*, New York: W.W. Norton and Company.

Wildasin, D. (1988), 'Nash Equilibria in Models of Fiscal Competition', *Journal of Public Economics*, 35, 229–40.

Index